THE PRINCIPLES OF MUSIK
IN SINGING AND SETTING

Da Capo Press Music Reprint Series
GENERAL EDITOR
FREDERICK FREEDMAN
VASSAR COLLEGE

THE PRINCIPLES OF MUSIK
IN SINGING AND SETTING

By Charles Butler

INTRODUCTION BY GILBERT REANEY
University of California at Los Angeles

DA CAPO PRESS • NEW YORK • 1970

A Da Capo Press Reprint Edition

This Da Capo Press edition of Charles Butler's
The Principles of Musik in Singing and Setting
is an unabridged republication of the first
edition published in England in 1636.

Library of Congress Catalog Card Number 68-13273
SBN 306 · 70939 · 2

INTRODUCTION

Charles Butler was not a musician pure and simple. He was, in fact, for a large part of his life a relatively poor country parson, in whom it is difficult to see the erudite author of *The Principles of Musik*, published in 1636. But his fourteen years at Oxford evidently stood him in good stead. We know that Butler entered Magdalen Hall in 1579 and was a Bible-clerk at Magdalen College, receiving his B.A. in 1583 and his M.A. in 1587. He finally left Oxford in May 1593 to become rector of the small parish of Nately Scures, east of Basingstoke, and two years later Master at the Holy Ghost School, in Basingstoke itself. From 1600 until his death on March 29, 1647, Butler led a peaceful life as vicar of Wootton St. Lawrence, west of Basingstoke, where he wrote most of his books.

Butler's *The Feminine Monarchie, or a Treatise Concerning Bees*, first published in 1609, was a major contribution to the knowledge of bees and beekeeping for its time. Curiously enough, the book involves music, but in a rather unusual way. Butler studied very carefully the sounds made by bees, both queens and drones, when they are swarming, and decided to compose a bee's madrigal or, as he calls it, a *Melissomelos*.[1] It is the final section

---

1. The first edition of *The Feminine Monarchie* (1609) provides a brief description of the bee's madrigal; the third edition (1634) provides the four voice parts. Other details and a score of the "final section" may be found in James Pruett, "Charles Butler—Musician, Grammarian, Apiarist," *The Musical Quarterly* XLIX/4 (Oct 1963), 498-509. Other articles which may be of interest to the reader include: Gerald R. Hayes, "Charles Butler and the Music of the Bees," *The Musical Times* LXVI [988] (June 1925), 512-15; George Sarton, "*The Feminine Monarchie* of Charles Butler, 1609," *Isis* XXXIV/6 [98] (Autumn 1943), 469-72; three articles by Nan Cooke Carpenter, "A Reference to Marlowe in Charles Butler's *Principles of Musik* (1636)," *Notes and Queries* CXCVIII/1 (Jan 1953), 16-18; "Charles Butler and Du Bartas," *Notes and Queries* CXCIX [New Series I/1] (Jan 1954), 2-7; "Charles Butler and the Bees' Madrigal," *Notes and Queries* CC [New Series II/3] (Mar 1955), 103-6.

of this four-voice setting which is in imitation of the bees, for it contains a great deal of repeated unison writing, and nearly all the notes are black ones in triplet minim groups.

The prince's (*i.e.*, young queen's) or "mean" part, contained entirely within the octave above middle *C*, is composed with the four upper "clefs" (*i.e.*, top notes *G*, *A*, *B^b*, and *C*). Butler's rhythm may appear arbitrary, but it is clear from his explanation that this is not really the case. The opening odd minim, followed by a semibreve, and the lengthy minim groups on a unison *A* or *B^b*, always ending with a minim, are intentional. The queen's part (*i.e.*, tenor) is also in triplet minims, but within the four lower "clefs" (from middle *C* up to the *F*, a fourth above) ; and the tune is continued for the length of nine or ten semibreves. The possible addition of a third and fourth prince's part completes the four-part harmony.

According to Butler, the bees' madrigal exemplifies the principles of music: first, the various types of rhythm; then the six solmization syllables; and finally, the six concords, namely, the minor and major third, fourth, fifth, sixth, and octave.

Apart from a defense of the marriage of cousins, occasioned by the marriage of Butler's son William to a cousin, Mary Butler, and published in 1625, his next important book was *The English Grammar* of 1633.[2] In it, Butler expounded his simplified system of phonetic spelling, based on the way English sounded at the time. Since Butler's *The Principles of Musik* and later editions of *The Feminine Monarchie* follow this system, it is necessary here to examine its principal features. Although it can be read quite easily, the immediate impact of the strange lettering is rather disturbing. This is what prompted the printer of *The Principles of Musik*, John Haviland, to insert a note at the beginning of the volume explaining that the aspirate signs, with which some of the readers were having difficulties in spite of Butler's extensive

---

2. The full text, with notes and commentary, is in Albert Eichler, *Charles Butler's English Grammar (1634)*. (Halle: 1910) [*Neudrücke fruhneuenglischer grammatiker*, IV.]

discussion of the new orthography in his *English Grammar*, were nothing more than an abbreviation of the letter plus the aspirate, indicated by a stroke through the letter in question. Thus *t*, *d*, *c*, k (hard *c*), *g*, *p*, *s*, and *w* plus an *h* are abbreviated by a horizontal or diagonal stroke through the principal letter. The only points to remember are that an *e* mute is shown as an apostrophe, and *q* is omitted entirely, since it is merely an abbreviation of *c* or *k* plus *u*.

Butler's *The Principles of Musik in Singing and Setting* is the work of a highly qualified and erudite musician. As the full title suggests, it considers music from two points of view, that of the singer or performer, and that of the setter or composer. Music is also divided into two large classes, secular and sacred, called civil and ecclesiastical music both by Butler and by Johannes de Grocheo, writing over three hundred years before Butler. Book I is mainly devoted to details of musical practice. Chapters 1 and 2 are concerned with the fundamentals of music, and are addressed to both singer and setter, while Chapters 3 and 4 go more into the detail of actual composition. This, of course, is the time-honored scheme of most earlier treatises, for the fundamentals were always given pride of place, even in Greek times, while composition as a separate subject began to take up more and more space in musical theory books from the late fifteenth century.

Chapter 1 deals with the "moods." Butler defines music, in the words of Augustine, as the art of modulating notes, and its strength, in the words of Boethius, as its ability to move the emotions of its hearers. Although the key system was beginning to crystallize in Butler's time, he still talks in terms of "moods" (meaning modes), of which, however, he acknowledges only five: Dorian, Lydian, Aeolian, Phrygian, and Ionian. Essentially, "mood" seems to have meant to Butler what it means to us, for he speaks of the Dorian as sober and slow in time, set mainly note-against-note, and suited to psalms or canticles in meter or rhythmical verse, while the Phrygian is manly and courageous, and good for marches, *almains*, and warlike music with trumpets, fifes, and drums. Some music, like the *Battle Galliard*, is compounded of all the moods.

The old idea that, as in medieval plainsong, the *final* defines the mood was well known to Butler, but he seems to have preferred the possibility of applying any mood to any key or tone. When he criticizes the distinction made between flat and sharp keys—for the flat keys are no more flat than the sharp ones—he undoubtedly has in mind the modern key system, where both flat and sharp keys are but transpositions of one basic scalar arrangement of tones and semitones.

The hexachords are still very much a feature of Butler's musical background. In Chapter 2 of Book I, he includes a drawing of an extended Guidonian scale of three octaves, with Greek note-names and Guidonian letters, ranging from the *F* immediately below the bass staff to the *f* at the top of the treble staff, followed by a similar scale according to the three types of hexachord. The organ and virginal have three extra notes below the basic three-octave scale and four above it, giving a four-octave scale from *CC* to *c₃*. In fact, the organ is allowed a further top note, namely *d₃*. For higher notes, the stops are used. It is of interest that, even though Butler talks in terms of hexachords, he differentiates between *F* and *B* in the octave on *C* as *fa* and *pha*.

The terminology is a little confusing for the twentieth-century reader. The word "key" means a note-letter for Butler, while Butler's note-names are the solmization syllables *ut, re, mi, fa, sol, la,* and *pha*. And when he speaks of the "tune" of notes, he means the arrangement of the scale by tones and semitones. He approves of the frets on the lute because they make it easy to locate the tones and semitones.

In the fourth section of his very extensive second chapter, Butler discusses rhythm, from the points of view of both note-shapes and values. The semibreve is the principal note-value and tactus, though the notes range in length from the *large* to the semiquaver. It is interesting to see that, where there are nine minims to the beat, the up-beat comes on the fifth minim. After discussing other notational signs, such as flats and sharps, in Section 5, Butler devotes the chapter's sixth and final section to sight-singing lessons, in order of difficulty: by step, by leaps of a third, by leaps of thirds and fourths, etc. It is not surprising that these were considered useful practice melodies, for as Butler points out, each of the first three lessons has two parts in one, *i.e.*, they can each be sung canonically, and they can also be sung in six parts.

Chapter 3, the first chapter on actual composition, deals with the various elements involved in musical composition. Section 1 considers the various parts (bass, tenor, contratenor, etc.) and their combinations. Living at a time when the verse anthem was very popular, Butler naturally liked the alternation of treble or countertenor solo with a chorus, or a duet alternating with two choruses.

Melody is treated in Section 2. Butler emphasizes that all parts of a song should be harmonious with each other, as well as melodious individually. Melodic movement may be attained either by step or by leap, but if by leap, the skip should be to a consonant interval.

In Section 3, Butler examines intervals and the division into concords and discords. His harmonic outlook is quite modern, for he points out that the proper place for the perfect consonances is in the lower part of the harmony, while thirds should be placed above. His lengthy footnote on the interval of the fourth is clearly due to this interval's ambiguous history, both in the theory and practice of music.

The fourth and final section of Chapter 3 deals with what Butler calls the four ornaments of melody: consecution (which chords should follow which), syncopation, imitation (called "fuge"), and formality (maintaining the key or mode by free means, *e.g.*, cadences, imitation, single notes, etc.). As regards consecution, consecutive perfect consonances are forbidden, while successions of imperfect consonances are permissible. Passing notes and rests do not conceal parallel perfect consonances. On the authority of Calvisius, whom he so often quotes, Butler points out that successions of parallel fourths are, though not desirable, satisfactory when used in the upper parts of parallel six-three chords. Evidently he is talking about *fauxbourdon*. As for the harmonic tritone, he admits it in passing, as Tinctoris had one hundred and fifty years earlier. Syncopation is treated systematically and in detail, and there is an interesting observation to the effect that the leading tone is always sharp at cadences, even when it is not expressly notated in the source.

According to Butler, there are two kinds of imitation, exact and by contrary motion. Like cadences, imitative passages should remain in the mode, or "air," beginning and ending on one of the four "air" notes. This refers to the four cadential finals (the final, 3rd (4th, and 5th). The section on formality clarifies this point. Only the primary cadence is used at the end of an important section. Elsewhere, the fifth is most important, and the third next, but they may not be used in modes where the leading tone cannot be sharpened in the conventional suspended cadence passage. The improper cadences are the 6th, 2nd, and 7th, but they may be used occasionally, providing they are followed by a principal cadence.

Chapter 4 is very straightforwardly divided into two sections, one on note-against-note setting (called "setting in counterpoint"), and the other on florid composition (called "setting in discant"). "Counterpoint" is used in setting psalms and other similar metrical pieces. Each strain or line is divided by a double bar and subdivided by a single bar (though, as usual, Butler's barring seems to adhere to this principle only in a general way). In discant, both kinds of imitation should be used. Slow phrases should alternate with quick ones, and contrapuntal phrases with homophony. Discant may employ a plain *cantus firmus*, or the plainsong may permeate all parts.

Finally, in the Epilogue to Book I, Butler sums up the qualities needed by the good composer. First of all, he must have

Nature's gifts—aptness and ability of wit and memory. Assuming that he possesses these qualities, he should study Morley's *Plaine and Easie Introduction*, especially the discussion of composition and counterpoint in two to six parts, and imitate such great models as Clemens non Papa, Orazio Vecchi, Lassus, Ferrabosco (probably A. Ferrabosco II), Marenzio, G. Croce, Fayrfax, Tye, Tavener, Parsons, Bull, Dowland, Tallis, Byrd, White, Morley, and the excellent contemporary masters, Thomas and John Tomkins. But even then, all the natural aptitude and study in the world will not help the composer unless he is inspired, like an organist playing a voluntary. This is certainly a very early testimony to the nineteenth and early twentieth century cult of inspiration. In this case inspiration seems to be connected with improvisation, for it causes a spontaneous musical flow which can be imparted best in a musical form like the voluntary, an essentially free composition which nevertheless in the seventeenth century was founded on such disciplinary techniques as imitation.

Book II of Butler's musical treatise is perhaps of lesser direct interest to the twentieth-century musician than Book I; yet it contains a great deal of information on musical life in the early seventeenth century. In listing the instruments of his time, Butler mentions that the cittern and gittern (probably the guitar) are different instruments. He also mentions the cymbal as a stringed instrument, probably the dulcimer in this case, and the claviorganum, a combination of organ and virginal played simultaneously. The addition of couplers to the claviorganum was apparently a new invention.

Butler thinks the good musician should also be something of a poet, for even when he does not write his own verse, he should be able to alter other people's texts to suit his own purposes. In fitting the mood of the music to the text, the composer should use simple, slow passages for serious or sad material; quick notes or triple time for cheerful texts; harsh short notes, quick suspensions, and concordant cadences for hard, manly, or cruel words; semitones, slow suspensions, and discordant cadences where the poem is lamenting, effeminate, or passionately sorrow-ful. Word-painting, by slow and quick notes for slow and quick motion, and by high and low pitch for ascent and descent, is another useful adjunct to textual expression. In discant, these elements may be applied individually, but in note-against-note settings it is enough to observe them in the principal part, called "cantus" or "tune" by Butler.

Other hints to the musician are designed to insure the clear enunciation of the text. For instance, imitation should be re-peated, the text should not be obscured by being set to tied notes or long groups of notes, rests should correspond to the punctua-tion of the text, and principal cadences to periods in the text. Similarly, singers should concentrate on clear pronunciation of every letter and syllable of the text, especially vowels, keeping each part even in volume, except where an imitative entry de-mands stress.

Finally, in the last section of his first chapter for Book II, Butler discusses "mixt musik." Music, he says, is more accept-able when voice, text, and instruments are combined. The instru-ments should not compete with the voices, but should sound quietly or in small groups by turn, so that the text will not be obscured; for although the musicians may enjoy the music with-out its text, the audience likes to hear the words.

Chapter 2 deals with music in the service of the church. Using the Bible as his authority, Butler shows that the principal use of music is in the divine service. Sometimes a special occasion requires voices and instruments, and this is confirmed by Psalms 33 and 98. Similarly, as in Old Testament times (*e.g.*, the deliv-erance from Egypt), the most solemn music with full harmony of voices and loud (wind) instruments is reserved for the most solemn times, places, and congregations, when praising God. Butler also notes that during the entire existence of the church of Christ as an established body, church music had flourished in the form of plainsong responsories, antiphons, and hymns. Once again, Butler's list of authorities is quite exhaustive; among others, he cites Isidore, Jerome, Athanasius, and Eusebius.

Living as he did in the age of the Puritans, it is not surprising that Butler felt compelled to answer objections against church music. Some people, he says, complain that music hinders consideration of the words, but Augustine realized that music was beneficial in church, because it raised weaker spirits to the love of piety. People also say, Butler goes on, that the worship of God does not consist in graces and ornaments. The Bible shows, however, that even though God may not have wanted to hear the music of Amos, He must certainly have been pleased with the psalms of David, for in composing them, David had performed an additional service to God, Whom he already worshipped in spirit. Another objection to church music in Butler's time was that ordinary people did not understand it, presumably because it was difficult to hear the words. Butler answers that many of the regular service texts are well-known to the congregation, and in other cases a soloist may sing, or a particular clear voice may help the choir, and of course, repetitions can make clear what is not understood the first time.

All this may sound very familiar, for the opponents of music in church bring up the same arguments today. Even if the congregation can understand what is sung, they cannot join in its complex music. Some people cannot read music, others do not have good enough voices, and some can neither read nor sing. Butler believes that members of the congregation should probably restrict themselves to lessons and prayers, but if they must sing more difficult pieces, let them learn how to do it! After all, they often amuse themselves at home with the most ingenious vocal and instrumental music. The critics claim that the most elaborate music cannot be performed in all churches, yet it is possible to be content with vocal music, either in parts, or if this is not practicable, just as a melody. But harmonized tunes should be the aim of every church.

In the final section of his second chapter, Butler advises performers as to how they should behave. Once again, he asks them to sing the words clearly and not too loudly. They should avoid much ornament and trilling, and should not try to sing too high or too low. All these habits make the words more difficult to hear. Church musicians should be men of good character so that their lives match their art. Common wind players should not be admitted into the church, for God does not like loud noises. But if they are needed for a particular piece of music, they should forego their wretched ways and be ordained and sanctioned by proper authority before setting foot in the choir.

This long exposition on music and its place in church, which was evidently very much a part of Butler's life as an Anglican vicar, is followed by a chapter on secular music. Here again the discussion is very reminiscent of Johannes de Grocheo, though behind it one sees lurking the shadow of Puritan extremism. Secular music is for man's comfort, it is agreeable to Nature and to God, and so why do men object to it? They say it is but vanity, but then all is vanity. In Butler's opinion, secular music is a blessing if performed decently and at suitable times. Even more relevant to the twentieth century is the objection raised that "debauched Balad-makers and Dance-makers" corrupt youth. Butler, however, is of the opinion that the way to reform young people is by finding fault with them, and shaming them. Happily, he sees a better generation coming along in his time.

Secular music in Butler's time resembles sacred music in that it could be entirely vocal, or for voices and instruments; but wholly instrumental music was less common in church, even if it appears that consorts occasionally penetrated into the church to accompany anthems. Butler shares with Byrd the beliefs that singing is good for one's health, and that vocal polyphony outshines purely instrumental music. Once again, however, the combination of voices and instruments seems best to him.

The blending of erudite musician and country parson is everpresent in Butler's *The Principles of Musik*. The Bible is always his prime source book, but his knowledge of Latin and Greek enables him to quote from the ancients with authority, and he quotes equally well from almost any of the more recent musical theorists. He nearly always gives his source in a marginal note, which indicates that he is not working at second hand. His footnotes contain a wealth of additional material which is often extremely valuable. But perhaps most important is the clarity with which Butler writes, for the present-day musician often has to grapple with concepts that have been lost, or can only be understood dimly at a distance of three hundred years. Butler's phonetic script has often prevented scholars from reading his treatise on music, but it is not too much to say that this is one of the most important treatises of the century that followed Butler's own revered authority, Thomas Morley.

Gilbert Reaney
University of California at Los Angeles
July, 1967

THE
PRINCIPLES
OF MUSIK,
In
SINGING AND SETTING:
WITH
The two-fold Use therof,
[*Ecclesiasticall* and *Civil*.]

By
CHARLS BUTLER Magd. *Master of Arts*.

LONDON,
Printed by *John Haviland*, for the Author:
1 6 3 6.

TO
THE MOST'NOBLE
AND GRACIOUS LORD,
CHARLS,
BY THE GRACE OF GOD,
PRINCE OF GREAT BRITAIN,
FRANCE AND IRELAND.

SIR,

THere is nothing that more conduceth to the prosperiti and happines of a Kingdom, than the good education of yuthe and children : In which the * Philosopher requireth three Arts especially to be taught them [*Grammar, Musik, Gymnastik:*] this last for the exercise of their lims in activiti and feats of Arms ; the other two for the ordering of their voices in Speech and Song. Meerly to Speak and to Sing, ar of Nature : and therefore the rudest Swains of the most barbarous Nations dœe make this dubble use of their articulate voices : but to speak well, and to sing well, ar of Art : so that

among

Polit. l. 8. c. 3.

¶ 2

among the beſt Wits of the moſt civilized people, none may attain unto perfection in either facultie, without the Rules and Precepts of Art, confirmed by the practice of approoved Authors.

I have been induced, (My GRACIOVS LORD) for the furtherance of the ſtudious, to ſet foorth the Principles of both theſe vocall Arts, [Grammar and Muſik.] The firſt hath, not long ſince, been graciouſly received by your Graces ſacred hands : the other modeſtly higheth after hir Siſter, hoping for the like acceptance : that ſo, both beeing ſafely ſhrouded together vnder the wings of your Princely protection, may daily grow into the loov and favour of the Studious : and ſo be admitted to ſerv, (the one with matter, the other with form, the one with hir words, the other with hir Tones) not only for the inſtruction and recreation of Men ; but alſo, for the ſervice and praiſe of God, who is the Author of them both, as of all other Arts in the † Columns of Heber.

That theſe two ſhoold not be parted in the diſcipline of children, Quintilian ſheweth, where he ſaith, that Grammar cannot be perfect without Muſik. *Nec citra Muſicen Grammatica poteſt eſſe perfecta, cùm ei de Metris Rhythmiſq; dicendum ſit. And again, that Grammar is under Muſik, & that the ſame men formerly taught them both: †Architas atq; Ariſtoxenus ſubjectam Grammaticen Muſicæ putaverunt, et eoſdem utriuſq; rei præceptores fuiſſe. And for Muſik it ſelf, the Philoſopher concludeth the ſpeciall neceſſiti therof in breeding of Children, partly from its naturall delight, and partly from the efficacy it hath, in mooving affections and vertues.

The

† Notes wittily
and learnedly,
than poetically,
explaned by di-
vine Du Bartas,
and his worthy
Interpreter Jo-
ſua Sylveſter.
*Inſtit. Orat.
l. 1. c. 4.
† Ibid. c. 10.

DEDICATORIE.

The firft Reafon he propofeth thus: *Habet Mu-* * Polit. l.8. c. 5.
fica naturalem voluptatem, per quam illius ufus cunctis
ætatibus cunctifq; moribus eft acceptus : the fecond
thus : † *Sunt autem in Rhythmis & Melodijs fimilitu-* † Ibidem.
dines, maximè penes veras naturas Iræ, & Manfuetu-
dinis, ac fortitudinis, & temperantiæ, atq; contrariorum his, & aliorum omnium quæ ad mores pertinent.
Upon which two Reafons he inferreth his Con-
clufion: *Quòd fi hoc poteft Mufica, clarum eft quod ad
puerorum difciplinam eft adhibenda, & in ea pueri funt
inftituendi.*

Befides thefe and * fundry other civill ufes of * L. 2. c. 3. § 2.
this Art, it hath one (above all other Arts) much
more excellent : which Venerable † *Beda* noteth in † In Mufica
practica.
thefe words: *Nulla Scientia aufa eft fubintrare fores
Ecclefiæ, nifi ipfa tantummodo Mufica : per hanc Plaf-
matorem mundi collaudare debemus, & benedicere.*
No Science, but Mufick, may enter the Dores of
the Chyrch. By this we praife and bleffe the Crea-
tor of the world.

This ufe did that religious, wife, valorous, and
victorious King of the holy Land, [the man after
Gods own heart] make of it : who was a skilfull
practicer both of vocall and inftrumentall Mufik,
fet to thofe facred, eloquent, and Majeftik Mee-
ters, which himfelf compofed, both for the pre-
fent Service of his gracious God, who had don fo
great things for him ; and alfo to remain, for In-
ftructions, Devotions, and Patterns, to be learned, exercifed, and imitated of Gods people, in all
ages, and languages, to the worlds end.

The Example of which devout and zelous King,
many Chriftian Princes, Kings, and Emperours,

¶ 3   did

did follow with like zele and devotion. *Constantine the Great*, that most blessed Emperour, for the more honour of divine service, began the Chyrch-song : * *Constantinus cantare primus cœpit.* The pious Emperour † *Theodosius* in the mids of the Congregation, did likewise lead, in singing the Hymns unto God. The Emperour * *Justinian* himself did make a Song ; which began, *The onely begotten Soon and word of God :* and gave it to the Chyrch of *Constantinople* to be sung. And, after them, that incomparable Prince, the most Puissant, Politik, Fortunate Conquerour; the most Prudent, Magnificent, Religious Governour, C H A R L S, sirnamed the G R E A T, his zele was such, that † whensoever he came to any Cittí, he went to the *Psalmodi*, and sang himselt : appointing to his Soons and his other Princes lessons to be sung, &c. A worthy precedent for all Christian Potentates !

Eusebius l. 4. de vita Constantini.

† Niceph. Ecclef.hist.l.1.c.3. *Pius Imperator Theodosius, ipse medius hymnis canendis præiit, habitu privato incedens.*

* Niceph.l.17. c.28. *Post Synodum, Imperator cantilenam [cujus initiū est, Vnigenitus Filius et verbum Dei] composuit: atq; eam ecclesiæ, inter psallendum, usurpandam tradidit.* † Carion Chronic. l.4. *Quandocunq fuit in urbibus, accessit ad psalmodiam, & una cecinit ipse : & filiis ac principibus distribuit lectiones canendas : & precationem suam, cum pius serio conjunxit :* To wie Narration our Autor addet dis Epiphonema, *Quàm pulchrum exemplum fuit toti orbi terrarum, tantum principem, acie jam dimicaturum, stare in templo, & se, & ecclesiam, & imperium, Deo commendare!*

This Divine use of *Musik*, together with the Civil, * St *Chrysostom* dœth thus recommend unto us : *Principale ejus lucrum est, ad Deum Hymnos dicere, Animam Expurgare, Cogitationem in altum tollere, de præsentibus & futuris Philosophari. Habet autem cum his & multam Voluptatem, & Consolationem aliquam, et Recreationem: & facit eum qui canit Gravem, & Venerandum.* For which special Vertues, is this Art worthily preferred before all other, *Theologi* onely excepted. *Planè judico* † (sayth one) *nec pudet asserere, post Theologiam, esse nullam Artem, quæ possit*

*In Psal. 134.

† Luth. in Epist. ad Senfelium Musicum, cited by Calvisius.

DEDICATORIE.

possit Musicæ æquari : nam ipsa sola, post Theologiam, id præstat, quod alioqui sola Theologia præstat : scilicet Quietem & animum lætum. Hence is it, that *Musik* alone, of all the sevn liberall Sciences, is honoured with the highest Degree of Schooles. * Hence is it, that the learnedst of Kings [your most Noble Progenitor] hath graced the Professors of this profound Mystery, with an Emblematicall Coat of Armes : and made them a free Company of the great *Citti*, or third Universiti. Hence is it, that *Charls* the Ninth of France, mooved with the like loov and affection to his intended Musicall Academi, did, with his own hand and great Seal, confirm both it and the Constitutions thereof: professing himself the Protector, and first Auditor of the same. *Mersennus in C. 4. Genes. V. 24. Articulo 15.*

Most Gracious Prince, these two sociated Sisters [*Musik* and *Grammar*] these two liberal Arts, necessary in the liberal education of yuthe, prostrating themselvs at your Highnes feet, humbly pray, that, by your safe conduct, they may freely passe to the ingenuous *Tyroes* of this Land, for the furtherance of Gods Service, and the Godly Solace of good Men ; [the two scopes of these two, and all other the Blessings of our heavenly *Father* :] Who therewith so fill your Heroïk spirit, that, to

the

the Glorie of the Giver, the Happines of the Re-
ceiver, and the Joy of all thoſe that lœv the Peace
and Proſperitie of *Sion*, you may equalize, or rather exceedᶜ even the worthyeſt of your moſt re-
noumed Anceſtors.

Your Highnes

devoted Servant,

CHARLS BUTLER.

THE PREFACE
To ðe READER.

* Vide lib. 2.

E Art of Muſik, (Muſical Reader) for ðe important and manifold * Uſes ðer`c`of, is found ſo
neceſſari in ðe lifᶜ of Man ; ðat even in ðeſᶜ
giddy and nuᶜfangled timᶜs, it is ſtil reteined by
ðe beſt, and in ſoom meſurᶜ reſpeᶜted of all. But
ðe elder wiſer ages, as ðey acknowledged ðe Art to
bǣ ðe moſtᶜ ancient, ſo did ðey higly reverencᶜ ðe Profeſſors ðer`c`of,
eſteeming ðem as Propets and wiſᶜ men among ðem. T imagines

† l. 1. c. 10.

author eſt (ſaiꞇ † Quintilian) omnium in literis ſtudiorum
antiquiſſimum Muſicen extitiſſe : quæ tantum antiquis illis
temporibus, non ſtudii modò, verùm etiam venerationis
habuit, ut ijdem, Muſici, & Vates, & Sapientes, judicaren-
tur. To ðis purpoſ ſpeaket Eccluſ of ðe ancient woordiᶜs of his

* c. 44. v. 4

v. 5.

Nation. * Ðat ðey werᶜ leaders of ðe people by ðeir coun-
ſels, and by ðeir knowledg of learning mæتᶜ for ðe people:
wiſᶜ and eloqent in ðeir inſtructions : ſuᴇ as found out
Muſical Tunᶜs, and recited Verſes, in writing. Suᴇ werᶜ

† vid. l. 2. c. 2.
§ 1. (a) in Not.

Davids ᴄief Muſicians, [† Aſaph, Heman, and Jeduthun, bæing alſo Propets :] of wᴑm ᶜ Heman was ðe Kings Sᴇᴇr : yea ſuᴇ

* 2 Sam. 23. 1.
† Eccluſ. c. 47.

was ðe King himſelf, [*ðe ſweetᶜ Singer of Iſrael:] wᴑmᶜ for ðis
cauſ † ðe ſamᶜ Auᴛor dᴑ`c`t ðus commend.

v. 8. In all his woorks hǣ praiſed ðe Holy Onᶜ moſtᶜ hig, wiᴛ
woords of glori : wiᴛ his wolᶜ hart hǣ Sung ſongs, and loov-
ed him ðat madᶜ him.

9. Hǣ ſet Singers alſo beforᶜ ðe Altar, ðat, by ðeir voices,
ðey miᴦt makᶜ ſwæᴇᶜ Melodi, and daily ſing praiſes in ðeir
Songs. And ſuᴇ werᶜ, among ðe Greekᶜs, ðoſᶜ famous Muſicians and Poëts, Orpheus, Linus, Amphion, Arion, Terpander, Timotheüs, and oðers, men of greᴀt power amᴑng ðe people ;
wᴑmᶜ by ðeir art and wiſdom, ðey browᴦt from a wildᶜ and bru-
¶ ¶   tiſ

The Preſac

tif manner of living, to *Civiliti* and *Moralili.* And der'for' oder
learned men, renowmed for deir wiſdom, wie coold' not attein to
de perfeČtion of deſ', woold' yet bee *Students* of dis divin' *Art'*;
dat, at de leaſt, dey migt hav' ſoom competent knowledg der'of. *Claros nomine Sapientiæ viros, nemo dubitaverit ſtudioſos
Muſices. Of dis number † *Plutark* teſtifyet divin' *Plato* to
bee on' : wo was inſtruČted der'in by two eoic' *Skool'-maſters,*
[*Draco* and *Metellus.*] Studioſiſſimus Muſices fuit Plato :
ut qui Draconem audiviſſet Athenienſem, & Metellum
Agrigentinum. And * *Quintilian,* dat Socrates [*Plato's*
maſter, de † wiſeſt of *Piloſopers*] was an oder : wo having neg-
leČted de ſtuddi of dis profitable and neceſſari Art (as himſelf callet
it) in his yut', was fain to learn it in his old' ag'. * Socrates
jam ſenex inſtitui Lyrâ non erubeſcebat : and himſelf ſait
dat † Connus was his *Maſter,* wo taugt him *Muſik* : for de-
fenc' wer'of hee mad' dis anſwer ; * Dat it was not unmeet' for
him to learn kings wie befor' hee had not known, beeing ſo profitable for dis lif'. Objurgantibus reſpondit, nequaquam abſur-
dum eſſe ea diſcere, quæ prius neſciviſſet communi vitæ tam
utilia & neceſſaria eſſe.

 Neider hat dis profitable and neceſſari Profeſſion been mor'
acceptable unto de *Wiſ'* and *Learned,* dan to de great and migty
Potentat's of de world. *Elfred or Alfred a *Saxon King,* [de
mirrour of Princes, Founder of de moſt' famous Univerſiti] beſid's
his knowledg in oder Arts, his many *Moral* and *Divin' Vertu's,*
was moſt' skilful in *Muſik* : wer'of in his greateſt *Extremiti,* hee
mad' greater uſ', dan of all his oder bot' inward and outward *Helps.*
†*Hadrian* de *Emperour* was an excellent *Poet,* and *Muſician,*
bot' for de *Theori* and de *praČtic'.* De *Emperour* * *Alexander
Severus,* renowmed for his *Vertu'* and *Pieti,* was learned in de
Matematiks, and eſpecially in *Muſik.* De warlik *King* † *Henri*
de *Eigt* of *England,* did not on'ly ſing his *Part'* ſur', but himſelf
compoſed a *Servic'* of 4, 5, and 6 *Part's* : as *Eraſmus* teſtifyet
of his own knowledg. * De *Duk'* of *Venoſa,* an *Italian Princ',*
of lat' yeer's, compoſed many rar' ſongs ; wie Mr. Peacham
affirmet himſelf to hav' ſeec'n. But † de *Landgrav'* of *Heſſen,* in
deſ' days carryet away de *Palm* for excellenci, not on'ly in *Muſik,* but in watſoever is to bee wiſed in a brav' *Princ'.* I hav'
ſeec'n

* *Quintil. l. 1. c. 10.*

† *De Muſica.*

* *Q. Ibidem.*

† *So judged by de Oracle of Apollo. v. Academic. Quæſt. l. 1.*

* *Quint. ibid.*
† *Plato in Menexeno. Connum habeo præcepto-rem Muſices.*

* *Eraſm. lib. 3. Apophthegm. 92.*

* *Speed' Chron. lib. 7. c. 36.*

† *Idem lib. 6. c. 17.*
* *ibid c. 27.*

† *Mr. Peacham in his Complet' Gentleman.*

* *Idem ibidem*

† *Ibidem.*

ſecᵉn (ſaiꝺ ꝺis Autor) 9 or 10 Sets of Motets, and ſolemn Muſik, ſet purpoſᵉly for ꜧis own Cappel : werᵉ, for ꝺe morᵉ ꜧonour
of ſᴍm Feſtival, and ſᴍmtimᵉs, for ꜧis Recreation onᶜly, ꜧee is
ꜧis own Organiſt.

De loov and honour wiᴇ, for ꝺe profitable and neceſſari Uſes of
ꝺis Art, ꝺe ᴄief of Men [as wel ꝺe Wiſᵉ and Learned as ꝺe Princes
and Monarks of ꝺe eartꜧ]ꝺᴍᶜ giv unto it, Ulyſſes, in Homer,
for ꝺe ſamᵉ reaſons, reqireꞇ from all men.   * Odyſſ. Θ

> * Πᾶσι γὰρ ἀνθρόποισιν ἐπιχθονίοισιν, Ἀοιδοὶ
> Τιμῆς ἔμμοϱϱι εἰσι, κỵὶ αἰδ ὅς.

Omnibus enim hominibus mortalibus, Muſici
Honore digni ſunt & Reverentia.

Hencᵉ is it, ꝺat as for ꝺe excellenci of Homers Poeſi, ꝺe † Colophonii, Chii, Salaminii, Smyrnæi, and oꝺer peoples did
all ᴄallengᵉ Homer to bee ꝺeir Countriman ; ſo, for ꝺe ſamᵉ cauſ,
divers Countris ꝺᴍᶜ claim ꝺe Inventer of ꝺis Art to bee ꝺeirs.
Sᴍm wil havᵉ Orpheus, ſᴍm Linus : [two ancient famous
Poets and Muſicians:] of wꝺomᵉ, Virgil, Eclog. 4.

> Non me Carminibus vincet nec Thracius Orpheus,
> Nec Linus ; huic mater quamvis, atq; huic pater adſit :
> Orphei Calliopeia, Lino formoſus Appollo.

And ſᴍm wil havᵉ Amphion, him woſᵉ Muſik dreaw Stonᵉs
to ꝺe buildingᷤ of ꝺe walls of Thebᵉs ; (* Movit Amphion la-
pides canendo) as Orpheus tamed wildᵉ Beaſts, and madᵉ
Trees to dancᵉ after his Harp :

> † Mulcentem Tigres, & agentem Carmine Quercus.

By wiᴇ, ꝺe ſamᵉ Poet, in * an oꝺer placᵉ, ſeweꞇ an oꝺer ꞇing
to bee ment : to wit, ꝺat by ꝺe vertuᵉ of ꝺeir wiſ and pleaſing
Muſicall Poems, ꝺe onᵉ browᷤꞇ ꝺe ſavagᵉ and beaſt-likᵉ Thra-
cians to humaniti and gentlenes ; ꝺe oꝺer perſwaded ꝺe rudᵉ and
carᶜles Thebans to ꝺe fortiſying of ꝺeir Citti, and to a Civil converſation.

> Sylveſtres homines ſacer interpreſq; Deorum
> Cædibus, & victu fœdo deterruit Orpheus :
> Dictus ab hoc lenire Tigres, rapidoſq; Leones,

‡ Cicero pro Ar-
chia. Homerum
Colophonii Ci-
vem eſſe dicunt,
ſuum : Chii ſu-
um vendicant :
Salaminii repe-
tunt : Smyrnæi
verò ſuum eſſe
contendunt. &c.
But Gellius l. 3.
c. 1. reciteꞇ 7
Citti's ꝺat did
ᴄalleng his
birꞇ. Septem
urbes certant de
Stirpe inſignis
Homeri : Smyr-
na, Rhodos, Co-
lophon, Salamis,
Chios, Argos.
Athenæ.
* Horat. Carm.
l. 3. Ode 11.
† Georg. 4.
* In Arte Po-
etica.

Dictus & *Amphion*, Thebanæ Conditor arcis,
Saxa movere sono.Teſtudinis,& prece blandâ
Ducere quò vellet.

Alþoug þat wiᴄ is ſpoken of þe wildᶜ beaſts, Tulli affirmᵉ̃
to bee truᶜ in þe proper ſens. † Beſtiæ ſæpe immanes cantu
flectuntur, atq; conſiſtunt. Þis þing teſtifyeþ Henricus Stephanus * werᶜ hœ ſaith, þat hee ſaw in London, a *Lion* þat left
his meat to hear *Muſik* ; qui Muſicen audiendi gratiâ epulas
ſuas deſereret. Cælius Rhodoginus noteþ out of Strabo, þat
*Elepᵃts ar delighted wiþ Singing, and þe ſound of Tabrets : and
out of* Plutarch *in* Sympoſiacis, *þat moſt brutᶜ beaſts ar pleaſed
and affected wiþ Muſik : as þe Harts wiþ Pipes, and Dolphins
wiþ Singing, and þe Harmoni of þe Harp. And þe* Pythagoreans
(*as* † Ælianus *writeþ*) *affirm, þat of all beaſts þerᶜ is nonᶜ þat
is not delighted wiþ Harmoni, but onᶜly þe Aſ.* Pythagorei affir-
mant ſolum, ex omnibus animalibus, Aſinum ad harmoniam factum non eſſe.

Oþers aſcribᶜ þe Invention of þis Art to Mercuri : becaus hee
found out þe * firſt Inſtrument by þe Tortois-ſel. Oþers to þe
Muſes, of wom it haþ its namᶜ. And oþers to Apollo,[þe Preſident
of þe Muſes :] wo ſayþ of himſelf, þat bee invented boþ Poeſi and
ſtring-inſtruments :
† Per me concordant Carmina Nervis :
as ſœm ſay þat *Pan was þe Inventer of windᶜ-inſtruments :*
* Pan primus calamos cerâ conjungere plures
Inſtituit.————andſœm,*Minerva :* † Antiqui aiunt
Minervam Tibiæ repertricem. All wiᴄ and oþers migᵗ
haply bee, in þeir ſeveral countriᶜs, eiþer Autors or auctors of Muſik and muſical Inſtruments : for wiᴄ þey werᶜ in þeir timᶜs ad-
mired. But þe people of God dœᶜ truᶜly acknowledg a far morᶜ ancient Inventer of þis divinᶜ Art : [Jubal þe ſœn of Lamech
þe ſixt from Adam :] of wom it is ſaid, þat * hee was þe Faþer
of all þat handle þe Harp and Organ : i. of all Inſtruments,
† boᵗᶜ Entata and Empneuſta : wiᴄ Inſtruments dœᶜ neceſſarily impliᶜ þe Voicᶜ,[þe Ground and foundation of þem boþᶜ.]And
St. Auguſtinᶜ goeþ yet farþer : ſewing þat it is þe gift of God
himſelf, and a Repreſentation or Adminition of þe ſweetᶜ Concent
and

† Pro Archia
Poëta.

* In his Prefacᶜ
to Poëtæ prin-
cipes, ſet out by
himſelf.

† Hiſt. anima-
lium, l.10 c.29.

* V. l. 1. c. 2.
§ 2. (f)

† Metam. l. 1.
in fine.

* Virgil Ecl 2.

† Ariſt. Polit.
l. 8. c. 6.

* Geneſ. 4. 21.

† Vide l. 2. c. 1.
§ 1. (a) (b) in
Notis.
Muſica Dei do-
num.

to Þe READER.

and *Harmoni, wiꞓ his wisdom hað madꞓ in ðe Creation and Administration of ðe world.* * Non enim fruſtrà per Prophetam (qui hæc divinitus inſpirata didicerat) dictum eſt de Deo, † qui profert numeroſè ſeculum. Unde Muſica, [i. Scientia benè modulandi] ad admonitionem magnæ rei etiam, mortalibus rationales habentibus animas, Dei Largitate, conceſſa eſt. &c.

> * *Epiſt.* 28. *ad Hieronymum.*
> †*Eſai.* 40. 12. 26. *and* 28.

But aldowꞡ Muſik bee ðe **gift of God ; yet, likꞓ oðer his graces and benefits, it is not given to ðe Idle : ðey ðat wil havꞓ it, muſt reaꞓ it to ðem wið ðe hand of Induſtri.   To put in practicꞓ ðe Inꞓentions, and woorks of skilful Artiſts, [i. to Sing and to Play wel] (by reaſon of ðe many Accidents of ðe Notꞓs, ðe ſudden ꞓanging, or riſing and falling, of ðe voiꞓꞓ, and ðe truꞓ & reddy Fingering and Stopping of ðe Inſtruments, in ſo many ſundry Leſſons) is noꞓ Eaſy matter : but artificially to ſet ðoſꞓ Leſſons to voices and inſtruments, is a woork ſo ful of Difficulti and deepꞓ ſpeculation, (by reaſon of ðe multitudꞓ and great varieti of Rulꞓs and obſervations, and of ſecret Myſteriꞓs, wiꞓ lyꞓ hid in ðis profound Matematik) ðat a skilful and expert Compoſer († aldowꞡ hee bee firſt furniſhed wit a moſtꞓ excellent Wit, Memori, and Judgment, and a naturall Aptnes and procliviti unto it ; and morꞓover bee wel Seeꞓn, and exerciſed, in ðe coiſeſt patterns of ðe beſt Muſicians) ſall findꞓ ðe Proverb verifyed in his woork, χάλεπα τα Καλα : Difficilia quæ pulchra.*

> **Vid. l.* 2. *c.* 3. § 1.
>
> †*V. Epil. lib.* 1.

Sæing ðerefoꞓ (Ingenuous Reader) ðis myſterious and cœleſtiall Art, for ðe Antiqiti, for ðe Autors, for ðe various Uſes and effects ðerꞓof, trooꞡ its various Moodꞓs, Melodi, and Harmoni, wit ðeir ſweetꞓ Ornaments, (boꞓ in humanꞓ and divinꞓ offices)haꞓ been, is, and deſerveꞓ eꞓer to bee, eſteemed and affected of all men ; wꞓat remaineꞓ, but ðat ðey wꞓo ar capable of it, dooꞓ Studdi and Practicꞓ it ; and ðat ðey who ar not, dooꞓ Honour and Reverencꞓ it, and ðe Profeſſors ðerꞓof ; ðe ſweetꞓ fruit of woſꞓ ſerious Studdiꞓs, and ſacred Rapturꞓs, in ſo many good Uſes, ðey happily enjoy ?   Wootton, April 4. 1636.

CHAR. BUTLER.

TO
His friend Mr *Charls Butler*,
Upon his Book^e of Muſik.

S I R, I am ſatisfi'd: ſinc^e you hav^e ſown,
By ðis Book^e, all ðe former wer^e your own.
Ðis is ðe Syſtem : doſ^e ðe Praktik Parts
Of Natur^es rarer Muſik, and of Arts.
For wæt, Grav^e Butler, is ðy Syngeni,
But Natur^es two-part-Song ? Wat is ðy Bee,
[Ðat little, buſi ðing wee ſo admir^e]
Wat is it els, but Natur^es complet^e Qir^e ?
As for ðy Grammar, ðer^e I earmed bý^e
Wit Conſonants and Vowels Harmoni^e.
Wen ðoſ^e ſweet^e Accents hav^e my Senſes ſtol^e,
Ðy Rhetorik ðen robs mee òf my Sowl^e.

Enoug, good Butler : Stay ðy Qil : and her^e
Writ^e not ta raviſ, but t'inſtruct our ear.

HUM. NEWTON Bac. Mag. Col.

Pythago. in
Macrob. de Som.
Scip. Lib. 2. c. 1.

IN Mri. *CAROLI BVTLERI* Muſicam.

Sydereis alii referunt ſua Carmina Gyris,
Et geminis accepta Polis modulamina. Sunt qui
   Stridente, in vacuis, Euro aut Aquilone, Cavernis,
   Edidicere ſonos : ſic olim Fiſtulá nata eſt,
   Dum *Pan* inſequitur Syringa, &, murmure ducto
   Ad numerum, mediis ſuſpirat anhelus avenis.
Vulcano tribuunt alii primordia, & Artem
   Multiſonos duræ revocant Incudis ad ictus.

Inter Apes didicit *Butlerus* amabile Carmen :
Concentuſq; avidâ dum captat ab aure, canoros
Deprendit Litui fremitus : dumq; applicat acres
   Alveolis ſenſus, graviorem Tympana pulſum
   Edunt ; & miſto fervent præſepia Cantu.
Verùm audiſſe parum eſt, tam te communia tangunt
Commoda : quin repetens *Hyblæ* murmura Gentis,
Imprimis : & toti proſtat Symphonia Plebi.

Attica Melliflui non ultrà Terra *Platonis*
Jactet in ore favum, & teneræ Cunabula Prolis
Plena thymo : *Butlere,* tibi par gratulor Omen:
Namq; tuis etiam ſedêre Examina Labris.

S AM. E V A N S. *Nov. Col. Soc.*

To de learned Autor.

ONe Imp has made Iov's brain admir'd :
   Din has teem'd ſix, yet is not tyr'd :
Thy *Grammar, Rhet'rik, Monark,* c,
   Muſik, Orator, Syngene c.

Touching dy preſent Book, I'le ſay,
   D'aſt turn'd our Muſiks nigt to day :
Wat erſt was Diſcant, it may bee
   Heer learn'd as Plain-ſong nou from dee.

      Butler, d'aſt drawn all Muſik drie,
      De Learners firſt to ſatisfie.

Jo. P I N C K Art. *Mag. Nov. Col. Oxon.*

Ðe
Printer to Ðe READER.

Aldowg ðe Antiqiti, Certainti, and Faciliti, of ðe Ortogra-
pi or tru᷄ writing, uſed in ðis and oðer Bok᷄s, bee ſufficiently
demonſtrated in ðe Engliʒ Grammer ; yet, becaus ðe Aſpirat᷄s (ꝫ ie in-
deed᷄ ar moſt᷄ eaſy) ſæm᷄ to ſom, at ðe firſt ſigt, difficult and obſcur᷄ ; I
ꝧowgt it not amis, in ðis vacant pag᷄ to explan᷄ ðem, by ðeir ſim-
ple Conſonants and ðe Letter of Aſpiration [H:] of ꝫ ie ðey ar noting
els, but Abbreviations.

Theta, or *Thau*.	ꚋ		th, lik᷄ Θ or Ꮒ : *as in* ꚋiſſel, ꚋank.
Dhaleth.	ꝺ		dh, lik᷄ ꝩ : *as in* ꝺis, ꝺat.
	ꞓ		ch, ———— *as in* ꞓain, ꞓapter.
Khi, or *Khaph*.	k	is	kh, lik᷄ χ or Ɔ : *as in* karaꞓter, Tikicus.
Ghimel.	g		gh, lik᷄ ꝫ : *as in* hig, migti.
Phi, or *Phe*.	p		ph, lik᷄ φ or Ꙫ : *as in* pyſik, piloſoper.
Shin.	ſ		sh, lik᷄ ꙍ : *as in* ſall, ſibbolet.
	w		wh, ———— *as in* wat, wen.

Not᷄ heer᷄, ðat, of all ðe 8 Aſpirat᷄s, Ꞓ and W ar peculiar to ðe
Engliſ : ðe reſt ar common to oðer Languages wiꝺ ours : You may
bee pleaſed alſo to obſerv, ðat E Sonant and E Silent, becaus different in
poꙴer and uſ᷄, ar for ðe Readers eaz, differenced in Figur᷄ alſo. And ðat
Q beeing (as ðe Nam᷄ importeꝺ) an Abbreviation of C or K and V, an o-
ðer V after it, having no᷄ uſ᷄, is ðer᷄for᷄ omitted, as ſuperfluous. See ðe
Prefac᷄ to ðe Grammar, and eac᷄ Letter in his plac᷄.

J. HAVILAND.

DE
PRINCIPLES
OF
MUSIK.

LIB. I. CAP. I. *Of* ðe Mood's.

USIK is ðe (ᵃ) Art of (ᵇ) modulating Not's in (ᶜ) voic' or inſtrument. Đe wie, having a great (ᵈ) power over ðe affections of ðe mind', by its various Mood's producet in ðe hearers various effects.

Đeſ' Mood's ar (ᵉ) fiv' : [Dorik, Lydian, Æolik, Prygian, and Ionik.]

(ᶠ) Đe Dorik Mood' conſiſtet of ſober ſlow-timed Not's, generally in Counter-point, ſet to a Pſalm or oder pious Canticle, in Mæter or Rhytmical vers : ðe not's anſwering ðe number of ðe Syllables. Đis moovet to ſobrieti, prudenc', modeſti, and godlines. *Vide* (ᵉ) *in Notis.*

(ᵍ) Đe Lydian Mood' is a grav', ful, ſolemn Muſik in Diſcant, for ðe moſt part', of ſlow tim', ſet to a Hymn, Antem, or oder ſpiritual ſong in proſ', and ſoomtim' in vers, ðe not's exceeding often ðe number of ðe ſyllables : wie trœg his heavenly harmoni, raviſhet ðe mind' wit a kind' of ecſtaſi, lifting it up from ðe regard' of early ðings, unto ðe deſir' of celeſtiall joyz : (*Vid.* (ᵉ) *in Notis*) wie it doo't liv'ly reſemble. *Vid.* ☞ *in cap.* 3. § 1.

A

Đe

(ᵃ) (ᵇ)

(ᶜ)

(ᵈ)

(ᵉ)
Quinq; Modi Muſices.
Đe 5 Mood's.

1
Dorik.
(ᶠ)

2
Lydian.
(ᵍ)

3
Æolik.
(h)

De (h) *Æolik* Mood' is dat, wi-e, wit its soft pleasing sounds, pacifyet de Passions of de mind', and wit instruments or dittiles *fa-la's,* in continued discant, deligting de sens, and not intending de mind' of de hearer, like Mercuri's *Caduceus,* earmet affections and car's, and so lullet him sweet'ly a sleep'. *Vid.* (e) *in Notis.*

4
Prygian.
(i)

De (i) *Prygian* Mood' is a manly and coorragious kind' of Musik, wi-e, wit his stat'ly, or loud and violent ton's, rouset de spirit, and inciteth to arms and activiti : sue ar Marees, Almains, and de warlike sounds of Trumpet, Fif's, and Drum. *Vid.* (e) *in Notis.*

5
Ionik.
(k)

De (k) *Ionik* Mood' is contrary to de Prygian : an effeminat' and delicat' kind' of Musik, set unto pleasant songs and sonnets of loov, and sue lik' fanci's, for honest mirt and deligt, ciefly in feasting and oder merriments. *Vid.* (e) *in Notis.*

(l)

And soom Musik is compounded of soom or all of des' : as de Battel-galliard. For all wi-e various effects, dis (l) Matematical Art and sevnt liberal Scienc', hat ben always re-

(m)
(n)

spected, and used, of all sorts of people, as wel (m) learned and ingenuous, as (n) ignorant and barbarous.

* *Vid.* (e) *in
Notis.*
† *V. c. 3. § 4.
¶ 4. &* (d)
in Notis.
(o)
* *V.* (b) & (c)
in c. 3, § 4, ¶ 4.
† *Ibidem.*

Des' 5 Mood's, wi-e *Cælius Rhodoginus* (out of *Cassiodorus,* or rader King *Theodorius* Epistle to *Boetius*) rigtly descritbet * by de Effects, soom Defin' and Distinguif (as dey doo' de Airs) by de final Key of de Bas' : or † rader by its (o) Constituted Ton') but Skilful Musicians know hou to form any Mood' in any Key or Ton' indifferently : so it be * conformable to de Air of the † Subject.

ANNOTATIONS to CAP. I.

* *Politic. l.* 8.
c. 3.

(a) AN *Art.* So *Aristotle* : * *Veteres inter Disciplinas Musicam collocaverunt, ex eo quòd Natura quærit non solùm in negotio recte, verum etiam in otio laudabiliter posse versari.* And *Boetius* : *Cùm sint quatuor Mathesios disciplinæ ; cætera quidem ad investigationem veritatis laborant : Musica verò non modò speculationi, verùm etiam moralitati conjuncta est.*

† *De Musica,
l. 1, c. 2.*

(b) *Modulating.* So doo't † S' *Augustin'* defin' it : *Musica est scientia bene modulandi.* De proper differenc' wer' of he doo't dus der' maintein.

Modulatio

Modulatio *poteſt ad ſolam Muſicam pertinere ; quamvis* modus, *unde fle-xum verbum eſt, poſſit etiam in aliis rebus eſſe.*

(c) *Voic' or inſtrum.* Þus in effect doo't þat holy *Faðer divid' : Sonus triplex eſt : aut in voce animantis, aut in eo quod ſtatus in Organis faceret, aut in eo quod pulſu ederetur.* By þe firſt, meaning vocal Mu-ſik ; (wie is þe eief) by þe ſecond, þe muſik of Organs and oðer wind-inſtruments ; by þe third, þe Harp or Lute, or oðer inſtrument þat ſoun-deþ by touꞓ or ſtrok'.

† Tom. 1. de ordine l. 2.

( ) † *Tullius. Aſſentior ego* Platoni, *nihil tam facilè in animos teneros atq; molles inſtuere ; quam varios canendi modos : quorum dici vix poteſt, quanta ſit vis in utramq; partem. Nam & incitat languentes, & langue-facit excitatos ; & tum remittit animos, tum contrahit : civitatumq; hoc multarum in* Grecia *interfuit, antiquum vocum ſervare modum ; quaru mores lapſi ad mollitiem, pariter ſunt immutati cum cantibus.* Þus Plato : and after him * Ariſtotle. *In melodijs ipſis ſunt imitationes morum : & hoc eſt manifeſtum : ſtatim enim † harmoniarum diſtincta eſt natura ; ita ut qui audiunt aliter diſponantur, nec eodem modo ſe habeant ad unamquanq; ipſarum : ſed ad quaſdam flebiliter & contractè magis, ad quaſdam molliùs ſecundùm mentem : ad aliam verò mediocriter & compoſitè plurimùm : ut videtur* Dorica *facere ſola omnium* harmoniarum. Þeſ' various effects were lik'wiſ' obſerved by † Macrobius. *Omnis habitus animi, cantibus gu-bernatur : nam dat cantus ſomnos, adimitq; : nec non curas immittit, & retrabit : iramſuggerit, & clementiam ſuadet : &c.* And by S⁺ * Iſidor'. *Omnes affectus noſtri, pro ſonorum diverſitate, vel novitate (neſcio qua oc-culta familiaritate) excitantur magis, cùm ſuavi & artificioſa voce canta-ur.* Alſo by *Caſſiodorus,* or raðer King † *Theodorius,* mor' at larg'. *Mu-ſica cum de ſecreto Naturæ, tanquam ſenſuum Regina, tropis ſuis ornata pro-ceſſerit, reliquæ cogitationes exiliunt ; omniaq; facit ejici, ut ipſam ſolum-modo delectet audiri. Triſtitiam noxiam jucundat : tumidos furores atte-nuat : cruentam ſævitiam efficit blandam : excitat ignaviam, ſoporantemq; languorem : vigilantibus reddit ſaluberrimam quietem : vitiatam turpi amore, ad honeſtum ſtudium revocat, caſtitatem : ſanat mentis tædium bo-nis cogitationibus ſemper adverſum : pernicioſa odia convertit ad auxilia-tricem gratiam : & (quod beatum genus curationis eſt) per dulciſſimas vo-luptates expellit animi paſſiones : incorpoream animam corporaliter mulcet, & ſolo auditu ad quod vult deducit.*

† De legibus l. 2.

* *Polit. l. 8. c. 5.*
† *I. Modorum.*

* *Seu modorum.*
† *L. 2. de Som-nio.* Scip.
* *De Eccleſiaſt. officiis. lib. 1. cap. 5.*
† *Epiſt. ad Boe-tium Muſicum :* wie is þe 40. Epiſt. in *Caſſio-dorus.*

(e) Fiv'. As * *Cœlius Rhodiginus* obſerveþ out of þe abov-cited E-piſtle. *Quid Caſſiodorus (ſait hee) ſuper modis* Muſicæ *prodat, attenden-dum magnopere.* Modus *Dorius prudentiæ largitor eſt, & caſtitatis effector :* Phrygius *pugnas excitat, votum furoris inflammat :* Æolius *animi tempe-ſtates tranquillat, ſomnumq; jam placatis attribuit :* Lydius *intellectum ob-tuſis acuit, & terreno deſiderio gravatis cæleſtium appetentiam inducit, bonorum operator eximius. Adjicitur à pleriſq;* Ionicus, *quem floridum in-telligunt ac jucundum.* But † *Martianus Capella,* making 3 degre'es of cæ of þeſ' fiv', accounteþ in all 15. D O R I U S, Hypodorius, Hyper-dorius : L Y D I U S. Hypolydius, Hyperlydius : Æ O L I C U S, Hy-poæolicus, Hyperæolicus : P H R Y G I U S, Hypophrygius, Hyperphry-gius :

* *Variarum l. 9. c. 3.*

† As *Glareanus* haþ *Dodeca-cordi. l. 1. c. 21.*

gius : IONICUS, Hypoionicus, Hyperionicus. In all wie *Hypo* signifieꞇ a defeꞔt, and *Hyper* an exceſ of ðe Mœdͨ principal.

Sœm ancient Muſicians madͨ but two Mœdͨs, [Dorik and Prygian:] referring all oðer unꞇo ðem. † *Quidam in harmoniis poſuerunt duas ſpecies, [unam Doricam, alteram Phrygiam:] cæteras omnes vel ad Doricam, vel ad Phryg am referunt.*

† *Ariſt. Pol. l. 4. c. 3.*

Ðe fivͨ Mœdͨs by wie ðoſͨ various effeꞔts ar wrowgꞇ, * *Caſſiodorus* ſewex to havͨ ðeir ſeverall appellations of ðe Countriͨs, in wie, according to ðeir ſeverall manners and diſpoſitions, ðey werͨ invented and praꞔticed. *Hoc totum* (ſaiꞇ hee) *quinque modis agitur : qui ſinguli provinciarum, ubi reperti ſunt, nominibus vocitantur :* as likͨwiſͨ * *Boetius : Modi Muſici Gentium vocabulo deſignati ſunt. Quo enim unaquæꝗ gens gaudet, eodem Modus ipſe vocabulo nuncupatur.*

☞ * In ðe abovͨ-cited Epiſt.

* *Muſic. l. 1. c. 1.*

Ðe firſt haꞇ his namͨ of *Doria* a civil part of Græcͨ, neerͨ Aꞇens : ðe oðer 4 had ðeir beginnings and namͨs from certain Regions of Aſia minor, wie bordering upon Græcͨ werͨ peopled by Græcian Coloniͨs.

1 Dorik.

Ðe *Lydian* Mœdͨ was ſo called of *Lydia*, famous for ðe golden River *Paꞔtolus*, and ðe winding reꞇrogradͨ *Mæander :* ðe onͨ reſembling ðe treaſurͨ and glorious matter of ðe Ditti ; ðe oðer ðe pleaſing Reports and Reverts, wiꞇ oðer admirable varietiͨs of ðe Muſik. Ðe ꞔief citties ar *Piladelpia*, and *Sardis* [the royall ſeat of rich *Cræſus*.]

2 Lydian.

Ðe *Æolik* of *Æolia* [ðe Kingdom of *Æolus*] wencͨ hee is feined to ſend his ruſſling windͨs : ðe wie dœͨ heerin reſemble ðis Mœdͨ, ꝺaꞇ ðey alſo havͨ a ſopiting faculti.

3 Æolik.

Ðe *Prygian* Mœdͨ of *Prygia*, a region bordering upon Lydia and Caria : in wie is *Cios* ꝺat martiall Marꞇ-toun, and ðe moſt high hil *Ida*, famous for the Trojan war.

4 Prygian.

Ðe *Ionian* of *Ionia*, wie lyeꞇ between *Æolia* and *Caria* ; for ðe gœdnes of aier and ðe commodious ſituation, inferiour to nonͨ of ðe Aſian Regions : woſͨ plenty and idlenes turned ðeir honeſt mirꞇ into † laſcviouſnes : as *Athenæus* obſerved in his timͨ : * *Noſtra ætate Ionum mores deliciis ſunt perditiſſimi : eorumꝗ itidem Cantus ab iꝇo vetuſto multùm diverſus.* It was adorned wiꞇ 12 great cittiͨs werof *Epheſus* and *Miletus* werͨ two.

5 Ionik.

† *Vide l. 2. c. 3. §4.* (b) *in Notis.* * *Deipnoſophiſt: l. 14.*

Ðis Mœdͨ is alſo called *Modus Chromaticus* [*i. coloratus, fucatus,*] of *Chroma, color :* becaus as piꞔturͨs ar beautifyed wiꞇ trim livͨly cœllors, to pleaz ðe wanton ey ; ſo ðis kindͨ is as iꞇ werͨ cœllored wiꞇ delicaꞇ livͨly ſounds to pleaz ðe wanton ear.

1 Dorik.

(f) Of ðe *Dorik* Mœdͨ ar ðe Pſalms in Meeter : and all gravͨ and honeſt ſongs : ſuͨe as is, *Like to ðe Damask-roſe we ſee,*———&c. ðe Auꞇor werͨ of is Mͬ F. *Quarles*: wo haꞇ written many excellent Divinͨ Pœems. Ðe wolͨ bookͨ of Pſalms was latͨly ſet forꞇͨ in 4 Parts by Mͬ *Thomas Ravenſcroft,* compoſed by Iohn *Farmer,* Th. *Morley,* G. *Kirby, Thomas* and *Iohn Tomkins, R. Alliſon, I. Milton,* and ſundry oðers : but ðe greateſt partͨ by him ꝺat ſet ðem out.

Of ðis Mœdͨ werͨ ðoſͨ ſober feaſt-hymns, wœnt to bee ſung in ðe praiz

praiz of honourable men: wie * *Tulli* remembreth. *Vtinam extarent* † 38.
illa carmina quæ multis seclis ante suam ætatem in epulis esse cantitata à
singulis conviviis, de clarorum virorum laudibus, in Originibus scriptum
reliquit Cato. In † an oðer plac', to ðe voic' is added ðe Recorder or †*Tuscul. Quæst.*
Shalm. *Gravißimus anthor in Originibus dixit Cato. Morem apud Majo-* *lib. 4.*
res hunc epularum fuisse, ut deinceps qui accubavent, canerent ad tibiam
clarorum virorum laudes: alðowg ðe *Pytagoreans* seemed raðer to affect
ðe Harp or other string-instruments, becaus every on' by himself might
sing and play upon *Entata* togeðer. Ðis Mœd', for ðe Moraliti and Me- * *V. l. 2. c. 1. § 1.*
diocriti ðer'of (I may ad for faciliti) ðe Pilosoper adviset to bee first † *Polit. l. 8. c. 7.*
learned of yung beginners. † *Manifestum* (inquit) *quòd Doricam præ* 2
cæteris decens est junioribus addiscere. *Lydian.*

( ) Of ðe *Lydian* Mœd' ar ðos' solemn Hymns and oðer sacred
Chyre-songs, called *Moteta, à motu:* becaus ðey mœv' ðe harts of ðe
hearers, striking into ðem a devout and reverent regard of him for wœs'
praiz ðey wer' mad'. Ðes' Motets requir' most' Art, of all Musik, in Setting: fitly to take Discords and Bindings, using plain, soft, sweet' Discan-
ting, wiɛ freqent, grac'full Reports and Reverts. Agreeable unto ðe art
of ðe *Setters* sœld' bee ðe art of *Singers:* sweet'ly and plainly to expres
ðe words and syllables of ðe Ditti, ðat ðey may bee understœd of ðe
Congregation: and beeing lik' ðeir *Motets* [grav', sober, holy] to sing
wiɛ a grac' to ðe Lord in ðeir harts. *V. l. 2. c. 1. § 2.* ꝗ and *c. 2. § 5.*

Of ðis Mœd' seem' ðos' religious vouz of ðe *Romans* in ðeir sacrifices;
and ðeir grav' Canzons at ðe solemn feasts of ðeir Magistrat's: of wie
† *Tulli; Neq; verò illud non eruditorum temporum argumentum est, quòd in* † *Tuscul. Quæst.*
Deorum pulvinaribus, & epulis Magistratuum, fides præcinunt. And lik' *lib. 4.*
wis' ðos' funeral Elegi's of Noble men, commanded in ðe old' Roman * *Cicero de le-*
Lawz. " *Honoratorum virorum laudes in Concione memorantor: easq; e-* *gib. l. 2.*
tiam ad cantum tibicinis prosequuntur, cui nomen Nænia: *quo vocabulo*
etiam Græci cantus lugubres nominant.

Of ðis Mœd' is ðat passionat' Lamentation of ðe good musical King,
for ðe deaɛ of his *Absalom:* Composed in 5. Parts by M' *Th. Tomkins,*
nou. Organist of his Majesti's Chappel. Ðe melodious harmoni wer'of,
wen I heard in ðe *Musik-skœl',* weiðer I sœld' mor' admir' ðe sweet'
wel governed voices (wiɛ consonant Instruments) of ðe Singers; or ðe
exqisit Invention, wit, and Art of ðe Composer, it was hard to determin.

Ðes' *Nænia* or funeral Elegi's, seem' to hav' been ðe first us' of ðis
Mœd': as *Cælius Rhodoginus* observet in ðe plac' of *Caßiodorus* befor'
cited. *Prima Lydii modi constitutio fletus lamentationisq; causâ facta est.*
Nam Aristoxenus in primo de Musica, Olympum tradit in Pythonis sepul-
tura cecinisse tibiâ, secundùm Lydium modum, funeralia.

Ðis stat'ly Mœd' ðe Pilosoper preferret befor' all. † *LYDIA* † *Polit l. 8. c. 7.*
maximè omnium Harmoniarum ornatum simul, doctrinamq; affert. 3

(h) Of ðe *Æolik* Mœd' * was that Enchanting Musik of ðe Harp, *Æolik.*
provided for King *Saul,* wen ðe evil spirit trubbled him: wie Musik * I Sam. 16.
beeing mad' by on' ðat was cunning, and cœld play well, so charmed ðe
evil

evil spirit; ðat *Saul was refreſed, and was wel; and ðe evil spirit departed from him.*

Of ðis Mood' was ðe Patetical ſong of ðe god Biſhop *Flavianus:* wʒ iʒ moved pitti in ðe Emperour *Theodoſius,* and procured Pardon for ðe peoples oſſenc'.

† Soʒomen hiſt. Eccleſ. l.7. c. 23. † *Populus Antiochenus Theodoſi Imperatoris iram metuens ob ſeditionem exortam, Deo melodiis quibuſdam lugubribus ſupplicabat. Flavianus quoq, epiſcopus, cùm pro civibus apud Imperatorem adhuc offenſum intercederet, perſuadet adoleſcentibus, qui ad menſam Imperatoris canere ſolebant, ut pſalmodias canerent quæ in Supplicationibus Antiochenorum uſurpabantur. Quo facto, ferunt Imperatorem miſericordiá ſuperatum, confeſtim iram poſuiſſe & urbi reconciliatum.*

Of ðis Mood' was ðat calm Symponi wer' wiʒ *Achilles* appeaſed his own Paſſions againſt *Agamemnon:* as *De Muſica.* own Paſſions againſt *Agamemnon:* as * *Plutarch* notes out of *Homer. Oſtendens enim Muſicam multis in rebus eſſe conducibilem, introduxit Achillem, qui iram adverſus Agamemnonem ſuam concoqueret Muſicæ operâ, quam didicerat à ſapientiſſimo Chirone, Muſicæ ſimul, & juſtitiæ, ac Medicinæ Doctore.*

Of ðis Mood' also was ðe Pytagorean Evn-ſong, mentioned by *† Lib. 9. c. 4.* † *Quintilian. Qui cum ſomnum peterent, ad Lyram prius lenire mentes ſolebant; ut, ſiquid fuiſſet turbidiorum cogitationum, componerent:* And by ** Tuſc: Quæſt. lib. 4.* * *Tulli: Mentes ſuas Pythagorei à cogitationum intentione, cantu fidibuſq; ad tranquillitatem traducebant,* For conſopiting Car's and Paſſions, Inſtruments *Entata ſymphona (v. l. 2. c. 1. § 1.)* ar generally mor' fit, ðan oðer inſtruments, or voices.

4 Prygian. † Pol. t. l 8. c. 5. Ibid. c. 7. (¹) Ðus dœ'ʒ ðe Piloſoper deſcrib' ðis Mood': † *Phrygia diſtrahit ac rapit animum, & quaſi extra ſe ponit.* And againe; * *Habet eandem vim Phrygia in Harmoniis, quam habet tibia in Inſtrumentis: ambæ enim concitant animos, & in affectus impellunt.* Ðe Prygian Mood' dœ'ʒ diſtract and raviſ ðe mind', and dœ'ʒ as it wer' ſet it beſides it ſelf: having ðe ſam' forc' among ðe Mood's, ðat ðe Pip' or Fiſ' haʒ among Inſtruments: for boð' of ðem dœ' rouz up mens mind's and driv' ðem into paſſions. Wiʒ ðing ðe skilfull Muſician *Timoteus* prœved in ðe great *Alexander:* Wom', wiʒ his Prygian Flut', hæ did ſo incens, ðat ðe King ran preſently to take up Arms: Wiʒ beeing dœn, Suʒ (qoʒ *Timoteus*) ſœld' bæ ðe Muſik of Kings. * *Timotheum aiunt Tibiá ludentem ſui Carminibus adeo perturbaſſe Alexandrum, ut inter audiendum ad Arma confeſtim corripiendum accurreret:* ** Suidas in litera T.* *Timotheum verò dixiſſe, Talia oportere eſſe Regia Tibiarum carmina.* Ðe lik' dœ'ʒ † *Marſenius* report of ðis Hyper-prygian Mood', in ſundry Examples.

But ðe ſtori of * *Ericus* Muſician paſſeʒ all: wo having given ſœrʒ ðat hæ was able by his Art to driv' men into wat affections hæ liſted, *† In Geneſ. c. 4. verſ. 24. Artic. 15.* [even into anger and furi;] and bæing reqired by ðe King to put his ** King of Denmark ſirnamed Bonus.* skil in practic', harped ſo long, not upon on' ſtring, (as ðe proverb is) but upon his Polykord Lyr', wiʒ ſuʒ effectual Melodi and Harmoni, in varieti of Proportions, Figur's, Conſecutions, Syncope's, Fuga's, Formaliti's, in his different Airs and Mood's; ðat his Auditors began firſt

to hœ mœved wiᵗ ſœm ſtrangᶜ and contrari Paſſions: and at laſt wiᵗ his
Prygian mœdᶜ hœ ſet ðe King into ſue a Frantik mœdᶜ, ðat in a ragᶜ hœ
fel upon his moſtᶜ truſty friends, and, for lack of weapon, ſluᶜ ſœm of ðem
wiᵗ his fiſt : wiᶜ wen hœ camᶜ to himſelf, hœ did mue lament. Ðis is
recorded at largᶜ by *Krantzius lib 5. Daniæ, c. 3.* and by *Saxo Gramma-
ticus l. 12, Hiſtoriæ Daniæ.* Ðerᶜforᶜ is ðis mœdᶜ fit for ðe warz: bœing
ſo uſed by ðe *Lacedæmonians, Romans, Germans,* and oðer warlikᶜ Nations, wiᵗ divers Inſtruments. † *In bellis ſuis tuba utuntur Hetruſci,
fiſtulá Arcades, Siculi *Pyctidibus, Cretenſes lyrá, Lacedæmonii tibiá, Cor-
nu Thraces, Tympano Ægyptii, & Arabes cymbalo, ac Troes lituo:*
of wiᶜ *Virgil.*

† *Clemens Alex.*
4. *Padag.*
* *Fidiculis.*

> * *Miſenum Æoliden, quo non præſtantior alter*
>   *Ære ciere viros, Martemq; accendere cantu:*

Ac ibid.   *Et lituo pugnas inſignis obibat, & haſtá.*

* *Æneid. 6.*

† *Exercitus Lacedæmoniorum Muſicis fuiſſe accenſos modis traditum.
Quid autem aliud in noſtris legionibus Cornua ac tubæ faciunt? Quorum
concentus quantò eſt vehementior, tantò Romana in bellis gloria cæteris
præſtat.* Sue was our Anceſtors Mœdᶜ: of wiᶜ * *Tacitus* ſayᵗ, *Cantantes ibant ad bellum.*

† *Quint. lib. 1.*
cap. 10.

* *In deſcriptio-*
ne Germaniæ.

Of ðis Mœdᶜ alſo (ðowg not ſo violent) was the Pyᵗagoreans Huntſ-
up or Morhitig-Muſik; to waken and rouz up ðeir ſpirits to ſtuddi and
action. Of wiᶜ † *Quintilian. Pythagoreis certè moris fuit, ut cùme vigi-
laſſent, animos ad lyram excitarent, quò eſſent ad agendum erectiores.*

† *L. 9. c. 4.*
5
Ionik.
* *Il ad. Σ.*

(ᵏ) Of ðe *Ionik* Mœdᶜ, werᶜ ðoſᶜ *Epithalamia,* or *Hymens,* mentioned
by * *Homer,* in his deſcription of ðeir Nuptial Ritᶜs :

> Νύμφας δ' ἐκ θαλάμων δαΐδων ὑπὸ λαμπομενάων
> Ἠγίνεον ἀνὰ ἄςυ πολὺς δ' ὑμέναιος ὀρώρει.
> Κέροι δ' ὀρχεςῆρες ἐδίνεον· ἐν δ' ἄρα τοῖσιν
> Αὐλοι φόρμιγγές τε βοἡν ἔχον———

> *Sponſas autem ex thalamis, tedis ſubaccenſis,*
> *Ducebant per urbem : Multuſq; Hymenæus excitatus fuerat.*
> *Iuvenes autem ſaltatores in orbem agebant : interq; hos*
> *Tibia citharæq; ſonum edebant.*

Alſo ðoſᶜ Lov-ſonnets, of wiᶜ * *Tulli: Nec dubitari debet, quin fuerint ante Homerum Poetæ: quod ex iis Carminibus intelligi poteſt, quæ a-
pud illum in * Procorum epulis canuntur.* † And generally all pleaſant
ſongs at Feaſts: unto wiᶜ *Ecolus* (in praiſing gœd men) compareᵗ ðe
ſweetᶜ memorial of King *Joſias.* * *Ðe remembrancᶜ of Joſias is as ſweetᶜ
as hœnni in all mouðs; and as Muſik at a Banqet of Winᶜ.*

* *Brut.* ¶ 36.

* *Iliad.* A.
† *V. l. 2. c. 3.*
§ 2. II.
* *C. 49. v. 1.*

Ðe Abuſᶜ of ðis Mœdᶜ is reformed by ðe ſober Tonᶜs of ðe *Dorik,*
as *Boetius* ſeweᵗ out of *Tulliᶜs* Fragments: *Cum vinolenti adoleſcentes,
tibiarum etiam cantu, ut ſit, inſtincti, pudicæ mulieris ſores frangerent;
admonuiſſe*

admonuiſſe Tibicinam ut Spondæum caneret, Pythagoras dicitur : quod cùm illa feciſſet ; tarditate Modorum & gravitate canentis, illorum furentem petulantiam conſediſſe. Inde Chromaticum, quòd adoleſcentum remolleſcerent eo genere animi, Lacedæmones improbáſſe feruntur.

Of ðis Mɷd ar *Madrigalz* and *Canzonets.*

Madrigal.

Ðe *Madrigal* is a Kromatik Mɷd in Diſcant, woſ not's dɷ often exceed ðe number of ðe ſyllables of ðe Ditti ; ſomtim in Duple, ſomtim in Triple Proportion : wiþ qik and ſweet Report's, and Repeats, and all pleaſing varietiz of Art, in 4, 5, or 6 Part's : having, in on or mor of ðem, on or mor Reſts, (eſpecially in ðe beginning) to bring in ðe Points begun in an oðer Part.

Canzonet.

A Canzonet (as ðe nam importeþ) is a leſ or ſorter ſong, of ðe ſam Mɷd : woſ not's, for ðe moſt part in Counterpoint, dɷ ſeldom exceed ðe number of ðe ſyllables, beginning and ending togeðer ðe Lin's of eaþ vers, commonly in 4 part's : ſo ðat ðe Canzonet is to ðe Madrigal, as ðe Canticle to ðe Motet.

Ðe cief autors hærof were *Alfonſo Ferraboſco, Luca Merenzo, Horatio Vecchi,* and *Jo. Croce.*

Of ðis ſort ar Pavins, invented for a ſlow and ſoft kind of Dancing, altogeðer in duple Proportion. Vnto wiþ ar framed Galliards for mor qik and nimble motion, alwais in triple proportion : and ðer for ðe triple is oft called Galliard-tim, and ðe duple, Pavin-tim.

In ðis kind is alſo comprehended ðe infinit multitud of Balads (ſet to ſundry pleaſant and deligtfull tun's, by cunning and witti Compoſers) wiþ Country-dances fitted untɷ ðem. But boþ in Madrigalz and Canzonets, Counterpoint wiþ Diſcant, and Diſcant wiþ Counterpoint, ar ſomtim enterþangeably and artificially mixt.

☞

All wiþ ſurly, migt and wɷld bee mor freely permitted by our Sages ; wer ðey uſed, as ðey owgt, only for healþ and recreation ; and not corrupted, as ðey ar, wiþ dangerous immodeſti, and filþy obſceniti, to ðe offenc of God and gɷd folk, and to ðe hurt boþ of body and ſowl. (*Vid. lib. 2. c. 3. § 3.* and 4.)

Of ðe uſes and abuſes of Muſik and Verſes, at feaſts, weddings, and oðer meetings, ðis is * *Martyrs* ſentenc : *Omnia hæc (ſi moderatè ac tempeſtivè agantur) & ferri & commendari poſſuunt. Nam huc tria bonorum genera concurrunt,* [*Honeſtum, Vtile, ac Iucundum.*]

* *Loc. com. claſſis 3. c. 13. § 25.*

(1) *Vid.* (a)

† *Tuſc: Quæſt. l. 1.*

(m) As well learned, &c. † *Cicero, Summam eruditionem Græci ſitam cenſebant in Nervorum vocumq; cantibus. Igitur & Epaminondas, princeps meo judicio Græciæ, fidibus præclarè ceciniſſe dicitur : Themiſtocleſq; , aliquot antè annis, cùm in epulis recuſaſſet Lyram, habitus eſt indoctior. Ergo in Græcia Muſici floruerunt, diſcebaniq; id omnes : nec qui neſciebat ſatis excultus doctrinâ putabatur.*

* *In Somnium Scipionis. l. 2. o. 3.*

(m) (n) * *Macrobius. Non ſolùm qui ſunt habitu cultiores, verùm univerſæ quoq; barbaræ Nationes, cantus, quibus vel ad ardorem virtutis animentur, vel ad mollitiem voluptatis reſolvantur, exercent : & ita delinimentis canticis occupantur, ut nullum ſit tam immite, tam aſperum pectus,*

pectus, quod non oblectamentorum talium teneatur affectu. And † *A-*   † *Deipnosophist.*
thenæus: Ad exercendam acuendamq; mentem confert & Musica: quo- *lib. 14.*
circa apud singulas Nationes tum Græcorum tum Barbarorum, quoium
nobis innotuerunt leges ac instituta, in pretio est. Itaq; (ut non inscitè Da-
mon Atheniensis dixit) agitato prorsus animo, cantiones atq; saltationes
fieri necessarium est : liberales ac speciosas ab animis ejusmodi ; contrari-
as ab iis quibus animus diversus est.

(o) Aldowg eae Key havᶜ in it divers Tonᶜs ; yet, đe Mi-clief
bæing known, onᶜ onᶜly is taken. For in *Scala duralis*, đe Constituted Tonᶜ of *G-sol-re-ut* is *Vt* : in *Scala naturalis*, it is *Sol* : in *Scala*
mollaris it is *Re*. Likᶜwisᶜ in *Scala duralis* đe constituted Tonᶜ of
C-sol-fa-ut is *Fa*, in *Scala naturalis* it is *ut*, and in *Scala mollaris* it is
Sol. And so of đe rest : Sæ đesecond Scalᶜ *in c. 2.* § 2. and (f) *in No-*
tis.

CAP. 2. Of Singing.

§ 1. Of đe *Number of* đe *Not*ᶜ*s.*

MUSIK consistet eider in (a) Singing, or Set-   *De Parts of*
ting.   *Musik.*
In Singing ar considered fivᶜ tings : [đe Number, (ᵃ)
đe Namᶜs, đe Tunᶜ, đe Timᶜ, and đe 7 extern
Adjuncts of đe Notᶜs.]

Witin đe ordinari compas of humanᶜ voices [i. from đe   *De Number of*
lowest Notᶜ of a Mans Basᶜ, unto đe higest of a Boyz Tre- đe *Not*ᶜ*s.*
ble.] ar conteined (b) 3 Septenariz of Musical Notᶜs : (ᵇ)
aldowg derᶜ ar found sœm Bases đat reach below , and
sœm Trebles đat arisᶜ abœv đis ordinari compas. And in
Instruments đe Notᶜs ar extended farder, botᶜ upward and
dounward : as in đe *Virginal* to *C folfa* abœv *eela*, and to *C C*
fa ut below Γ*amut* : (in wiє compas is conteined fowɪ
Eigts, or a *Tetrakisdiapason*) werᶜunto is also added *A A re*
placed upon đe lowest of đe narrow or fort Keyz : (of wiє
sortᶜ all đe rest ar *Hemitonia*, serving for đe farping and
flatting of đe ordinari Notᶜs of đe Scalᶜ) all wiє ordinari
Notᶜs ar exprest in đe broad keyz alonᶜ. But đe *Organ* goet
yet a far greater compas : as reaєing onᶜ wᵒlᶜ Septenari

be-

* V. [hand] in Notis ad § 2. post (8) in (f)

[hand]

(c)

Rul's and Spaces.

(d)

(e)

below C C faut, and fifteen Not's or a *Diſdiapaſon* aboov de * *Hyperbolæan C ſolfa* : [in all 51 Not's in the direct and natural order of de Scal':] beſid's de 20 extraordinari *Hemiton's*, and de ſecond Set bot' of *Principals* and *Diapaſons.*

De number of Not's Muſical is der'for' divided by Septenariz ; becaus der' ar in Natur' but (c) 7 diſtinct ſounds, expreſt in Muſik, by 7 diſtinct Not's, in de 7 ſeveral Cliefs of de Scal'. For de 8th and 15th Not's hav' de ſound or tun', and der'for' de nam', and clief, of de firſt : de 9th and 16th of de ſecond : de 10th and 17th of de tird : de 11th and 18th of de fowrt : de 12th and 19th of de fift : de 13'h and 20th of de ſixt : de 14th and 21th of de ſevnt.

Deſe tric' ſevn Not's (as de Cliefs wer'in dey ſtand) ar diſcerned by deir Places. A Plac' is eider Rul' or Spac'. In elevn Rul's wit deir Spaces is comprehended de wol' Scal'. Of wic Rul's in de pricking or ſetting doun of any Part', (d) fiv' ar commonly uſed : becaus dat number of Rul's and deir Spaces ar Places enou for as many Not's as de ordinari compas of a Part' dœ't reac unto. If any Not' happen to exceed' dis compas ; his Plac' is to bœ notifyed by (e) a ſort Rul' drawn for de nonc', eider aboov or below, as you ſall hav' caus. Aboov, as in de Baſ', and below, as in de Countertenor, of de *Dial. V.* (h) *in Notis ad C.* 3. § 1.

ANNOTATIONS to CAP. II. § I.

(a) BEcaus Singing is de beſt expreſſing of Muſical ſounds ; der'for', by a *Synecdoche,* de word *Cano* [to Sing] is enlarged, and ſignifyet commonly, as wel to play on Inſtruments, as to Sing wit voices : as *Tuſc. Quæſt. l.* 1. *Epaminondas fidibus præclarè ceciniſſe dicitur.* (vide (m) c. 1.) and *Eclog.* 2. *Imitabere Pana canendo.* So Met. 1. *Structis cantat avenis.* Vid. Rhet. l. 1. c. 2. Singing alſo by a *Metonymia effecti,* ſignifyet heer' as wel de knowledg of de præcepts, as de practic' : for de practic' alon' dœ't not mak' a Muſician : as *Ornithoparchus* out of *Guido. Muſicorum ac Cantorum magna eſt differentia : illi ſciunt & dictant ; iſti faciunt quod dictatur. Eſt itaq; Muſicus ad Cantorem, quod Prætor ad Præconem.*

(b) Deſe

* De Oratore
perfecto.
† Mean, Tre-
ble, and Baſ^e.
* L. ς. c. 10.

(ᵇ) Deſ^e ðræ Septenariz or Orders of Not^e s and Sounds *Tulli* did obſerv. *Mira eſt quædam natura vocis: cujus quidem è tribus omnino ſonus [↑ Inflexo, Acuto, Gravi] tanta ſit & tam ſuavis varietas perfecta in Cantibus.* And * *Quint.* mentionez, wer^e hæ likenez Rhetorik to Muſik. *Muſicorum etiamſi aliò ſpectent, Manus tamen ipſa conſuetudine, ad Graves, Acutos, Medioſq; ſonos fertur.*

(ᶜ) Deſ^e 7 natural diſtinct Sounds or Not^e s, ð e Poet ſewez to hav^e been obſerved and uſed, even by *Orpheus*, [the fað er of Muſik] bo^t in voic^e and inſtrument : wer^e, in recounting ð e pleaſant exerciſes of ð e *Elyſian* fields, hæ ſayz,

> † *Pars pedibus plaudunt choreas, & carmina dicunt.*
> *Nec non Threicius, longá cum veſte, ſacerdos*
> *obloquitur numeris ſeptem diſcrimina vocum :*
> *Iamq; eadem digitis, jam pectine pulſat eburna.*

> Sœm fœt^e ð e danc^e, ſœm verſes dœ^e recit^e;
> And *Orpheus* ð e 7 ſev'ral Not^e s ðer^e ſings
> In Numbers : and ð e ſam^e dœ^t ſwæt^e ly ſtrik^e
> Nou on ð e Harp-, nou on ð e Cittern-ſtrings.

Alð owg *Boetius* affirm ð e perfect Septenari to hav^e been found out afterward by degræs. *Vide* § 2. (ᶠ) *in Notis.*

(ᵈ) Fiv^e ar commonly. For Plain-ſong, it bæing but of little compas, fowr Rul^e s hav^e ſufficed : for Inſtruments (wie go^e beyond ð e compas of voices) ſix ar reqired : and for ð e Virginals and Organs two Sixes : on^e for ð e left hand, or lower keyz ; and ð e oð er for ð e rigt, or upper keyz. De wie two Senariz (wen *gg* is ſet in ð e higeſt of ð e lower ðræ Rul^e s of ð e rigt hand, and): in ð e loweſt of ð e higer ðræ of ð e left hand) dœ^e contein al ð e *Gam-ut* : ð e loweſt of ð e rigt hand, and ð e higeſt of ð e left hand bæing ð e ſam^e : [to wit ☰.]

(ᵉ) But if many Not^e s exceed^e, (ſo ð at ð e ſet pi ð e of ð e ſong bœ altered) Tranpoſition of ð e Clief is permitted : by wie means alſo a general miſtaking of ð e places in pricking is wont to be amended : as

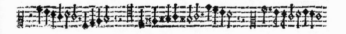

C A P. II. § II.

Of de Nam's of de Not's.

De Nam's of de Not's.
(ª)

DE Nam's of de Not's wer' (ª) invented for de mor' eafy and fpædy inftruction of Skollars in Tuning dem : dat bæing taught de Nam's and Tun's togeder ; wen dey ar perfect in dof', dey migt, by de help of dem, know def' de mor' reddily.

For de 7 Not's, der' ar but fix feveral Nam's : [*Ut, re,* M I, *fa, fol, la.*] De fevnt Not', becaus it is but a half-ton' aboov *la*, as de fowrt. is aboov *M I*; (wer'as de reft ar all

De fecond Fa *or* Pa.
(º)

wol' ton's) is fitly called by (ᵇ) de fam' Nam' : de wie bæing added, de next Not' wil bæ an Eigt or Diapafon to de firft ; and confeqently placed in de fame Letter or Clief, and called by de fam' Nam'.

† *See de free* M I*-cliefs.*

Of def' fevn Not's dus Named, *M I* is de principal, or Mafter-not' : wie † bæing found, de fix fervil Not's doo' follow , (bot' afcending and defcending) in deir order. As in example.

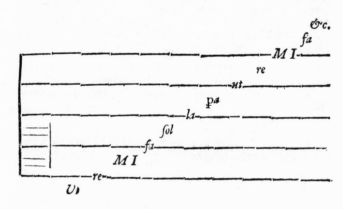

But de perpetual order of de Not's in de *Gam-ut* (as
of

of đe Mꝺnts in đe yœrᶜ) is moſtᶜ fitly exemplifyed in đat
Figurᶜ, ꝺiᴇ hatᶜ noᶜ endᶜ.

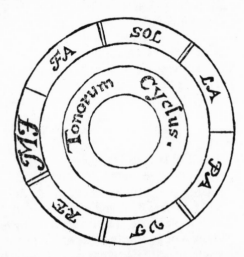

Đesᶜ Namᶜs đowᵹ đey bœ ſtil taugt in Skꝺlᶜs, (according to đe firſt inſtitution,) among ođer Principles of đe
Art; yet đe modern vulgar praᶜtiᶜ đꝺᶜt commonly ᴇangᶜ
ut and *re*, đe onᶜ into *ſol*, đe ođer into *la*: ſo đat, for đe 7
ſeveral Notᶜs, đey uſᶜ but 4 ſeveral Namᶜs: (ᶜ) ꝺiᴇ đꝺᶜt
not a little hinder đe Learners boᵗᶜ in Singing and in Setting. But ɪf you wil nœdᶜs retein đis ᴇangᶜ; đen take đis
ſort Direᶜtion. After *M I*, ſing *fa, ſol, la* twiſᶜ upward;
and *la, ſol, fa* twiſᶜ dounward; and ſo cꝺm you boᵈᶜwᴀys
to *M I* again, in đe ſamᶜ Clief.

Anſwerable unto đesᶜ 7 diſtinᶜt Notᶜs, ar 7 ſeveral Cliefs
or keyz, called by đe Namᶜs of đe firſt 7 Letters of đe Alpabet, [(ᵈ) *G, A, B, C, D, E, F* :] and đerᶜforᶜ as đe ⋆ 7
Notᶜs, ſo đe 7 Cliefs ar tripled: ((ᵉ) đe firſt Septenari
ꝺherᶜof is noted wiᴇ Capitals, đe ſecond wiᴇ vulgar letters, and đe ᴇird wiᴇ dübble vulgar) ꝺiᴇ ᴇrœ Septenariz,
for đe reaſon after-mentioned, (*vide* (ᵈ) *in Notis,*) ar called đe (ᶠ) *G A M-U T* : [đe ground and foundation of all
Muſik, boᵗᶜ Vocal and Inſtrumental.]

　　　　Đe

đe *Gam-ut* or
Scalᶜ.
(ᵈ)
⋆ *Vid.* (ᶜ) *in*
§ 1.
(ᵉ)

(ᶜ)

(ᶠ)

Ðe olde *Gam-ut* or Scal's woſ's higeſt Clief was *ee-la*, wanted one Cliefof de ſræ Septenariz : aldowg ðe Trebles of many ordinari Songs dœc reac a Not's higer ; as deir Baſes dœc to F *fa-ut*, below *Gam-ut*.

( )   In de Scal's or *G A M-U T* , ar (a) 3 ſigned-Cliefs :
Thræ Signed   wie hav's certain Sign's or marks , wer'by dey may bee
Cliefs.   known. And deſ's ar de higeſt of de loweſt, [or ðe Baſ's F ;] de loweſt of the higeſt, [or de Treble G ;] and de middle- moſt of de middlemoſt, [or de Mean C :] one of wie ſræ is prefixed to every part's of a ſong : ðat by it aſcending and deſcending in Alpabeticall order, you may certainly find's

(h)   all de reſt. Ðe (h) mark of de Baſ's F is this) : of de
*For want of de Mean *C*, dis 𝔢 : of de Treble *G*, dis * *gg.*
common Karaċter, wee ar fain to ſubſtitut's gg, wer'of it was made.

    Beſid's deſ's Signed Cliefs, ðer's ar alſo in de Scal's to be
(i)   noted (i) 3 MI-cliefs : [*B, E,* and *A :*] ſo called, becaus
3 MI-cliefs.   in one of deſ's 3, is placed de Maſter-not's *M I*, by wie de nam's of all oder Not's (as befor's is ſewed) ar known.

    To know wie of deſ's 3 Cliefs hat de *M I* in de preſent ſong, Firſt, by ðe Signed clief, look's out de next *B* : wer's, if
†*Vid. c. 2. § 5.* you find's not a † Flat, is his place : if de Flat put him out dence's ; look's him in *E* : wer's you fall hav's him ; unles de Flat lik'wiſ's (wie happenet ſeldom) dœc remœv's him : and den his plac's is certainly in *A. U.* (i) *in Notis.*

    Ðe rul's of de *Mi-clief,* and de order of de Not's bæing
(k)   known, it is enoug to learn, for de *Gam-ut,* de (k) tric's 7 letters forward and bakward : obſerving eſpecially, de ſræ ſigned Cliefs, [de Baſ's *F*, de Mean *C*, and de Treble *G*.]

ANNOT. to CAP. II. § II.

(a) **D**E Autor of dis uſ'full Invention, was *Guido Aretinus* [a famous Muſician :] of wom's *Ornithoparchus l. 1. c. 3* give't dis
larg's teſtimoni : *Guido Aretinus, Muſicus acutiſſimus, poſt Boe-
tium ſolus apud Latinos, Muſicam illuſtravit, voces reperit, claves ordi-
navit, ac ex mirâ quadam induſtriâ, facillimum quendam praċticandi modum invenit.* And in ðe 2. cap. hæ ſettet doun ðe ſtrang's manner of
ðe Invention : *Guido Aretinus, divinâ inſpiratione duċtus, Hymnum di-
vi Ioannis Baptiſtæ devoté examinans, verſuum ſex capitales Syllabas,
[ſcilicet,* Ut, re, mi, fa, ſol, la,] *Muſicis conſonantiis convenire perpen-
dit.*

dit. Quare eas in Introductorü ſui chordis applicavit. Quod Ioannes 22.
Romanæ urbis Pontifex, approbavit.

Deſ^c famous Syllables hæ found in ðe firſt *Saphik* of ðe Hymn.

> *VT queant laxis REſonare fibris,*
> *MIra geſtorum FAmuli tuorum;*
> *SOLve polluti LAbij reatum.*

Wie ſix nam^cs wer^c ðenc^cfoort^c generally taugt and practiſed, in ðe
ſam^c order, aſcending and deſcending : as in witty *Owens* conceited
Epigram.   *Epigr.* 171.

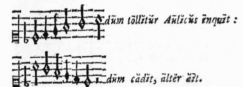

. . . dūm tōllītūr Aulīcūs ēnqūit :

. . . dūm cādīt, āltēr āīt.

(b) De ſam^c Nam^c. Yet ſoom, becauſ ðe ſevn^t Not^c hat a diſtinct
ſound from all ðe reſt, ðowgt gœd lik^cwiſ^c to giv it a diſtinct nam^c, and   * *Merſennus.*
call it.* Sy : † *Ericius Puteanus,* admitting alſo *Guido*^cs 6 Nam^cs, calle^t   † *In ſua Muſa-*
ðe ſevn^t *Bi* : And a certain * *Duic-c-man* tœk^c upon him not on^cly to   *thena.*
giv a diſtinct Nam^c to ðe ſevn^t Not^c, as ðey; but alſo to nu^c-nam^c all ðe   * *Keplerus Har-*
reſt, ðus : *Bo, Ce, Di, Ga, Lo, Ma, Ni.* All ðeſ^c agree, to call ðe ſevn ſe-   *mon.* l 3. c.10.
verall Not^cs by 7 ſeverall Nam^cs : † as ſoom ſay ðe Grœk^cs did by ðeir   † *Merſennus.*
ſevn vouels, [α, ε, η, ι, ο, ω, υ.] But becauſ (as is abœv ſaid) ðis ſe-
vn^t Not^c is but a *Semitonium* from his inferior *La,* as ðe fowr^t is from
his inferior *M I* ; queſtionles it is beſt, and moſt eaſy for ðe Learners,
to call ðem bod^c (as ðe manner now is) by ðe ſam^c Nam^c : aldowg ðe   *Pa.*
ſecond Half^c-not^c may, for differenc^c from ðe firſt, bœ written *Pa :*
wie is ðe firſt ſyllable of *Pharos,* ðe nam^c of an hig tour, and of an upper garment ; as ðis ſecond *Hemitonium* is ðe uppermoſt and higeſt of
all ðe ſevn Not^cs.

(c) Dat ðis eang^c is a Let to ſpeedy and certain Singing, appœre^t
by ðis ; ðat *Sol* bee^{ij}ng fowr not^cs abœv *ut,* and *ut* 3 abœv *Sol* ; *la* 4 not^cs
abœv *re,* and *re* 3 abœv *la* ; acquainting our ſelvs wit ðeir proper Nam^cs,
in ðeſ different riſings and fallings, wee ſall, by ðat means eaſily hit
upon ðe rigt Sounds of ðe Not^cs, in ðoſ^c divers diſtances : (like as paſſing from *la* to *M I,* and from *M I* to *la,* wee dœ^c readily giv ðem ðeir
rigt tun^cs, by reaſon of ðeir divers nam^cs : wer^cas (ðis eang^c beeing
mad^c) from *ſol* to *ſol,* and from *la* to *la* wil bœ ſœmtim^c 3, and ſœmtim^c
4 Not^cs : ſo ðat ðe ſo naming of ðem, dœ^ct not help to ðe different
ſounds of ðeſ^c different diſtances.

De lik^c certainti is betwœen^c *re* and *ſol,* and betwœen^c *ut* and *fa* ; wie
by ðis eang^c is loſt in bod^c : for ðen aſcending from *ſol* to *fa,* and lik^c-
wiſ^c from *la* to *ſol,* ðe diſtanc^c is ſœmtim^c 3 not^cs, and ſœmtim^c 2.

For

For ðis cumberſom eangꞗ ðey havꞗ two Excuſes:onꞗ ðat RE and Ut ar not ſo facil and fluent ſounds (eſpecially in qik timꞗ) as *La* and *Sol* : ðe oðer ðat ðey can ſing as reddily and as truꞗly wiꞇ deſꞗ 4, as wiꞇ all.

To ðe firſt I ſay, Conceipt is muꞇe : but wo ſo tryeꞇ, ſall findꞗ ðat *Re* is a ſyllable as facil and fluent as any ; running ſmœdꞗly and joyning fitly, even in ſwifteſt timꞗ, to any Notꞗ, eiðer ſuperior or inferior : ſo ðat ðerꞗ is no cauſ of eanging ðat at all.

And for *ut,* wen wee deſcend unto it or aſcend from it, ſpecially werꞗ it is onꞗ of ðe loweſt Notꞗs of a Partꞗ, iꞇ is yet commonly reteined ; and if elſwerꞗ it ſœmeꞇ not ſo fluent and facil a Namꞗ, ðe eieſeſt cauſ of it is Diſuſꞗ. But wen it ſall return, *quaſi poſtliminio,* into its own rigꞇ, and havꞗ poſſeſt it a wilꞗ in Peacꞗ ; it wil bœ found as fitting as his Supplanter *Sol :* and ðat, in ſwifteſt notꞗs tœ, if (*T*) his final conſonant be eliſꞗ

ſo

dꞗd, as (*L*) in *ſol* is wœnt, in likꞗ caſꞗ, to be : as in example :

But houſoever, ðe great uſꞗ and benefit, wil moꞇꞗ ðan makꞗ amends for a little inconveniencꞗ.

And for ðe oðer Excuſe, Expert Singers indeedꞗ, ðat inſtantly know ðe tunꞗs of ðe Notꞗs by ðeir places, may call ðem at ðeir pleaſurꞗ : ðey may ſay *Mi* for *fa* and *fa* for *Mi* ; and, if ðey will, *ut* for *ſol* and *re* for *la,* as wel as *ſol* for *ut* and *la* for *re* : ðey may call any Notꞗ by any namꞗ, and all Notꞗs by onꞗ Namꞗ : els hou cœldꞗ ðey ſing Ditti, according to ðe Notꞗ, at firſt ſigꞇ ? But unto Learners (for woſꞗ help ðis fit Number of fit Namꞗs was invented) ðe ſtrict obſerving of ðem in ðeir proper places, will prœvꞗ no ſmall furðerancꞗ boꞇ in Singing and Setting : In Singing, as to a morꞗ ſpœdi and truꞗ tunꞗing of ðat wiꞗ ðey ſœ pricked; ſo to a ſpœdi truꞗ pricking doun of ðat wiꞗ ðey hear tuned : And in Setting (belœvꞗ it) ðey ſall muꞇe morꞗ reddily diſcern ðe Concords and Diſcords by obſerving ðeſꞗ diſtinct Namꞗs of ðe Notꞗs ; ðan by marking ðe diſtances of ðe Cliefs.

¶ If you ꞇink ðat ðe *Metatheſis* of ðe Letters will makꞗ ðis namꞗ morꞗ facil ; ſo alſo is it onꞗ of ðe † capitall ſyllables of ðe ſamꞗ firſt vers : and ſo dœꞗꞇ it begin wiꞇ a Conſonant and endꞗ wiꞇ a Vouel, as all oðer Namꞗs dœꞗ, but onꞗ ; woſꞗ laſt is a half-vouel, fit enouꞡ to precedꞗ any of ðe oðer Namꞗs : ſavꞗ onꞗly in very qik timꞗ, werꞗ it is wœnt to loſꞗ his final Conſonant. *V. ſupra.* But if you lœv ðe Eaꞇ and Spœdꞗ of ðe Learners; in any caſꞗ diminiꞡ not ðe juſt number of ðe Namꞗs, [ðe principal help to certain and reddy Tunꞗing.]

Nou for ðe paſſing from *fa* to *fa,* (betweenꞗ wiꞗ ðe diſtancꞗ is ſœmtimꞗs of 3, ſœmtimꞗs of 4 notꞗs) becauſ it cannot bœ helped, (* bœing ſo ordered upon gœd reaſon at ðe firſt) it muſt bœ tolerated : and onꞗ ſꞇꞗe uncertain riſing and falling, among ðe reſt, wiꞗ ar certain, cannot muꞗ hinder.

(d) *G, A, B, C, &c.* ðe uſe of ðeſꞗ 7 Letters in ðe Scalꞗ, anſwerable to ðe 7 eſſentiall or natural Sounds, † *Franchinus* ſayꞇ to havꞗ been ðe Invention

Invention of Sᵗ *Gregori. Septem tantùm essentiales chordæ septenis literis à Gregorio descriptæ sunt.* Wer⁶ not⁶ ðat aldowᵹ G bæ ðe sevnᵗ letter of ðe Latin Alpabet, yet, bæing ðe firſt letter in ðe word GREEC⁶,
it is set in ðe firſt plac⁶ of ea⁶ Septenari: and in ðe firſt Septenari reteinet ðe nam⁶ and form of ðe Greek⁶ *Gamma* Γ; in remembranc ðat ðe
Art of Muſik, as oðer learned Arts, cam⁶ from ðat ſeat of ðe Muſes: as
* *Ornithoparchus* notet out of *Berno* Abbas: *Græca litera in graviori In-*
troductorii parte locatur, ad Græcorum reverentiam; à quibus Muſica de-
fluxit ad nos. Inquit enim Berno lib. I. *Muſicæ ſuæ, Græcam literam ma-*
lucrunt ponere moderni, quàm Latinam; ut Græci innuantur hujus Artis
Authores. To ðis purpoſ⁶ ſpeaket † *Glareanus: Veteres Muſici Voces*
pthongos, Claves Chordas ſeu nervos *appellabant. Has claves in ordinem,*
tanquam in Scalam quandam, ad Græcam olim chordarum diſpoſitionem,
redegit Guido Aretinus, [*eximiæ eruditionis vir:*] *quem noſtra ætas ſe-*
quitur: ita ut in infimo gradu in linea parallela poneret vocem Uᵗ, *præ-*
ſcriptâ tertiâ Græcorum literâ Γ: *nempe ut haud immemores eſſemus hanc*
diſciplinam, ut alias omnes, à Græcis eſſe.

(e) Ðe firſt Septenari. *Sunt* Claves *naturâ diſtinctæ ſeptem, totidem*
literis notatæ, hoc diſcrimine à Muſicis pictæ: [*majuſculis formis primæ*
ſeptem, ſequentes 7 *tenuibus, & ſupremæ geminatis.*] Glareanus Dodecachord. *l.* 1. *c.* 2.

(f) Ðe *Gam-ut* was ðe Invention of * *Guido Aretinus,* about ðe
yer⁶ 960. For ðe Greek⁶s, and ancient Muſicians befor⁶ him, named ðe
ſevn Cliefs and Kords according to ðe order of ðeir Places: (1) Hypate, Parhypate, Lichanos, Meſe, Parameſe, Paranete, (2) Nete. Unto
wi⁶ perfect number ðey cam⁶ ðus by degree⁶s. † It is recorded by Homer, ðat Mercuri finding a Tortois, woſ⁶ nervs or Kords, being dryed
and ſtrained in ðe Sun, yeelded, wiᵗ a toxe, a pleaſing ſound, did ðer⁶-
upon mak⁶ an (3) Inſtrument lik⁶ unto it, wi⁶, after ðe nam⁶ of ðe Tortois, hæ called *Chelys,* [*Teſtudo:*] and ſtrung it wiᵗ fowr Strings or Kords
of 4 diſtinct Not⁶s: ðe loweſt *Nete,* ðe next *Paranete;* ðe Higeſt *Hy-*
pate, and ðe next *Parhypate,* ðus:

(4) *Tetrachordon MERCVRII* {
———Hypate———
——Parhypate——
——Paranete——
———Nete———
}

(5) Betwixt ðeſ⁶ fowr, *Chorebus* [ðe ſun of *Atys* King of *Lydia*]
did interpoſ⁶ a fift: wi⁶, of his middle plac⁶, was called *Meſe. Hyagnis,* a
Prygian, added a fixt: wi⁶, bæing placed next aboov *Meſe,* is fitly called
† *Lichanos;* becaus as ðe for⁶finger is ðe fowrᵗ, beginning at ðe loweſt;
ſo is ðis String or Not⁶, beginning at *Nete.* And laſt of all *Terpander* of
Leſbos, finding yet an oðer Not⁶ differing from all ðe former in ſound,
perfected ðe ſingle Scale⁶, by adding a ſevnᵗ Kord: wi⁶, bæing placed
next under *Meſe,* is *Parameſe.* And ſo hat *Meſe* his middle plac⁶ in ðe
Sevn, (as at ðe firſt in Fiv⁶) wi⁶ it loſt in ðe Six, becaus ðat hat no⁶
middle

C

* *Lib.* I. *c.* 2. *de*
Clavibus.

† *Dodecachord.*
l. I. *c.* 2.

* *V.* (ᵃ) and (ᵈ)

(1)
(2)

† *Vid.* (4) *in "*
Notis.

(3)

(4)

(5)

† *Index, i.* ðe
for⁶finger.

middle number. But *Lichanos,* by ðis mean's is raiſed to ðe fift plac⟨,
[ðe place of *Anticheir* or *Pollex* :] wer⟨ yet it ſtil holdeð ðe nam⟨ *Lichanos.* And ſo, ðis is ðe form of ðe Greek⟨ *Heptachordon.*

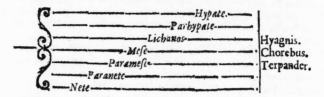

(6)

Ðus ðis firſt Inſtrument obteined, at ðe laſt, his ſevn Strings, accor-
ding to ðe ful number of ðe ſevn diſtinct Muſical Not⟨s. But (6) *Pytha-
goras,* obſerving ðat ðe two extrem⟨ Kords wer⟨ diſcordant, and ðat
neiðer *Diateſſaron* nor *Diapente* did mak⟨ ſo good a *Symponi* wiþ ðeir
Ground, as if ðey wer⟨ conjoyned in a Diapaſon, aſſumed unto ðeſ⟨ ſevn
Kords, an Eiʒt, (wic is ðer⟨for⟨ called * *Proſlambanomenc*) to mak⟨a
Diapaſon to *Hypate* [ðe ſevnþ or higeſt ;] as wee commonly aſſum⟨
F F *fa ut* below *Gamut,* for a *Diapaſon* to ðe Signed *F faut.* And ſo ðe
Greek⟨ *Heptachordon,* and ðe Latin Septenari of *Letters* wiþ ðeir Not⟨s,
bæing tripled, (according to ðe ordinari compas of Voices) ðis wil bee
ðe Skem⟨ or Figur⟨ of ðeir and our Scal⟨, in (7) 22 Cliefs.

* *Aſſumpta,* of
προσλαμβάνω
*accipio præte-
rea, aſſumo.*

(7)

		Hypate	fff a		
		Parhypate	æ la		
	Hypatæ ſummæ	Lichanos	dd la ſol	acutæ Treble	
		Meſe	cc ſol fa		
		Parameſe	bb fa b mi		
		Paranete	aa la mi re		
		NETE	gg ſol re ut		
		Hypate	f fa ut		
		Parhypate	e la mi		
Chorda	Meſæ mediæ	Lichanos	d la ſol re	media Mean	Claves Keyz.
		MESE	c ſol fa ut		
		Parameſe	b fa b mi		
		Paranete	a la mi re		
		Nete	g ſol re ut		
		HYPATE	F FA UT		
		Parhypate	E LA MI		
	Netæ limæ.	Lichanos	D SOL RE	gravæs Baſſ.	
		Meſe	C FA VT		
		Parameſe	B MI		
		Paranete	A RE		
		Nete	GAMVT		

Proſlambanomene F F *fa ut.*

But

But if ðe rigt Nam's of ðe Not's wer' affixed to ðeir Keyz in ðeir natural order, as ðey follow *Mi* in every of his 3 Cliefs, [B, ♮, and A;] ðen wœld' ðis bee ðe tru' form of ðe Scal'.

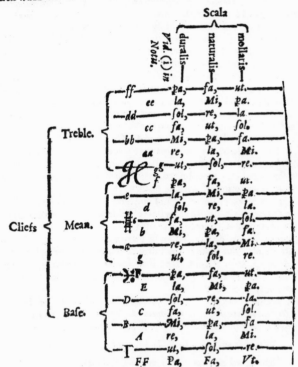

In wie you may not', ðat wat nam' ðe Not' of any Clief hat, ðe sam' nam' (8) properly hat his Eigt: *Fa* in ðe Mean *C*, and *Fa* bot' in ðe Treble and Bas' *C: Re* in ðe Bas' *A*, and *Re* in ðe oðer two.

Vnto ðis Scal' of a Trisdiapason, may bee added (for ðe * *Virginal* and *Organ*) ðe rest of ðe 4 † *Hypobolæan*, or dubble Bas'-cliefs, [EE La Mi, DDfol Re, and CC faVt ;] wiþ ðe 4 * *Hyperbolæan*, or Hig Treble- Cliefs [G, A, ♮, C,] wie mak' up a Tetrakisdiapason : and (for ðe Or- gan) D. For ðe *Organ* hat but ðis on' Key, mor' ðan ðe *Virginal*: all ðe oðer transcendent Not's, [bot' Grav' and Acut'] even unto Pentakis- diapason, Hexakisd. and Heptakisd. ar mad' by ðe Stops.

Not's upon ðe Not' (f.)

(1) *Hypate* (2) *Nete.* ὕπατ⊕· of ὑπέρτατ⊕·, ðe Superlativ' of "ὑπέρ *fupra* : *as ὑ πατοϛ ὄεοϛ altiſſimus mons, † ὕ πατ⊕· Ζεὺϛ *fupremus* "*Iupiter* :

(8)

☞
*Vid. (♭) in §1.
† Of ἐπιβάλλω *ſubiicio.*
* Of ἐπιβάλλω *ſuperiniicio.*

* *Homer Epigr.*
† *Iliad* T, Ἰcω νῦν ζεὺς πρῶτα θεῶν ὕπατ⊕· κỳ ἄεισϛ.

"Iupiter: ſo ὑπάτη χορδὴ, and ſimpliciter ὑπάτη ſuprema chorda, ðe
"higeſt Kord. Lik⁽ᵉ⁾wiſ⁽ᵉ⁾ νήτ Θ-, of νέατ Θ-, of νεώτατ Θ-, noviß.mies,
"ultimus,imus;wenc⁽ᵉ⁾ νήτη, ultima ſeu ima chorda, ðe loweſt Kord : ſo

* V. ☞ in (ᶜ)
in Notis ad
c. 2. § 4.

"Stephanus, * Ariſtotle in Probl. Vitruvius l. 5. c. 4. Martianus Capella,
"Schoħaſtes,Plutarch de Muſica,and Boetius himſelf : (Vide infra) And
"yet ðe ſtream of neoterik Muſicians runne⁽ˢ⁾ an oðer way ; making
"Hypate ðe loweſt, (as if ðey derived it from ὑπὸ, wie yet ha⁽ˢ⁾ no⁽ᶜ⁾
"ſu⁽ᵉ⁾ Superlativ⁽ᵉ⁾) and Nete, vice versâ, ðe higeſt. Wer⁽ᵉ⁾of I can
"conceiv no⁽ᶜ⁾ oðer ground, but ðe miſtaking of ðe meaning of ðis wœrd

* L. I. c. 20.

"[graviſſima] in * Boetius; wer⁽ᵉ⁾ hœ ſay⁽ˢ⁾, Inq; his quæ graviſſima e-
"rat, vocata eſt Hypate. For alðowg among Muſicians, gravis bœ
"generally taken for low or Baſ⁽ᵉ⁾, as acutus for hig; (as wer⁽ᵉ⁾ it is ſayd,

† Ariſtoxenus
Harmonico-
rum element.
l. I.

"† Acumen eſt quod conficitur per Intenſionem, Gravitas quæ per Remiſ-
"ſionem: quando Chordas, ut congruæ ſint, Intendimus aut Remittimus)
"yet it is manifeſt ðat onr Au⁽ᵗ⁾or in ðat Chapter, dœ⁽ˢ⁾ not ſo under-
"ſtand it : partly by his Epexegeſis of ðe wœrd ; [quaſi major atq; hono-
"rabilior : unde Jovem etiam Hypaton vocant] but ſpecially, for ðat in
"ðe ſam⁽ᵉ⁾ Chapter (according to ðe tru⁽ᵉ⁾ meaning of ðe wœrds, and ðe
"common acception of ancient Au⁽ᵗ⁾ors) hœ name⁽ˢ⁾ Hypate ðe fiꝛſt of
"ðe 4 Superiors, (Vide (6) infra) and Nete ðe loweſt of ðe Inferiors :
"(v.(5)) as alſo in ðe Diagram bo⁽ᵗ⁾ of his Heptachordon and Octochor-
"don, in ðe ſam⁽ᵉ⁾ Chapter, is expreſſed.

(3) Wie was ðe fou⁽n⁾dation of Harp andLut⁽ᵉ⁾, and other String-
"inſtruments. But weiðer ⁽ᵗ⁾is Inſtrument did mor⁽ᵉ⁾ reſemble ðe Lut⁽ᵉ⁾

† Horat. Carm.
l. I. Ode 10.

"or ðe Harp, is uncertain. De † Poet ſpeake⁽ˢ⁾ for ðe Harp, wer⁽ᵉ⁾ hœ
"calle⁽ˢ⁾ Mercuri, Curvæ lyræ parentem : alðowg Chelys or Teſtudo bœ
"commonly taken for ðe Lut⁽ᵉ⁾.

(4) Octochordon. † Muſica quatuor nervis tota conſtabat : idq; uſq;

† Boct. l. I. c. 20.

"ad Orpheum duravit, ad imitationem Muſicæ Mundanæ, quæ ex quatuor
"conſtat elementis. Cujus Quadrichordi Mercurius dicitur Inventor.

Homer. in Mer-
curium.

Ἔνϑα χέλυν εὑρὼν ἐκτήσατο μύϱιον ὄλϐον

Ἑρμῆς, τὰ σϱώτισα χέλυν τεκτήνατ' ἀοιδόν.

Intus teſtudinem invenies poſſedit inſinitas opes

Mercurius : utiq; primam Teſtudinem fabricatus eſt canoram.

* Boct. l. I. c. 20.

(5) * Quintam verò Chordam pòſt Chorebus, Athis filius, adjunxit, qui
"fuit Lydorum rex. Hyagnis Phryx ſextum his appoſuit Nervum. Sed ſep-
"timus Nervus à Terpandro Leſbio adjunctus eſt, ſecundùm ſeptem ſcilicet

Vid. (1) & (2)

"Planetarum ſimilitudinem. Inq; his quæ * graviſſima erat vocata eſt Hy-
"pate: Parhypate ſecunda, quaſi Iuxta Hypaten : Lichanos tertia, quæ
"eſt quarta à Nete, ut Index ab imo digito : quarta Meſe, quoniam inter
"ſeptem ſemper eſt media : Quinta eſt Parameſe, quaſi Iuxta mediam col-
"locata : ſeptima autem dicitur Nete quaſi Neate,id eſt inſima:inter quam
"& Parameſen eſt ſexta, quæ vocatur Paranete, quaſi Iuxta Neten loca-
"ta : Parameſe verò, quoniam tertia eſt à Nete, eodem quoq; vocabulo
"Trite, i. tertia nuncupatur.

(6) † Hujus

(6) † *Hujus Lyræ heptachordæ* Pythagoras *concentus rationem &* †*Georgius Valla.*
" *proportionem excogitâſſe primus fertur. Is cùm intueretur, in ſeptem ner-*
" *vorum Lyra, extremos nervos prorſus inter ſe eſſe ecmeles; exiſtimavit*
" *non modò quarto & quinto, nervos ipſos eſſe conſonos efficiendos; ſed eti-*
" *am inter ſe invicem componendos : proinde octavum adjecit: (quâ idea*
" *dicitur Proſlambanomenos) atq; ex Heptachordo fecit Octochordon. In*
" *Heptachordi & Octochordi diſpoſitionibus, (inquit* Boetius) *Hepta-*   *L. I. c. 20.
" *chordum quidem dicitur Synemmenon, quod eſt conjunctum; Octochor-*
" *dum verò Diazeugmenon, quod eſt disjunctum. In Heptachordo eſt u-*
" *num Tetrachordon,* [Hypate, Parhypate, Lichanos, Meſe;] *aliud verò*
" *Meſe, Parameſe, Paranete, Nete : dum Meſen chordam ſecundò nu-*
" *meramus; atq; adeo Tetrachorda per Meſen conjunguntur. In Octochor-*
" *do autem (quoniam octo ſunt chordæ) ſuperiores quatuor* [Hypate, Par-
" *hypate, Lichanos, Meſe] unum Tetrachordum explent: ab hoc verò diſ-*
" *junctum inchoat à* Parameſe, *progrediturq; per* Paraneten, & Neten,
" *ac finitur ad ultimam, ſeu Proſlambanomenen.*

(7) 22. De number of 22 Cliefs in ꝺe Scal' † *Franchinus* require t, as † *L. I. c. 1.*
" neceſſari : aldowg *Guido* ſet doun but twenty.

(8) *Properly.* To wit, wen ꝺe directorder of ꝺe Not's is obſerved.
" For ſomtim' it happene t ꝺat *Mi,* having his certain Clief appointed
" torrow all Part's, is yet in ꝺis or ꝺat Part's, for a Not' or two, changed
" into *Fa. Vid.* § 5.

(g) *Thrꝫ ſigned Cliefs.* Wie 3 ar ſufficient for Song : dowg, at ꝺe
firſt, wer' marked *Gam ut* alſo, and *Ddla ſol :* (vid (h)) as nou ꝺey ar in
Virginal- and Organ-leſſons of exorbitant compas.

(h) De marks of ꝺe Signed Cliefs wer' at ꝺe firſt ꝺe Karacters of
ꝺeir Letters : as in *Gam-ut* it is Γ, and in *Ddla ſol, dd:* wie two bæing
little uſed, had little occaſion to bæ ꝺanged, as ꝺe oꝺer by often tran-
ſcribing, had. De ſign' of *F fa ut* bæing at ꝺe firſt a plain *F,* cam' in
tim', by degræs, to ꝺeſ' figur's 𝄢 𝄢 𝄢 : ꝺe ſign' of *C ſol fa ut*
bæing a plain *C* was ꝺanged by degræs, into ꝺeſ' ▯ ▯ ▯ :
and ꝺe ſign' of *G ſol re ut* bæing a dubble *G, gg,* as of *D la ſol* it
is a dibble *D, dd,* (becaus all ꝺe Treble Cliefs uſed to bæ written
wiꝺ dubble Letters) is turned into 𝄞 : and now again, in printed   *Vid.* (e)
Copi's, into a capital Roman *G.* Likwiſ' ꝺe flat and ſarp (wie ar boꝺ'
in *B fa B mi*) ar marked, ꝺe on' by a round ♭, wie doꝺ' t yet remain; ꝺe o-
ꝺer by a ſqar' ▯, wie by little & little, is ꝺus altered : ♭ , ♯ , 𝄪 .

(i) Of ꝺe 3 *Mi-cliefs,* ꝺe Scal' is ꝺreefold'.   (i)

Scala { *Duralis.*
          Naturalis.
          Mollaris.

De Dural, or ſharp, haꝺ no' Flat marked : and his *Vt* is in *G.* De
Natural haꝺ on' Flat : and his *Vt* in *C.* De Mollar or Flat haꝺ 2 Flats

and his *Vt* in F. As it is in ðe oldᵉ Vers:

In G Dural, in C Natural, F quoq; Mollar.

Alðowg yet, ðe Mollar, wiᵉ haᵵ 2 Flats marked in it, [ðe onᵉ in *B*, ðe oðer in *E*] is no morᵉ flat indeeᵈ, ðan ðe Dural, wiᵉ haᵵ nonᵉ: for ðe Dural wiᵉ is ſarp in boðᵉ ðoſᵉ Cliefs, haᵵ yet 2 Flats in onᵉ Heptakord, [*C* and *F :*] and ðe Mollar haᵵ no morᵉ; becaus ðoſᵉ 2 Flats [*C* and *F,*] by ðe flatting of *B* and *E*, becom wolᵉ notᵉs, [*ſol* and *ut.*] And ðowg onᵉ woldᵉ flat ðe ðird Mi-clief alſo, (wiᵉ ſom, profeſſing to make an extraordinary flat ſong, havᵉ don) and ſo ſet *Mi* in *Dla-ſol-re*, *Re* in *C-ſol-fa-ut*, and *Vt* in *Bfa-Bmi*; yea if hee woldᵉ goᵉ furðer, and flat *D* too; yet all woldᵉ beᵉ onᵉ: ðe ſong woldᵉ prœvᵉ noᵉ morᵉ flat wiᵵ all ðeſᵉ flats, ðan wiᵵ nonᵉ of ðem.

(ᵏ) Weiðer you learn ðe Letters alonᵉ, or ðe Notᵉs wiᵵ ðem; ((if, for ðe help of Memori, you will account ðem (as ðe manner is) on ðe fingers))ðey ar ðus moſtᵉ fitly placed. Set *Gam-ut* in ðe firſt joint of ðe forᵉ finger, next ðe palm: ðencᵉ aſcending, ſet *Are* in ðe ſecond, *Bmi* in ðe ðird, and *C fa ut* in ðe top: ðen deſcending on ðe bak-ſidᵉ, ſet *Dſolre* in ðe ðird joint, *Elami* in ðe ſecond, and *F fa ut* in ðe firſt: and ſo havᵉ you don onᵉ Septenari. In likᵉ manner placᵉ ðe ſecond Septenari on ðe Middle finger, and ðe ðird on ðe Ring-finger.

Cᴀᴘ. II. §III.

Of ðe *Tunᵉ* of Notᵉs.

Cᴏncerning ðe Tunᵉ of Notᵉs, From *Mi* to *fa*, and likᵉ wiſᵉ from *la* to *pa*, is but (ᵃ) Half a tonᵉ: betweenᵉ any oðer two Notᵉs is a wolᵉ Tonᵉ: as from *fa* to *ſol*, from *ſol* to *la*, likᵉ wiſᵉ from *pa* to *ut*, from *ut* to *re*, and from *re* to *Mi*: wiᵉ ðing is manifeſted in a Lutᵉ: werᵉ from fret to fret is but half a Tonᵉ, and from any onᵉ fret to ðe next ſavᵉ onᵉ is a wholᵉ Tonᵉ, or Notᵉ. But, in Singing, hou to tunᵉ eaᵉ Notᵉ and Half-notᵉ to his fellow, cannot be declared by precept; but is to be learned eiðer by ðe livᵉly voicᵉ of ðe Teacher, or by ſom Inſtrument rigtly tuned: as if ðe firſt baſᵉ Lute-ſtring, ſtrokᵉ open, beᵉ *M I*; ðe ſamᵉ ſtopt at ðe firſt fret ſoundeᵵ *fa*, at ðe ðird *ſol*, at ðe fift (wiᵉ is all onᵉ wiᵵ ðe ſecond ſtring open) *la*: at ðe firſt fret of ðe ſecond ſtring *pa*, at ðe ðird *ut*, at ðe fift *re*, at ðe ſevnᵵ, or ðe ſecond of ðe ðird ſtring, *Mi* again: &c.

Aɴɴoᴛ.

ANNOT. to CAP. II. § III.

(a) HALf a Tone. Desc Half-tons weiꝺer ꝺey bee Eqal or Uneqal, it is a Qestion. *Aristoxenus* ꝺe Mufician (according to ꝺe judgment of ꝺe Ear) teaꝼeꝺ ꝺem to bee eqal moꝺtiz of a Tone. * *Aristoxenus Muficus, judicio aurium cuncta permittens, hæc Semitonia non arbitratur esse, contractiora Dimidio; sed sicut Semitonia dicuntur, ita esse Dimidietates Tonorum.* But *Philolaus* (as ꝺe same Auꝺor haꝼ) divideꝼ ꝺe Tone into 2 uneqal Parts: werꝼof ꝺe one is more ꝺan Half, wie hee calleꝼ *Apotome*; ꝺe oꝺer les ꝺan half, wie hꝛ calleꝼ *Diefis*. † *Philolaus duas efficit partas: unam quæ dimidio sit major, eamq; A-potomen vocat; reliquam quæ dimidio sit minor, camq; Diefin dicit.* Wie Parts, wiꝼ ꝺeir Parts and Particles, hee doꝼ ꝺus defineꝼ.

† *Tonus duobus Semitoniis minoribus & Commate constat. Nam si totus Tonus ex Apotome constat ac Semitonio; [scilicet Minore;] Semitonium verò ab Apotome differt Commate; nihil est aliud Apotome, nisi Semitonium minus, & Comma.*

Diefis (inquit Philolaus) est spatium, quo major est Sesquitertia propor-tio duobus Tonis. Boꝺc wie hee doꝼꝼ afterward deſcribꝼ by ꝺe number of Comma's.

† *Minus Semitonium minus est quàm quatuor Commata, majus quàm tria.*

* *Apotome major est quàm quatuor Commata, minor quàm quinq;. Diaſchiſma est dimidium Diefios. i. Semitonii minoris.*

Comma est spatium quo major est Sesquioctava proportio duabus Diefi-bus.

Schiſma est dimidium Commatis.

Integrum verò dimidium Toni (quod est Semitonium) constat ex dua-bus Diaſchiſmatibus (quod est unum Semitonium minus) & Schiſ-mate.

Ꝺis opinion of *Philolaus*, concerning ꝺe uneqal partꝼs of a Tone, *Boetius* takeꝼ mue pains, by his qeint Ariꝼmetical Conclufions, to maintein. But ꝺat it is indeꝺ a meeꝼ fanci, forged onꝼly by Melan-kolik imaginations, ꝺer is noꝼ Mufician fo fimple, ꝺat knoweꝼ not: and ꝺat ꝺe Juſt Hemitonꝼ is that, wie naturally paffeꝼ in ꝺe Order or Series of ꝺe Notes in ꝺe Heptaꝼords or Septenariꝯ of ꝺe Scale. So ꝺat, according to *Aristoxenus*, ꝺe Diateffaron confifteꝼ of 2 Tones, and ꝺe Diapente of 3, wiꝼ one eqal Semitonꝼ: wie if it bee raiſed or depreſt from its juſt found, ꝺe quantiti of a Diefis, or *Diaſchiſma*, or a *Comma* or *Schiſma*, or les, if les may bee; it is out of Tune: and noꝼ gꝺd Mu-fik, or truꝼ Concord can bee madꝼ wiꝼ it, til it bee reꝼtifyed, anꝺ browgꝼ ꝺe perfeꝼt *Hemitonium*.

CAP. II.

Margin notes:
* Boet. l. 3. c. 1.
† Ibid. c. 5
† Boet. l. 3. c. 6.
Apotome.
Diefis.
‡ L. 3. c. 14.
* Ibid. c. 15.
Diaſchiſma.
Comma.
Schiſma.
Semitonium integrum.

C A P. II. § IV.

Of de *Tim* *of Not's* : ¶ I. *Of Figur's.*

4
De *Tim* of
Not's.
(ᵃ)

TO signifi de differenc of Tim, de Not's hav (ᵃ) eigt different Figur's and Nam's : a Larg ⊏⊐ , a Long ⊏⊐ , a Brief ⊏⊐ , a Sembrief ◊ , a Minim ◊ , a Croeet ♩ , a Qaver ♪ , and a Semiqaver ♪ .

(ᵇ)
De *Sembrief* is
de *Mefur*-not.

(ᵇ) De principal *Tim-not* is de *Sembrief* : by wol Tim, de tim of all Not's is known : and it is mefured by *Tactus* or de Strok of de Hand, in a certain fpac or diftanc : de wie, Imitation and Uf will make you perfect in.

Thefis & *Arfis.*

De part's of *Tactus* ar two : [*Thefis* and *Arfis*:] i. de Depreffion or Fall, and de Elevation or Rif of de Hand.

Dis conftant tim of de Mefur-not doo't contein 2 Minims, 4 Croeets, 8 Qavers, and 16 Semiqavers : and, on de oder fid, de Brief conteinet 2 of def Tim's, de Long 4, and de Larg 8 : as is hær expreffed.

So dat, every greater comprehending his lef two tim's, on *Larg* is as much as 8 *Sembriefs*, or 128 *Semiqavers.*

---

§ IV. ¶ II. *Of Proportion.*

Proportions to
de *Mefur*-note.
(ᶜ)
I
Duple.

De *Sign* of
Duple.

DEr belonget to de mefur-not *Proportion* : wie is fowrfold : (ᶜ) [*Duple, Triple, Sextuple,* and *Noncuple.*]
Duple Proportion is, wen to a *Strok*, or *Sembrief-tim*, is fung 2 *Minims*, [or on *Sembrief* wie countervailet dem,] (and confeqently 4 *Croeets*, 8 *Qavers*, and 16 *Semiqavers*,) on to de *Thefis* or Fall, and de oder to *Arfis* or Rif of de Hand: de Sign wer of is dis : ₵.

Triple,

Triple Proportion is, wen 3 Minims [or a Sembrief and a Minim,] (and conſeqently 6 Croⱦeets and 12 Qavers) go⁶ to ðe Sembrief-ſtrok⁶ : 2 to ðe Fall, and ðe ⱦird to ðe Riſ⁶ of ðe Hand : (ᵈ) ðe proper Sign⁶ wⱦer⁶of is dis (· Unto wi∈ 3 Minims, 2 in *Dupla* ar⁶ eqivalent : and ðer⁶foꝛ⁶ may bæ ſung to ðem by an oðer Part⁶ : for in boð⁶ Proportions, ðe Hand fallⱦet in ðe ſam⁶ inſtant ; dowg it riſ⁶ a little ſooner in ðe *Dupla,* ðan in ðe *Tripla* : in ðat, wen ½ , in dis, wen ⅔ of ðe tim⁶ is paſt.

2
Tripla.

Ðe Sign⁶ of
Triple.
(d)

Sextupla is ðe *Triple* of ðe Minim in *Duple* Proportiꝋ : wen to eaⱦ∈ Minim in *Duple* Tim⁶, is ſung (ᵉ) 3 blak Minims [or a blak Sembrief and a Minim,] (and conſeqently 6 Croⱦeets, wi∈ muſt hav⁶, for differenc⁶, ðe form oꝼ Qavers) 3 to ðe Fall, and 3 to ðe Riſ⁶ of ðe Hand : [or, if you will kæp⁶ † Minim-tim⁶, 3 to on⁶ ſtrok⁶, and 3 to an oðer :] wi∈ *Triple* is ðer⁶foꝛ⁶ called *Sextupla* ; becaus 6 of ðeſ⁶ blak Minims go⁶ to on⁶ Sembrief-tim⁶.

3.
Sextupla.
(e)

† *V.* (b) *in Notis.*

Noncupla is ðe *Triple* of ðe Minim in *Triple* Proportion : wen to eaⱦh Minim in *Triple* Tim⁶, is ſung 3 blak Minims, 6 to ðe Fall, and 3 to ðe Riſ⁶ of ðe Hand : wi∈ *Triple* is ðer⁶-foꝛ⁶ called *Noncupla* ; becaus nin⁶ of ðeſ⁶ blak Minims go⁶ to on⁶ Sembrief-tim⁶.

4
Noncupla.

Ðe Sign⁶ of *Sextupla* is, wiⱦ ðe blak Not⁶s, his figured Number 6. 1 : and of ðe *Noncupla,* it is, wiⱦ ðe lik⁶ blak not⁶s, his figured number 9. 1.

Ðe Sign⁶s of
Sextuple, *and*
Noncuple.

Becaus *Sextupla* is ðe *Triple* of Minims in *Duple* Time, and *Noncupla* ðe *Triple* of Minims in *Triple* Tim⁶ ; ðer⁶-for⁶ wæ fall reddily out of *Duple* Proportion, into *Sextupla,* as in ðe *Kings Mask* : (aldowg in ðe *Medley,* dis *Sextupla* doⱦ⁶ⱦ immediatly ſucⱦæd⁶ ðe *Triple*) and out of *Triple* into *Noncupla* : as in ðe *G R O U N D* : wi∈ bæing ſet to ðe *Virginal,* ðe rigⱦ hand diſcantⱦⱦet in *Noncuple* uppꝋ ðe plain *Triple* of ðe leⱦt hand.

D

Examples

Examples of de 4 Proportions.

Not^e heer^e dat de blak Minim in *Sextuple* Proportion,
bœing ⅓ of a *Duple* Minim, and de Cro-chet in *Triple* Proportion, bœing ½ of a Triple Minim, ar bod^e, as of on^e form,
so of on^e tim^e; der^e going 6 of ea-c sort to a *Sembrief-strok^e* :
but dere is dis differenc^e, dat of de six blak Minim, de
sowr-t beginnet de Ris^e of de Hand, and is der^efor^e mor^e notably accented; as de First is, wi-c beginnet de Fall : and of
de six Cro-cets, de Fift beginnet de Ris^e, and is der^efor^e
mor^e notably ac cented ; as lik^ewis^e de First and Third is : so
dat de blak Minims go^e jumping by Thrœ^es, and de Cro-cets
by Two^es : wer^e-by de Melodi of de sam^e Not^es becom-
met divers : as in dis Example.

**Proportion of
Sounds.
(f)**
Besid^es des^e us^eful and necessary Proportions of Tim^e, in
Musicall Not^es, Speculativ^e Musicians tea-c also (f) Proportions of Sounds : specially in de trœ first-found Con-
cords, [*Diapason, Diapente,* and *Diate ssaron.*]

ANNOT.

ANNOT. to CAP. II. § IV. ¶ I and II.

Of Figur⁵s and Proportion.

(a)   AT ðe ſirſt, as in Syllables, ſo in Not⁵s, ðer⁵ wer⁵ but 2 Qantiti⁵s, [a Long and a Short, or Brief:] and ðen as *Syllaba brevis*, ſo *Nota brevis unius erat temporis, longa duorum*: But Muſicians finding afterward ðat in ðat ſort tim⁵ ðey migt paſ 2 Not⁵s, divided ðe Short into two Half-ſorts or Sembriefs ; joyning alſo 2 Longs into on⁵ Figur⁵, wie ðey called a Larg⁵ : [*Larga* or *Maxima*.]

De form of ðe *Short* or *Brief* was a Sqar⁵ □ : ðe wie having a ſank added unto it, (to ſigniſi⁵ his leng⁵) was ðe form of ðe *Long* |‾‾|, and ðe Sqar⁵ being dubbled, wiɩ ðe lik⁵ ſank added, was ðe form of ðe *Larg⁵* |‾‾‾‾|. De form of a *Sembrief* or [Half-ſort] was a Triangle or half of a ſqar⁵ divided from angle to angle : wie ſinc⁵, for qik and decent pricking, ðey hav⁵ canged into a *Rhombus* or Diamond-ſqar⁵ : ðus ◊.

Philippus de Vitriaco, not long ſinc⁵, divided ðe *Sembrief* alſo into two Not⁵s, wie hee called *Minims*, or leaſt of all : perſuading himſelf ðat ðis ſort or brief tim⁵ cœld⁵ not contein a greater number of Not⁵s ðan 4 : ðe form of ðe *Minim* was ðe form of ðe *Sembrief* wiɩ a ſank added unto it ◊̸. Deſ⁵ ſiv⁵ figur⁵s ar comprehended in ðis old⁵ *Pentameter* or ſiv⁵-ſooted vers :

Maxima, Longa, Brevis, Semibrevis Minima.

All wie *Glareanus* affirmeɩ to hav⁵ been in uſ⁵ ſœm 70 yeer⁵s heſor⁵ his tim⁵ : wo liv⁵d about ðe yeer⁵ of our Lord 1550.

De original ⁵ðeſ⁵ ſiv⁵ Figur⁵s or Tim⁵-not⁵s,* *Franch.* ðus delivereɩ.   * *L. 2, c. I.* *Poetæ atq; Muſici omne vocis tempus breve longumve poſuere, & unius temporis menſuram brevi ſyllabæ adſcripſerunt ¹ nge vero duorum temporum quantitatem. Sic Notularum alia brevis eſt, alia longa : naturaliter namq; correptio & productio ſonis ipſis, veluti & ſyllabis ineſſe noſcuntur. Quare Muſici Brevem primò Notulam quadrato corpore tradiderunt, hoc modo:* □ : [*Longam quoq; quadratā cum virgula in dextra deorſum vel ſurſum:* □ □. *Brevem inde quadratam duas in partes diametraliter partientes,*] *Semibrevē conduxerunt, dimidiam ei Brevis quantitatem adſcribentes, hoc modo ;* ◊. *Neoterici poſtremò Semibrevi temporis unius menſuram adſcripſerunt ; Theſin & Arſin, uniuſcujuſq; Semibrevis ſono, concludentes: & Semibrevem ipſam integrā temporis menſurā diſpoſitam duas in partes æquas diſtinxerunt ; quibus minimām vocis plenitudinem adſcripſerunt : ipſas inde Minimas nuncupantes. Minimæ figuram deſcribunt Semibrevem, appoſitā alteri acutorum angulorum virgulā hoc*

modo: ◊̸ *Deniq; † duplicem* Longam *ſuperduxerunt Muſici in Te-*   † *Seu Largam.*

norbus Motetorum *quatnor* Brevia *tempora continentem.* |‾‾‾‾| But

D 2.

But ſuccæding ages hav' gon far beyond *Philip*, wo towgt hæ was at ðe fardeſt. For ðey hav' mor' over deviſed not only a les ðan ðe leaſt, but alſo a les ðan ðe les ðan ðe leaſt, yea and a les ðan ðat tꝩ ðe firſt of ðeſ', wic is a *Half-minim*, had ðe form of a Minim wiꞇ a Crꝩk' added unto it

wer' of it hat ðe name *Crocet* [a diminutiv' of ðe Frenc *croc*, a hꝩk' or Crꝩk'] wic nam' it ſtil reteinet, ꝺowg it hav' loſt ðe form: for wen ðe *Qaver* [a half-Crocet] and *Semiqaver* [ðe qarter crocet] wer' invented; ðey, for mor' expedit pricking, diſtinguiſhed ðe *Crocet* from ðe *Minim* on'ly by blacking ðe ſqare, ðe *Qaver* (wic is not ſo freqent) from ðe *Crocet* by his crꝩk' and ðe *Semiqaver* from ðem boꞇ by his dubble crꝩk'.

And yet wen all is ꝺꝩn, ðey may ſæm' to hav' ꝺꝩn, in effect, as mue as noꞇing. For in ðeſ' Nu' Not's, ðey ar fain to kæp' Minim-tim': and ðat haply as long or longer ðan ðe old' Brief-tim': and ſo ðe Nu' *Qaver* wil bæ no ſwitter indæd', ðan ðe old' *Minim* was: and wer' ðey wil næd's uſ' *Semiqavers* tꝩ; ðey can bæ content to protract ðe Minim-tim', ſpecially, in ſinging, ðat ſo ðoſ' many Not's may bæ contained in it. For, as *Lyſtenius* ſayꞇ, ðe 3 Not's wic were invented ſinc' ðe Minim [   ], did ſerv raðer for Inſtrumental, ðan for

Vocal Muſik. † *Tres poſteriores ſpecies magis Muſicis inſtrumentis, propter nimiam celeritatem, quàm humanæ voci competunt.*

(b) As in former tim', wen ðe *Sembrief* and *Minim* wer' ðe leaſt Not's, ðe *Brief* was ðe Meſur'-Not', or principal Tim'-Not'; (by wic bæing meſured by ðe ſtrok' of ðe Hand, ðe juſt tim' of all oðer Not's was known) ſo ſinc' ðe inventing of ðe ſmaller Not's, (ðe *Brief* growing by little and little out of uſ') ðe *Sembrief* becam' Meſur'-not' in his ſtæd: as now in qik tim' ðe *Minim* beginnet to encroe' uppon ðe *Sembrief*.

† Dis *Tactus major* is ðe tim' ðat is ment in ðe Canons of *Fuga*'s: as *Fuga in uniſono, poſt duo tempora*: i. *poſt 4. Semibrevia.*

ðe Tim'-ſtrok' of ðe *Brief*, *Lyſtenius* termet † *Tactus major*, and of ðe *Sembrief Tactus minor*: ðe wic hæ ꝺꝩꞇ ꝺus defin': *Tactus major eſt, cùm Brevis Tactu menſuratur: Minor eſt, cùm Semibrevis ſub Tactum cadit integrum.* But now ðe Sembrief-tim' is our *Major Tactus*: and ðe Minim-tim' our *Tactus Minor.*

(c) ðeſ' 4 Proportions of 2, 3, 6, and 9 to on', (bæing peculiar to ðe Meſur'-not') as now ðey ar in reſpect to ðe *Sembrief-tim'*; ſo wer' ðey formerly to ðe *Brief* tim', wen ðat was ðe Meſur'-not': bæing ðen called ðe 4 Mꝩd's: [ðe Perfect and Imperfect of ðe mor', ☉, ℂ and ðe Perfect and Imperfect of ðe les, ○, ℂ.]

ðe Perfect of ðe mor' was, wen 3 Sembriefs went to ðe Brief-tim', and 3 Minims to ðe tim' of ðe Sembrief: lik' unto ðe Proportion *Noncupla*: in wic 9 blak Minims go' to ðe Sembrief-tim'.

ðe Imperfect of ðe mor', wen 2 Sembriefs went to ðe Brief-tim', and

3 Minims

3 Minims to ðe *Sembrief* : likᶜ unto our *Sextupla* : in wiᶜ 6 blak Minims goᶜ to ðe Sembrief-timᶜ.

Ðe Perfeƈt of ðe les, wen 3 Sembriefs went to ðe Brief-timᶜ, and 2 Minims to a Sembrief : likᶜ unto ðe *Triple* Proportion : in wiᶜ 3 Minims goᶜ to ðe Sembrief, [ðe nou mesurᶜ-notᶜ;] as 3 Sembriefs went to ðe Brief, wen ðat was ðe Mesurᶜ-notᶜ.

And ðe Imperfeƈt of ðe les, wen 2 Sembriefs went to ðe Brief-timᶜ, and 2 Minims to ðe Sembrief : wiᶜ seemeꝷ to bæ all onᶜ wiꝷ ðe Duple Proportion : neiðer of ðem altering ðe Natural and common valuᶜ of ðe Smaller Notᶜs, in refpeƈt of ðeir Integrals.

But now, ðe *Brief* bæing no longer ufed for ðe Mesurᶜ-notᶜ, ðe Mœdᶜs ar grown out of ufᶜ wiꝷ him. Never-ðeles, our Mafters ar pleafed, in honour of Antiquiti, to continuᶜ ðe teaᵹeing of ðefᶜ 4 Mœdᶜs among ðe firft Rulᶜs of ðeir Ifagog ; as if ðe Brief werᶜ ftil ðe Mefurᶜ-notᶜ.

I read of fundry oðer ftrangᶜ Proportions : as of 5 to 1, 7 to 1, 9 to 2, 10 to 1, &c : ðe wiᶜ (eiðer having never bæn in ufᶜ, or bæing nou out of ufᶜ) becaus of ðem ðerᶜ is no ufᶜ, but onᶜly to perplex ðe Setter and Singer, and to offend ðe Hearer ; (wofᶜ ear to pleaz is ðe endᶜ of Mufik) it is enouᵹ, if not tœ muᶜ, onᶜy to mention ðem.

(d) Sœm ufᶜ for a mark of *Triple* timᶜ, blak Sembriefs and Minims (and ðen ðe wiᶜ Sembrief cœmming among ðem takeꝷ up ðe ful Sembrief-timᶜ) but ðis makeꝷ a confufion of ðe Proportions : and fœm ufᶜ blak briefs and fembriefs : but ðefᶜ ar not fo proper : ðey had indeedᶜ ðeir ufᶜ, wen ðe Brief was ðe Mefurᶜ-notᶜ; but now ðerᶜ is no needᶜ of ðem at all : and fœm, to makᶜ furᶜ wœrk, ufᶜ ðe Mœd C, ðe blak notᶜs, ðe figured number 3. 1. and all.

(e) Ðe *blak Minim* in *Sextupla*, ðe *blak Minim* in *Noncupla* ; ðe Crœⱳet in *Dupla*, and ðe Crœⱳet in Tripla, having noᶜ differeneᶜ in form, ar ðus difcerned. Ðe *Crœⱳet* is ðe half of ðe Minim : wiᶜ, weiðer it bæ *Duple* or *Triple*, is known by ðe Mœd, [ℂ or (·]. Ðe *blak Minim* is a ðird part of his wiꝷ Minim : and is known boꝷ by ðe *blak Sembrief* accompanying him, and alfo by his figured number : wiᶜ, if ðe blak bæ ðe ðird of a *Duple Minim*, is, 6. 1. if of a Triple, 9. 1

(f) Ðis fuppofed Mufical Proportion is borrowed of ðe Aritmetical.   *Aritmetical*
Proportion in Aritmetik is of great ufᶜ : as bæing ðe ground of ðe   *Proportion in*
Rulᶜ of Þree, [ðat *Golden Rulᶜ* :] by wiᶜ even wœnders ar wrouᵹt.   *Numbers.*
And it is ꝷreefoldᶜ : [*Superparticularis,* Superpartiens, and Multiplex.]
Ðe fignᶜ of ðe firft is *Sefqui* : of ðe fecond, *Super.*   1

Sefqui, out of Proportion, fignifieꝷ onᶜ and a half : as *fefquihora* onᶜ   *Superparticula-*
hour and a half, *fefquilibra* onᶜ pound and a half : but, in Proportien,   *ris.*
bæing compounded wiꝷ ðe *Denominator* of any *Fraƈtion* , it fignifieꝷ
onᶜ entirᶜ, and alfo onᶜ for ðe *Numerator* of ðe *Fraƈtion* : as *fefquitertia,*
onᶜ and onᶜ ꝷird part [1, 1⁄3 :] as 4 is to 3 : but annexed to a Multiplex,
onᶜly onᶜ [ðe Numerator of ðe Fraƈtion :] as *Tripla fefquifeptima,* ꝷræ
and onᶜ fevnꝷ part, [3, 1⁄7] as 22 is to 7.

2
Superpartiens.

In likᵉ manner *Super*, compounded wiᵗ a woord of *Superpartient Proportion*, signifyeᵗ onᵉly onᵉ entirᵉ: afeer wiᵉ is expreſt ᵈe *Numerator* of ᵈe Fraction: and ᵈen ᵈe Denominator ᵈerᵉof : as *Superbipartiens tertias*, onᵉ and two ᵗird partᵉs [1, ⅔] jas 5 is to 3 : but annexed to a Multiplex, it ſignifyeᵗ noting; but ſerveᵗ onᵉly, as a *Copula*, to join ᵈe two Proportions in onᵉ : as *Tripla ſuperbipartiens tertias*, ᵗree and two ᵗird parts [3⅔] likᵉ as 22 is to 6.

3
Multiplex.

Multiplex haᵗ noᵉ common ſignᵉ; but every Sortᵉ is expreſt in its proper Term : as *Dupla* twofoldᵉ, twiſᵉ ſo mueᵉ : likᵉ as 4 is to two, 24 to 12.

1

Eaᵉ of deſᵉ ᵗree ſorts of *Proportion* haᵗ infinitᵉ *ſpecies. Superparticularis* haᵗ *Seſquialtera* 1, ½, *ſeſquitertia* 1, ⅓, *ſeſquiquarta* 1, ¼, *ſeſquiquinta* 1, ⅕, &c. in infinitum.

2

Superpartiens haᵗ *Superbipartiens, ſupertripartiens, Superquadripartiens*, &c in infinitum : and every onᵉ of deſᵉ haᵗ alſo his infinitᵉ partᵉs ; as *Superbipartiens tertias, ſuperbipartiens quartas, quintas, ſextas, ſeptimas, &c.* in infinitum : ſo *ſupertripartiens quartas, quintas*, &c. in infinitum : and ſo *ſuperquadripartiens quintas*, &c. in infinitum.

3

And *Multiplex* haᵗ *Dupla, Tripla, Quadrupla, Quintupla*, &c. in infinitum.

Muſical Proportions in Sounds.
*L. 1. c. 7.

Soom of deſᵉ *Proportions* * *Boetius* applyeᵗ to his Concords of Muſik : werᵉ hee ſayᵗ, *Illud tamen eſſe cognitum debet, quod omnes Muſica Conſonantiæ, aut in* Dupla, *aut in* Tripla, *aut in quadrupla, aut in* Seſquialtera, *aut in* Seſquitertia, *proportione conſiſtunt. Et vocabitur quidem quæ in numeris* ſeſquitertia *eſt*, Diateſſaronᵉ*in ſonu : quæ in numeris* ſeſquialtera *eſt*, Diapente *appellatur in vocibus: quæ in Numeris* Dupla *eſt*, Diapaſon *in* Conſonantiis : Tripla, Diapente *ac* Diapaſon : Quadrupla *autem*, Diſdiapaſon. By occaſion werᵉof, divers of our latᵉ Writers, to ſhew ᵈeir wit, (as *Glareanus* ſayᵗ) havᵉ taken mueᵉ pains in making largᵉ, tedious, and intricatᵉ Diſcoᵉrſes of ſundry oᵈer Proportions : wiᵉ hee finding to bee fruitles and impertinent to Muſik, doᵉᵗ ᵈus reprehend : †*Ars ut ars eſt tradi debet. At res ipſa nunc clamat, ſuperfluum eſſe tot Proportionum obſervationes : quarum Nemo, quamlibet cantu exercitatus, meminiſſe queat : quaſq; nullus ex doctiſſimis noſtra ætatis Muſicis dignatus eſt (præter pauculas) in Symphoniam aſciſcere : ut in quibus major labor in addiſcendo, quàm ſuavitas gratiæve in cantando eſſe conſtet. Teſtor itaq; diſplicere, quod magis hæc ad oſtentanda ingenia, quàm ad Muſices uſum inventa videantur.* And ᵈerᵉforᵉ hee reteineᵗ onᵉly ᵈoſᵉ few wiᵉ ar ſaid to bee in ᵈe Concords, *Diapaſon, Diapente*, and *Diateſſaron* : ᵈe wiᵉ hee doᵉᵗ ᵈus diſcribᵉ: Dupla *ut* 4 *ad* 2. Superparticularis *vocatur, quoties major numerus minorem in ſe habet totum ſemel, & præterea unam aliquam ejus partem. Si dimidiam; proportio eſt* Seſquialtera : *quæ etiam* ſeſcupla, *&* Græcè *hemiola vocatur: nt* 3 *ad* 2, 6 *ad* 4. *Si tertiam partem; ſeſquitertia dicitur : ut* 4 *ad* 3.

†*Dodecachordon,* Cap. 12.

De Original of Proportions Muſical.

Deſᵉ *Proportions*, *Pythagoras* is ſayd firſt to havᵉ found in ᵈe Smiᵗs Hammers, diſtinguiſhed by ᵈeir weigᵗs : as if ᵈe ſecond Hammer, wiᵉ ſounded upon ᵈe Anvil à *Diateſſaron* to ᵈe firſt, weiged ſo mueᵉ as it and a ᵗird partᵉ : ᵈe ᵗird, wiᵉ ſounded à *Diapente* to ᵈe Firſt, weiged ſo mueᵉ and halfſo mueᵉ : and ᵈe ſowrᵗ, wiᵉ ſounded a *Diapaſon* to ᵈe Firſt, weiged

weiged twif so mue: Wie ting Boetius doct dus delivet. * Pythagoras   * l. 1, c. 10.
dum inquirebat, quanam ratione firmiter & constanter Consonantiarum
momenta perdisceret; præteriens forte Fabrorum officinas, pulsos Malleos
exaudivit, ex diversis sonis unam quodammodo Concinentiam personare:
diuque considerans, arbitratus est diversitatem sonorum ferientium vires ef-
ficere: atque ut id apertius colliqueret, mutareat inter se Malleos imperavit.
Sed sonorum proprietas non in hominum lacertis hærebat, sed mutatos Malleos comitabatur. Ubi igitur id animadvertit; malleorum pondus examinat.
Et duplici reperti sunt pondere, qui sibi secundùm Diapason Consonantiam
respondebant. Eundem etiam, qui Duplus esset uni, Sesquitertium alterius
esse comprehendit: ad quem scilicet Diatessaron sonabat. Ad alium verò
quendam (qui eidem, Diapente consonantiâ, jungebatur) eundem superiorù
Duplum, reperit esse Sesquialterum. Duo verò hi, (ad quos superioris Du-
plex, Sesquitertius & Sesquialter esse probatus est) ad se invicem † Sesqui-   † Quia 9 con-
octavam proportionem perpensi sunt custodire. Quum igitur, ante Pythago-   tinent 8, & ⅛.
ram, Consonantiæ Musicæ partim Diapason, partim Diapente, partim Di-   * Nam Tertia
atessaron (quæ est consonantia * minima) vocarentur; primus Pythagoras   perfecta & im-
hoc modo reperit, qua proportione sibimet hæc sonorum chorda jungeretur.   perfectâ, (ut
Et ut sit clarius quod dictum est, Sint, verbi gratiâ, Malleorum quatuor   item Sexta)
pondera, quæ subscriptis numeris contineantur: [12, 9, 8, 6.] Hi igi-   tunc temporis
tur Mallei, qui 12 & 6 ponderibus vergebant, Diapason in Duplo Conci-   ignotæ erant.
nentiam personabant. Malleus verò 12 ponderum ad malleum 9, & Malleus
8 ponderum ad malleum 6 ponderum (secundùm Epitritam Proportionem)
Diatessaron consonantiâ jungebatur. Novem verò ponderum ad 6, & 12 ad
8, Diapente consonantiam permiscebant. Novem vero ad 8, in Sesquioctava
proportione, resonabant Tonum. All wie Proportions, as dey hav relation
on to an oder, ar expressed in dis Figur.

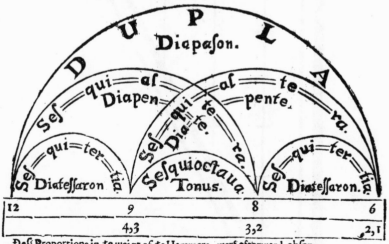

12	9	8	6
	4,3	3,2	2,1

Des Proportions in de weigt of de Hammers, wer afterward obser-
ved in de lengt of Nervs: as * Aristotle manifestet in his Triquetra.   * In Probl. Sect.
                                                   De 19, Quæst. 23.

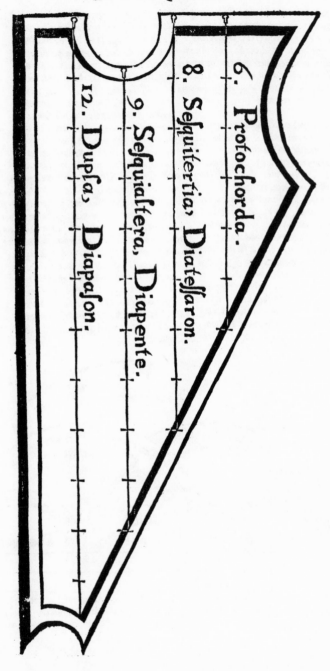

Et in Triquetris (sayꝼ hœ) *Nervi ,quorum alter longitudine* Duplâ,*al-ter subduplâ est, æquè intenti,* Diapaſon *Conſonantiam reddunt : genus autem concinendi, quod* Diapente *nominatur,* Seſquialterâ *conſtat : quod verò* Diateſſaron *vocamus, intervallo* Seſquitertio *continetur.* And after ꝼat in Magnitud͏ͤ alſo, Capaciti, and Craſſitud͏ͤ of oꝺer ꝼings : † as *Boe-tius* noteꝼ. Henc͏ͤ it is, ꝺat Concords ar ſaid to hav͏ͤ Proportions; Di-apaſon, à *Dupla*; Diapente, a *Seſquialtera* ;and Diateſſaron, a *Seſquitertia:* becauſ ꝺe ꝼings ꝺat yœld͏ͤ ꝺeſ͏ͤ Concordant ſounds, hav͏ͤ in ꝺem ſuꝼ Proportions : So ꝺat ꝺe knowledg of ꝺeſ͏ͤ myſteri͏ͤs ſeemeꝼ raꝺer to concern ꝺe Artificers ꝺat mak͏ͤ Inſtruments; ꝺan ꝺe Artiſts ꝺat uſ͏ͤ ꝺem: alꝺowg it may bœ, ꝺat ꝺey follow oꝺer Rul͏ͤs and Proportions in ꝺeir work, ꝺan ꝺeſ͏ͤ.

† *L. 1. c. 11.*

❧ Hœ ꝺat deſireꝼ to know ꝺe tru͏ͤ Proportions in all ſorts of Inſtru-ments [boꝼ͏ͤ Entata and Empneuſta] let him read ꝺe ingenious and ela-borat͏ͤ work of *Merſenɴus, De Harmonicis Inſtrumentis.* Wer͏ͤ hœ ſaꝇ find͏ͤ ꝺe various Forms of all Inſtruments, wiꝼ ꝺe Proportions of ꝺeir Not͏ͤs, moſt͏ͤ Artificially typifyed and deſcribed.

And ꝺis is ꝺe Doctrin͏ͤ of *Concord-proportions,* received from Anti-qiti. Unto wi͏ͤ † ſœm of our Neoteriks hav͏ͤ added Proportions of ꝺe oꝺer Concords, [to wit *Seſquiquarta* of *Ditonus,* *Seſquiquinta* of *Semiditonus,* *Superbipartiens tertias* of *Tonuſ-diapente,* and *Supertri-partiens quintas* of *Semitonium-diapente:* wꝇ haply ꝺey hammered out of ꝺe known differenc͏ͤ betwœn͏ͤ ꝺe Proportions *Seſquitertia* [1, $\frac{1}{3}$ and *Seſquialtera* [1, $\frac{1}{4}$] wi͏ͤ differenc͏ͤ is $\frac{1}{6}$: wer͏ͤunto ꝺe Diſtanc͏ͤ betwœn͏ͤ ꝺe Concords *Diateſſaron* and *Diapente* (wi͏ͤ is a wꝍl͏ͤ *Ton͏ͤ*) dœꝼ anſwer. So ꝺat $\frac{1}{6}$ in *Proportion* anſwereꝼ to a *Ton͏ͤ* in *Sound :* and $\frac{1}{12}$ in *Proportion,* to a *Hemitonium.*

† *Calviſius c.5.* and *Mutinen-ſis.*

By wi͏ͤ *Theſis* or *Maxim,* as by a *Lydius lapis,*all ꝺe *Proportions* in an Eigꝼ may bœ found and tryed.
For * ſœing ꝺat a *Diapaſon* is of ꝺe *Dupla* Proportion ; watſoever is ꝺe number of any Kord, ꝺe number of his *Diapaſon* muſt bœ ſo muꝼ mor͏ͤ: as if ꝺe Mean *Vt* bœ 12, ꝺe Baſ͏ͤ *Vt* [his *Diapaſon*] wil bœ 24. Lik͏ͤwiſ Pa bœing accounted 12, ꝺe ſam͏ͤ *Ground Vt,*haꝼ unto it ꝺe Pro-portion of 12 (wi͏ͤ is on͏ͤ entir͏ͤ)and $\frac{5}{6}$ of 12, [or 22.] So Sol or Re bœ-ing 12, ꝺe Ground haꝼ ꝺe Proportion, to ꝺe on͏ͤ, of 1, $\frac{3}{4}$, $\frac{1}{12}$ [or $\frac{1}{2}$ and $\frac{1}{12}$,] wi͏ͤ is 19; and to ꝺe oꝺer of 1, and $\frac{1}{6}$, [or 14 :] and ſo of ꝺe reſt.

* Ariſt. Probl. § 19, Quæſt. 35. *Cum* Nete *Dupla ad* Hy-paten *ſit ; quo-cunq; in genere* Nete *duo tenu-erit,* Hypate *u-num habebit : & ubi* Hypate *duo,* Nete *qua-tuor reſonabit.*

A Typ͏ͤ of all ꝺe Proportions of a Common *Ground* to ꝺe oꝺer Not͏ͤs in an Eigꝼ, boꝼ͏ͤ Ton͏ͤs and Hemiton͏ͤs, followeꝼ in 2 Examples.
Wer͏ͤ not͏ͤ, ꝺat ꝺe Number ſet after any Not͏ͤ, is ꝺe Proportion of ꝺe Ground to ꝺe ſam͏ͤ Not͏ͤ : as 1, $\frac{3}{4}$, [or 16] ſet after *Mi,* is ꝺe Proportion

of

of _Vt_ to _Mi_, not of _Mi_ to _Vt_: and $1, \frac{2}{8}, \frac{1}{12}$ is ðe Proportion of _Vt_ to _Fa_, not of _Fa_ to _Vt_. And likⁱwiſ ðat 12 ſet after ðe _Ground_, is ðe Proportion of every Notⁱ to ðe ſamⁱ _Ground_.

	Left scale	Right scale	
	Re: —1,— $\frac{6}{6}$ —24—	
	Ut: 1, $\frac{6}{6}$ 24	Ut: 1, $\frac{5}{6}$ 22	
	Pa: —1,— $\frac{5}{6}$ —22—	Pa: —1,— $\frac{4}{6}$ —20—	
	La: 1, $\frac{4}{6}, \frac{1}{12}$ 21	La: 1, $\frac{3}{6}, \frac{1}{12}$ 19	Diapente S.a.
Diapente S.a. Diateſſarö	Sol: —1,— $\frac{3}{6}, \frac{1}{12}$ --19--	Sol: —1,— $\frac{2}{6}, \frac{1}{12}$ --17--	Diateſſarö S.t.
S.t.	Fa: 1 $\frac{2}{6}, \frac{1}{12}$ 17	Fa: 1, $\frac{1}{6}, \frac{1}{12}$ 15	
	Mi: —1,— $\frac{2}{6}$ —16—	Mi: —1,— $\frac{1}{6}$ —14—	
	Re: 1, $\frac{1}{6}$ 14	Re: 12.	
	Ut: —12—		

By ðis it may appeerⁱ, ðat ðowg ðe _Intervallum_ or diſtancⁱ betweenⁱ _Diateſſaron_ and _Diapente_ (wⁱe is $\frac{1}{6}$) bœ rigt; yet ðe Diſtancⁱ boðⁱ of _Diateſſaron_ and of _Diapente_ from ðe _Ground_, is not exactly calculated: for ðe Proportion of _Diapente_ (wⁱe is of _Vt_ to _Sol_) is a _Seſquialtera_ and $\frac{1}{12}$: and ðe Proportion of _Diateſſaron_ (wⁱe is of _Vt_ to _Fa_) is a _Seſquitertia_ and $\frac{1}{12}$: ſo ðat ðe juſt _Seſquialtera_ is ðe half-ton betweenⁱ _Diapente_ and _Diateſſaron_: [an Irkſom Diſcord:] and ðe truⁱ _Seſquiteria_ is in _Mi_, [a Ditonus or perfect Third] half a Tonⁱ under _Diateſſaron_.

And ðerⁱforⁱ aldowg a _Diapente_ and a _Diateſſaron_ dœⁱ makⁱ a ful _Diapaſon_

paſon in Sound ; yet a *Seſquialtera* and a *Seſquitertia* wil not mak' a *Du-pla* in Proportion : wie ᵗing is evident by ðe for'cited Inſtanc' of our Autor : wer' 6 is ðe * *Set number,* 12 ðe *Dupla,* 9 ðe *Seſquialtera,* [as conteining 6 and ½ of 6,] and 8 ðe *Seſquitertia,* [as conteining 6 and ⅓ of 6.] For ſæing ðat ðe Differenc' or Exceſ of ðe *Seſquialtera* [9] to 6 is but 3, and ðe Differenc' of ðe *Seſquitertia* [8] to 6 is but 2 ; ðeſ' Differences wiᵗ ðe Set number 6, bæing but 11, cannot mak' a *Dupla,* wie is 12 : no mor' ðan ½ and ⅓ of a Sum, can mak' ðe wol'. De Proportion ðen anſwering to the Concord *Diapente,* is not a *Suſquialtera,* wie is *Superparticularis* ; but a *Superpartient* proportion : i. *Supertripartiens ſextas cum ſemiſſe,* or *Superſeptempartiens duodecimas.* And lik'- wiſ' ðe Proportion anſwering to *Diateſſaron,* is not *Seſquitertia ;* but *Superbipartiens ſextas cum ſemiſſe,* or *Superquinꝗpartiens duodecimas.*

* *Numerus propoſitus.*

And ðus ðe 2 Differences abꝏv ðe Set number, [wie ar $\frac{7}{12}$ and $\frac{5}{12}$ of 6] bæing added to ðe Set number 6, mak' ðe juſt *Dupla,* 12. De lik' Judgment is of ðe Proportions of ðe oðer 4 Concords.

But imagin wee ðeſ' Proportions to bæ not on'ly in ðe Inſtruments ; (as *Boetius* and *Ariſtotle* writ' from *Pythagoras* experiments) but alſo in ðe Sounds ðemſelvs , cauſed by ðe different proportions of Inſtruments ; and alſo ðat ðey ar rigtly examined, and applyed to ðe Concords ; [*Seſquitertia* to *Diateſſaron, Seſquialtera* to *Diapente,* and *Dupla* to *Diapaſon ;*] yet, unles our moſt' skilful Muſicians (wo ar nou grown to ðat perfeꝃion, ðat noᵗing neceſſary or uſ'ful to ðe Art is hid from ðem) can find' ſom uſ' of ðeſ' *Idea'*s ; let ðem reſt : and reſt wee contented wiᵗ ðe † proper proportions of Muſik, ſo uſ'ful and neceſſary ; ðat witout ðem, (ðowᵍ ðer' may bæ a kind' of Symponi) all Grac' and Efficaci of ðe Art is loſt.

† *Proportions of Tim'.*

Cap. II. § V.

Of ðe Not's external Adjuncts.

Der' belong to Not's [ðus deſcribed by ðeir Number, Nam's, Tun', and Tim',] ðeſ' 7 ᵗings : a Flat, a Sharp, a Ligatur', a Repet', a Pauz, a Direꝃ, and a Cloz'.

Not's Adjuncts.

A Flat ᴄangeᵗ *Mi* into *fa,* making him half a Ton' lower : and is ðus marked, ♭.

1
Flat.

A Sharp raiſeᵗ *fa* or *ut,* half a Ton' higer, not ᴄanging ðeir nam's : and is ðus marked, ✕.

2
Sharp.

A (a) Ligatur', deviſed for ðe Dittiᶜs ſak', is ᴡen 2
        E 2   or

3
Ligatur'.
(a)

or moᶜ Notᶜs ar ſung to onᶜ Syllable.   And it is eiđer oldᶜ, of đɇ Longer Notᶜs, [⌐, ⌐ ;] or nuᶜ, of đɇ ſorter, [◊ ♦ ♦ ♦.]

(b)   (b) Oldᶜ Ligaturᶜ haɇ ɇrɶſorts of Rulᶜs : 1, concerning Initial Notᶜs : 2, of Middle Notᶜs : and 3, of Final Notᶜs.

Rulᶜs,
Of Initial Ligaturᶜ, 4.

1
2   *Prima carens cauđâ* { *Longa eſt, Pendente ſecundâ.*
                { *Brevis eſt, ſcandente ſecundâ.*

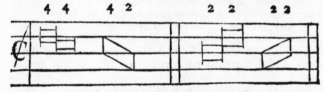

3 *'Prima manu lɶvâ Brevis eſt, cauđata deo ſum.*
4 *Semibrevis prima eſt, ſurſum cauđata* ‖ *ſequenſqჳ.*

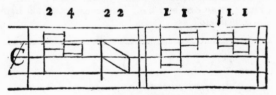

Rulᶜs,
Of Middle Ligaturᶜ, 2.

1 *Quælibet in medio Brevis eſt :* 2 ‖ *at proxima adhærens Surſum cauđatæ pro Semibrevi reputatur.*

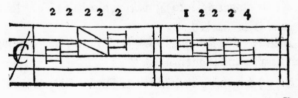

Rules

Rulᶜs,
Of Final Ligaturᶜ, 4.

1 *Ultima conscendens Brevis est quæcunq; ligata.*
2 *Ultima dependens quadrangula sit tibi Longa.*
3 *Est obliqua Brevis semper finalis habenda.*
4 ‖*Semibrevis, sursum caudatæ proxima primæ est.*

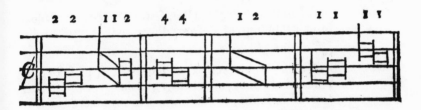

Ðe Ligaturᶜ of ðe ſorter Notᶜs is a ſemicircle, woſ 2 endᶜs point to ðe 2 Notᶜs conjoined: as ⎇, ⎇. Soomtimᶜ, (ſpecially wen ðe Notᶜs bæ many to onᶜ ſyllable) ðis Ligaturᶜ is ſignified in ðe Ditti onᶜly, by ſetting ðat ſyllable, wiꞇ a Hypen under ðe firſt Notᶜ, and ðe following ſyllable after ðe laſt.

Ðe middle and principal Notᶜ ◊, is conjoined by boðᶜ ðeſᶜ Ligaturᶜs. And wen any Notᶜ and his half-notᶜ in ðe ſamᶜ placᶜ ar conjoined for onᶜ ſyllable, ðe mark of ðe half-notᶜ, and of ðe Ligaturᶜ too, is a Point ſet by ðe Notᶜ: as ◊. ⌡. : for it is as muꞇe, as if wiꞇ ðe Notᶜ his half-notᶜ werᶜ expreſt, and conjoined by Ligaturᶜ.

A Repetᶜ is eiðer of ðe ſamᶜ notᶜs and ditti togeðer, having ðis mark (c) ꞃ; or of ditti wiꞇ oðer Notᶜs having ðis mark ; :‖: , or ðis, ÿ : befor wiꞇ ðe firſt woord of ðe Repeted ditti is commonly placed uuder his Notᶜ or Notᶜs : or of a wolᶜ Strain ; having at ðe endᶜ ðerᶜof 2 prickt Bars, toorrow all ðe Rulᶜs : ðus, :‖: .

4
Repetᶜ.

A Pauz is a mark of reſt or ſilencᶜ in a ſong, for ðe timᶜ of ſoom Notᶜ : werᶜof it haꞇ his namᶜ.

5
Pauz.

M 3   A linᶜ

A lin' depending from a fuperiour rul', and not toucing de rul' below, is a Sembrief-reſt : de lik' lin' riſing
from an inferiour rul', and not toucing de rul' aboov, is a
Minim-reſt : de fam' wit a crook' to de rigt hand, is a Cro-
cet-reſt, and to de left hand, a Qaver-reſt. Alfo a lin' rea-
cing from rul' to rul', is a Brief-reſt, or a Pauz of 2 Sembriefs : a lin' from a rul' to a third rul', is a Long-pauz,
or of 4 Sembriefs : and 2 of dem togeder mak' a Larg'-pauz,
or of 8 Sembriefs.

6
Direct.

A Direct in de end' of a lin', fewet wer' de Not' ſtandet
in de beginning of de next lin' : and is marked dus
,√, or dus ∫ .

7
Cloz'

A Cloz' is eider perfeſt, or imperfeſt. A perfeſt Cloz'
is de end of a Song, noted dus ⊙, or dus ⊙; or wit 2 Barz
aturt all de Rul's, or bod' ways. An imperfeſt Cloz' is de
end' of a Strain; or any plac' in a Song, wer' all de Part's
meet' and cloz', befor' de end' : and it is marked wit a ſingle
Bar.

ANNOTATIONS to § V.

L. 1. c. 2.

(a) **L**igatur'. Of *Ligare*, to bind' or ty' : becaus it tyet many
Nots to on' ſyllable of de Ditti. Wie Adjunct *Franchinus*
doo't dus defin' : *Omnis Ligatura , quanquam-multas complexa eſt notu-
las, unicam ſubtrahit ſyllabam pronunciandam.*

(b) In de Old' Ligatur's, de Ligatured Not's, [a Long, a Brief,
and a Sembrief] hav' on' form : bæing differenced on'ly by de Rul's :
wie dowg a man doo' know; yet in Practic', upon de ſuddain, hæ may
eaſily miſtak'. And der'for', for mor' certainti and faciliti, it wer' ex-
pedient, dat (as it is in de nu' Ligatur's) de Not's hær' wer' diſtinguiſhed by deir proper forms. But de uſ' of deſ' antiq' Ligatur's is
now wel nig antiqated.

(c) Dis Repet' *j* is uſed alfo for Not's alon', wer' der' is no'
Ditti.

CAP. II.

Cᴀᴘ. II. § VI.

A brief Synopſis of de Scalᵉ, and oder premiſſes reqiſit to Singing: wᵗⁱᵉ, wit de 5 Initial Leſſons, ar to begin de Learners Bookᵉ.

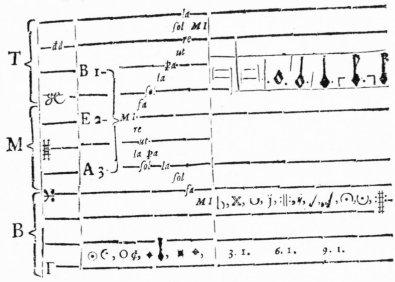

De fivᵉ Initial Leſſons.

De fivᵉ Initial Leſſons ſew de progreſ or paſſing of de Notᵉs botᵉ aſcending and deſcending, *per Gradus & Saltus :* [by Degrææſ and by Skippings.] — *Gradation & Skipping.*

De firſt Leſſon is de Duple *Ut-re :* conteining de Gradation [or paſſing by Degrææſ] of all de Notᵉs in a *Diapaſon*, botᵉ upward and dounward. — 1

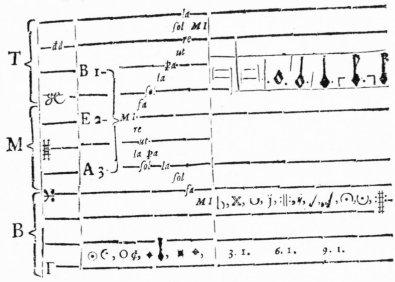

De ſecond Leſſon is de Skippings of Thirds, firſt upward and den dounward. — 2

De Third is de Skippings, firſt of Thirds dounward,
                                                  and — 3

and Fowres upward: and den of Thirds upward, and Fowres dounward.

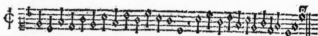

Deſᶜ 3 Leſſons havᶜ eaᶜ of dem 2 partᶜs in onᶜ : werᶜof every ſecond coomet in upon 2 Sembrief-reſts. All wie may bee fung ronnd in ſix Partᶜs : de tree leading Partᶜs beginning ſtil togeder, as likᶜwiſᶜ de oder 3 dat ſecond dem.

4

1 p.

DeFowre is de Prœfᶜ of de uſuall Skippings : in 2 Partᶜs.

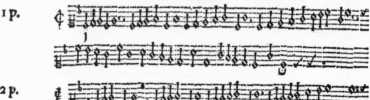

2 p.

5

De fift Leſſon is de Triple *Vt-re* : in fowr Partᶜs.

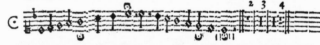

C A P III. Of Setting.

§ I.   *Of de Partᶜs of a Song.*

Vide(f)in No-tis. (a) (b) (c) (d) (e)

Etting is de framing of a Song in Partᶜs : wie, for de moſt part, (ſpecially in Counterpoint) ar * fowr [(a) Baſᶜ, (b) Tenor, (c) Counterrenor, (d) Mean:] of wie, in ſoom Songs, is wanting onᶜ or two : and in ſoom, for a voiᶜᶜ of an hig pitᶜe, is added (e) a Treble. Yea and in ſoom, (ſpecially of de Lydian Mœdᶜ, as in Talliſes and Birds *Cantiones ſacræ*) beſidᶜs de oder Partᶜs ſingle, ar 2 Baſes, or 2 Trebles, or Tenors, or Counterrenors : and den derᶜ ar ſix Partᶜs : ſoomtimᶜ 2 or 3 Partᶜs ar dubbled :

dubbled : and ſo ꝺerᶜ may bæ 7 Partᶜs, [as in Talliſes *Miſerere* ;] or 8, [as in Birds *Deliges Dominum :*] And ſoom, to ſew ꝺeir exorbitant ſkil, wil makᶜ (f) many morᶜ : but in ꝺeſᶜ caſes, ſoom Partᶜs muſt pauz wilᶜ oꝺer ſing ; or els ꝺey muſt needᶜs *coincidere.*

In ꝺis kindᶜ of Songs, ꝺe Muſik dooᶜꞇ morᶜ conſiſt in reportᶜs and ful Harmoniꞓ ; ꝺan in ꝺe Melodi of ꝺe ſeveral Partᶜs.

☞ But a ſolemn † Anꞇem, werᶜin a ſwæetᶜ Melodious Treble, or Countertenor, ſingeꞇ ſingle, and ꝺe ful Qirᶜ anſwereꞇ, (muꞓ morᶜ wen 2 ſuꞓ ſingle voices, and 2 ful Qirᶜs enꞇerchangᶜably repliᶜ onᶜ to an oꝺer, and at ꝺe laſt clozᶜall togeꝺer) is ꝺat *Hyperlydian* Muſik, wiꞓ (werᶜ ꝺe Sobrieti, Decenci, and Pieti of ꝺe Singers concur wiꞇ ꝺe Art and ſwæetᶜnes of ꝺe Song) makeꞇ ſuꞓ a heavenly Harmoni, aꞅ is pleaſing unto God and Man. *Vid.* l.2, c. 2, §1, III. and §2. (f) in *Notis.*

All ꝺeſᶜ Partᶜs ſet togeꝺer (ꝺowg for ꝺe dæepeſt Baſᶜvoicᶜ, and ꝺe loftieſt Treble-voice) ar conꞇained wiꞇin ꝺe compaſs of (g) 22 Notᶜs : wiꞓ is a *Triſdiapaſon,* or ꝺe ful extent of ꝺe ꞅam-uꞇ : but ordinarily ꝺey doᶜ not excædᶜ ꝺe number of 19 or 20. And generally, eaꞓ Partᶜ by it ſelf is to be kept wiꞇin his natural compaſs of (h) 8 Notᶜs : unles (for a Point or ſoom oꝺer ſpecial cauz) you bæ ſoomtimᶜ conſtrained to tranſgreſ ꝺeſᶜ bounds, a Notᶜ or 2, or 3, at ꝺe moſt.

(f)

† Græcè ᾽Αὐϑμα, of ἀνϑέω floreo , of ἀνϑος flos a Flour, of ἄνω ϑεῖν, *quod ſurſum aſcendat dum creſcit :* becaus ꝺe morᶜ it increaſeꞇ ꝺe morᶜ it aſcendeꞇ. For ꝺis is ꝺat fair flour, ꝺat *flos odorus,* or raꝺer *florea corolla,* wiꞓ, wiꞇ its ſwæetᶜ-ſmelling ſavour, aſcendeꞇ from ꝺe ground of an humble Hart, unto ꝺe higeſt Heavens : even to ꝺe Mercy-ſeat of ꝺe moſtᶜHig.

(g) (h)

ANNOTATIONS to §I.

(a) ꝹE Baſᶜ is ſo called, becaus it is ꝺe *baſis* or foundation of ꝺe Song, unto wie all oꝺer Partᶜs bæ ſet : and it is to be ſung wiꞇ a dæepᶜ, ful, and pleaſing Voicᶜ.

(b) Ꝺe Tenor is ſo called, becaus it was commonly in Motets ꝺe ditti-part, or Plain-ſong : wiꞓ * continued in ꝺe ſamᶜ kindᶜ of Notᶜs [uſually briefs] muꞓ after onᶜ plain faſhion : uppon wiꞓ, ꝺe oꝺer Partᶜs did diſcant in ſundry ſortᶜs of Figurᶜs, and after many different ways : or (if you will) becaus neiꝺer aſcending to any hig or ſtrained notᶜ, nor deſcending very low, it continueꞇ in onᶜ ordinari tenor of ꝺe voicᶜ : and ꝺerᶜforᶜ may bæ ſung by an indifferent voicᶜ.

(c) Ꝺe Countertenor or *Contratenor,* is ſo called, becaus it anſwereꞇ ꝺe Tenor ; ꝺowg commonly in higer keyꞅ : and ꝺerᶜforᶜ is fitteſt for a man of a ſwæetᶜ ſril voicᶜ. Wiꞓ Partᶜ ꝺowg it havᶜ littl Melodi by it ſelf ;

Baſᶜ.

* Tenor, of *teneo,* ſignifyeꞇ onᶜ continued order or faſion of aꞇing, held on wiꞇout eangᶜ.

Countertenor.

F

ſelfŭ (as conſiſting mue of monotoniˁs) yet in Harmoni it hat ðe greaveſt gracˁ : ſpecially wen it is ſung wiŧ a rigt voicˁ : wiε is tœ rarˁ.

Mean.

   (d) Ðe Mean is ſo called, becauſ it is a midling or mean hig part, betweenˁ ðe Countertenor, [ðe higeſt part of a man] and ðe Treble, [ðe higeſt part of a boy or woman :] and ðerˁforˁ may bœ ſung by a mean voicˁ.

Treble.

   (e) Ðe Treble is ſo called, becaus his notˁs ar placed (for ðe moſt pa t) in ðe ŧird Septenari, or ðe Treble cliefs : and is to bœ ſung wiŧ a hig clœrˁ ſwœtˁ voicˁ.

   (f) Many morˁ. *Partes aut voces in Harmonia, vel duæ, vel tres, 4, 5, 6, 7, 8, vel plures adhibentur : (nam hodie etiam vel quadraginta, vel interdum quinquaginta tales Partes & voces in unica Cantilena inveniuntur) Principales tamen tantum quatuor ſunt,* Calviſius Cap. 2.

   (g) 22 Notˁs. Dis compas of 22 Notˁs, or a Triſdiapaſon, is for Voices : for Inſtruments it may bœ muε larger. *Vide* C. 2 § 2. (f) & ☞ *in Notis.*

   ⟨ h ⟩ 8 Notˁs. Yet ðe Parts of ðat Dial-ſong (wiε is conteined in ðe ordinari compas of *Triſdiaˀaſon*) dœˁ all exceedˁ ðe ordinari limits of an Eigt : [ðe Tenor reaɕing 9 Notˁs, ðe ſecond Treble and ðe Countertenor 11, ðe firſt Treble and ðe Baſˁ 12 :] as hœrˁ you may ſœ.

I *TREBLE.*

COVNTERTENOR.

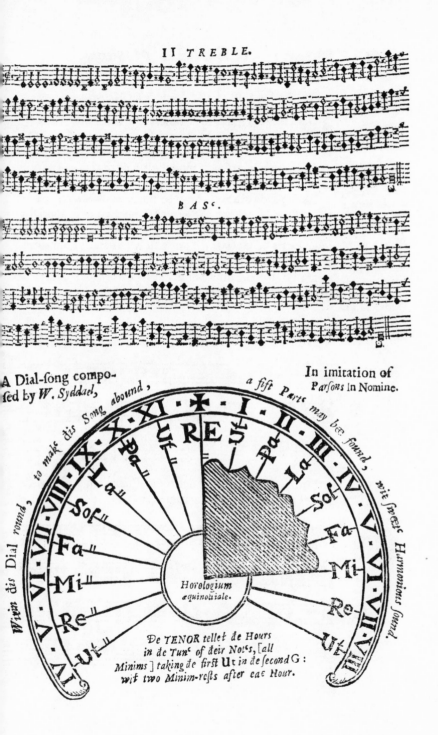

II TREBLE.

BAS.

A Dial-song compo-
sed by *W. Syddael,*

In imitation of
Parsons In Nomine.

Wiin dis Dial round, to make dis Song abound, a fift Parte may bee found, wit sweete Harmonies found.

Horologium
æquinoctiale.

De TENOR tellet de Hours
in de Tunᶜ of deir Notᶜˢ, [all
Minims] taking de first Ut in de second G:
wit two Minim-rests after eaᶜ Hour.

C A P. I I I. §I I.   *Of Melodi.*

IN Setting ar always to be observed (besid's de Rul's requisit' to Singing) *Melodi* and *Harmoni :* wit deir 4 Ornaments [*Confecution, Syncope, Fuga,* and *Formaliti.*

(a) *Melodi* is de fweet' modulation or tun' of ea·e part in it felf.

As de part's of a Song ougt to bæ *Harmonious* on' to an oder ; fo fwold' dey bæ *Melodious* ea·e on' in it felf : fpecially in de Mæters of de Dorik and Ionik Mood's. Su·e as ar all de fowr Part's of dat *Oxford* Tun' : de Mean and Tenor wer'-of, in de Pfalms fet out by *T ho. Eaft,* ar (for deir Melodi's) mad' two feveral Tun's, (under de nam's of Glaffenburi and Kentif Tun's) wit oder Part's fet unto dem.

Melodi, μελο·ſία carminis cantus ſeu Modulatio : of μέλ©· and ἀɗω, (V. § 3. ¶ 1. and (a) in Notis,) dowg ſœmtim' it bæ uſed for Harmoni, or Concent of many Part's. Vid. l. 2. c. 1. § 2.

Oxford Tun'.   M
    C
    T
    B

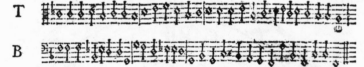

Unto wi·e you may ad deſ' oder Pfalm-tun's, fet to de voices and capaciti of yung beginners.

De Scottifh Tun'.   Tr
   M
   C
   B

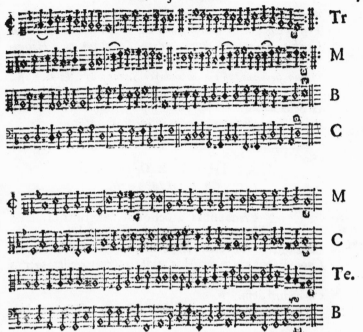

But hær onᶜ of đe upper Partᶜs is neceſſarily to havᶜ a ſpecial Melodi aboov đe reſt : ꝥiᴄ is called đe *Cantus* or *Tun*ᶜ : ſuᴄ as may deligt a Muſical ear, đowg it bæ ſung alonᶜ by it ſelf. Of đis ſort our * ſkilful Autors havᶜ deviſed infinitᶜ varieti, in đe *Ionik* or *Kromatik* Moodᶜ. Đe Melodi of ꝥiᴄ Partᶜ conſiſteꞇ muᴄ in reportᶜ : ſoomtimᶜ of fewer, ſoomtimᶜ of morᶜ Notᶜs ; ſoomtimᶜ of half a Strain, ſoomtimᶜ of a ᴡolᶜ Strain, in đe ſamᶜ vers : as in ſuᴄ Tunᶜs you may obſerv.

Modulations in Melodi ar morᶜ ſmoodᶜ, facil, and fluent, by Degræᶜs, đan by Skips : (and derᶜforᶜ even in many Partᶜs, đe ᴄief, as muᴄ as may bæ, ſooldᶜ obſerv Degræᶜs) and Skips ar better to Conſonant đan to Diſſonant Intervalls : as to a Third, a Fowrꞇ, a Fift, an Eigꞇ, and ſoomtimᶜ a Sixt : but ſeldom to a Sevnꞇ, or Ninᶜꞇ ; (and đat not wiꞇout ſoom ſpecial cauz) and to a *Tritonus* or *Semi-diapente*

* Suᴄ as ar *Nicolas Lanier*, *Henri Laws*, *Iohn Laws*, *Simon Iv*ᶜs, *Io. Wilſon*, &c.

diapente never. Agræable is de Doctrin^e of * *Calvifius.*
*Etfi maximè in id incumbendum eft, ut Modulatio potiùs per
Gradus, quàm per Saltus procedat ; (propterea quòd Harmonia inde generetur æquabilior, volubilior, & facilior) tamen cùm
id ubiq; fieri non poffit ; quando per Saltus progrediendum eft,
eligenda funt potius intervalla Confona, quàm Diffona.* Tritonus
& Semidiapente *prorfus vitanda funt : interdum Septima,
rarius Nona adhibetur : & non nifi certis de caufis.*

C A P. III. § I I I. *Of Harmoni :*
¶ I, *Of Intervalls.*

(a)
*^c Aῤμονία con-
gruentia, con-
centus: of ἀῤμό-
ζω congruo.

(a) * **H**armoni is a deligtful congruiti of all de
Part^es of a Song among demfelvs, trog de
Concordanc^e of certain Intervalls, wi-e G o d in Natur^e
(not witout a w onder) hat mad^e to agræ togeder ; wer^eas
oders doo^e found fo harfly on^e to anoder, dat no Mufical ear
can endur^e dem.

(b) Intervalls ar de different diftances of hig and low
founds.

And dey ar eider Simple, or Compound.

(c) Simple Intervalls ar de diftances of all de Sounds
witin de compas of a Diapafon, from deir Ground : de
wi-e, increafing by half-ton^es, ar in number twelv : [1
Semitonium, 2 Tonus, 3 Sefquitonium or Semiditonus,
4 Ditonus, 5 Diateffaron, 6 Tritonus or Semidiapente,
7 Diapente, 8 Semitonium-diapente, 9 Tonuf-diapente,
10 Semiditonuf-diapente, 11 Ditonuf-diapente or Semi-
diapafon, 12 Diapafon.

1. *Semitonium* is a Second imperfect : *i.* from *Mi* to *Fa*
or from *La* to *Pa.*

2. *Tonus* is a Second perfect : as from *Ut* to *Re,* from *Re*
to *Mi,* from *Fa* to *Sol,* from *Sol* to *La,* and from *Pa* to *Ut.*

3. *Semiditonus* is an imperfect Third , confifting of a
Ton^e and a Half-ton^e : as from *Re* to *Fa,* from *Sol* to *Pa,*
from *Mi* to *Sol,* and from *La* to *Ut.*

4. *Ditonus* is a perfect (d) Third, confifting of a Ton^e
and

and a Ton^c : as from *Ut* to *Mi*, from *Fa* to *La*, and from
Pa to *Re*.

5. *Diateſſaron* is a (d) Fowrt, of 2 Ton^{c}s and a Hemi-
ton^c : as from *Ut* to *Fa*, from *Re* to *Sol*, from *Mi* to
La, &c. (d)

6. *Tritonus,* or *Semidiapente,* is a Fift imperfe&t,
conſiſting of 3 wol^c Ton^{c}s, as from *Pa* to *Mi*; or of 2
Ton^{c}s and 2 Hemiton^{c}s, as from *Mi* to *Pa*. But *Calviſius*
(for doctrin^{c}s ſak^c) doo^{c}t diſtinguiſ dem : calling de
Interval of *Pa* to *Mi*, *Tritonus* ; and of *Mi* to *Pa*, *Semidiapente*. *Vid.* Conſecution of Diſcords.

7. *Diapente* is a perfe&t (d) Fift, of 3 Ton^{c}s and a He-
miton^c : as from *Ut* to *Sol*, from *Re* to *La*, from *Fa* to *Ut*. (d)

8. *Semitonium-Diapente* is an imperfe&t Sixt, of 3 Ton^{c}s
and two Hemiton's : as from *Re* to *Pa*, from *Mi* to *Ut*.

9. *Tonuſ-diapente* is a perfe&t Sixt, conſiſting of 4 Ton^{c}s
and a Hemiton^c : as from *Ut* to *La*, from *Fa* to *Re*, and
from *Pa* to *Sol*.

10. *Semiditonuſ-diapente* is a Sevn$\ddagger$ imperfe&t, of 4 Ton^{c}s
and 2 Hemiton^{c}s : as from *Ut* to *Pa*, from *Mi* to *Re*, from
Sol to *Fa*, and from *Re* to *Ut*.

11. *Ditonuſ-diapente* or *Semidiapaſon,* is a Sevn$\ddagger$ perfe&t,
or Eigt imperfe&t, conſiſting of fiv^c Ton^{c}s and a Hemiton^c :
as from *Pa* to *La*, from *Fa* to *Mi*, and from ♮ ſarp to ♭ ſlat in
de Eigt.

12. *Diapaſon* is a perfe&t Eigt, conteining (e) a *Diapente*, and a *Diateſſaron* ; or 5 wol^c Ton^{c}s and 2 Hemiton^{c}s:
[i. all de 7 * Naturall Sounds or Not^{c}s beſid^{c}s de Ground ;]
or briefly All de 12 Simple Intervalls : (wer^{c}of it ha$\ddagger$ his
$\dagger$ nam^c) as from *Ut* to *Ut*, from *Re* to *Re*, or from any Not^c
in any Clief to de ſam^c Not^c in de ſam^c Clief, in de next
Septenari.

(f) Compound Intervalls ar mad^c of de Simple, and
on^c or mo^c Diapaſons : as a Twelft, or a Diapaſon-fift, is
compounded of a Fift and a Diapaſon : a Fowrteen$\ddagger$ or a
Diapaſon-ſevn$\ddagger$, of a Sevn$\ddagger$ and a Diapaſon : as deir nam^{c}s
import^c. Lik^{c}wiſ^c an Eigteen$\ddagger$ or a Diſdiapaſon-fowrt, of
a Fowr$\ddagger$ and a Diſdiapaſon : a Twentit or a Diſdiapaſon-
ſixt,

(e)

* *V. c. 2. §1,*
and (c)

† *Diapaſon ex
omnibus aut per
omnia Inter-
valla.* *Vide* (i)
in Notis.

(f)
*Compound Ix-
tervalls.*

ſixt, of a Sixt and a Diapaſon.　And ſo a Triſdiapaſon-ſecond, or a Triſdiapaſon-tird, of a Second or Third and a Triſdiapaſon.

All wie Compounds, having de ſamᶜ Cliefs, de ſamᶜ Namᶜs of Notᶜs, and, in effeɛt, de ſamᶜ Sounds (derᶜ bæing, noᶜ oder differencᶜ in dem, but *Acumen* and *Gravitas*) wit deir Simple Intervalls; ar derᶜforᶜ, in Harmoni, uſed as de ſamᶜ: ☞ according to de common Maxim of Muſicians, *De Octavis idem eſt judicium. vide* ☞ in C. 2. § 1.

❡ II. *Of Concords and Diſcords.*

Of de 12 Intervalls 7 ar Conſonant, and 5 Diſſonant : doſᶜ ar called, in onᶜ woord, *Concords*; and deſᶜ *Diſcords.*

(g)　(g) A *Concord* is de mixturᶜ of a Gravᶜ and Acutᶜ ſound ſwæɛᶜly falling to de ear.

(h)　(h) A *Diſcord* is a jarring noiz of 2 permixed ſounds offending de ear.

Concords.　De ſevn Concords ar firſt (i) an Eigt, (wie * *Glareanus*, * Dodecachord. for perfeɛtion and ɛieſti, callet *Conſonantiarum Regina*) a l. 1, c. 8. Perfeɛt and imperfeɛt Third, (k) a Fowrt, a Fift, a perfeɛt (i) and imperfeɛt Sixt : wit deir Compounds. Unto deſᶜ In- (k) tervall-concords is added de (l) Uniſon : ſo called, becaus ſtanding in de ſamᶜ Clief dat de Ground dooᶜt, it yældet, in (l) an oder Partᶜ, ſuɛa ſound, as ſæmet onᶜ and de ſamᶜ wit it. De wie aldowg it bæ noᶜ Intervall ; (as all oder Con- cords ar) yet, de Ground and it bæing 2 individual con- cording ſounds, it may wel bæ called a Concord : and be- caus, likᶜ an Eigt, it dooᶜt ſwæɛᶜly reſound in Harmoni ; and wit its ſwæɛᶜnes, is ofttimᶜs neceſſari in contexing of Points, and oder melodious paſſages ; it is juſtly recko- ned among de Chief of dem.

Of Concords ſoom ar Primari, and ſoom Secundari.

(m)　(m) Primari Concords ar an * Uniſon or Eigt, a perfeɛt Primari Con- Third or *Ditonus*, and a Fift or *Diapente.* De wie of dem cords. ſelvs, witout de help of any oder, dooᶜ màkᶜ a ſwæɛᶜ ſym- * *Vid.* (l) in Poni. And derᶜforᶜ is dey ar good in de beginnings, and Notis. oder places ; ſo ar dey neceſſari in de Clozes : wencᶜ all Se- cundariᶜs ar excluded.

Secundari

Secundari Concords ar an imperfeƈt Third or *Semidito-*
nus, (n) a Fowrt or a *Diateffaron*, an imperfeƈt Sixt or *Se-*
mitonium-diapente, and a Perfeƈt Sixt or *Tonuf-diapente*. Wi€
becaus dey found not fo fweet'ly as de Primari doo€, nor fa-
tisfi€ de ear witout a fweeter following ; der€for€ non€ of
dem is admitted into de Cloz€ : and a Sixt or Fowrt fcar€€
alloued in de Beginning.

Intervalls ar alfo differenced by de Numberof de 7 Sounds:
(weider dey bee *Ton€s* or *Hemiton€s*) as dey follow on€ an
oder in de Scal€. A Second, a Third, a Fowrt, a Fift, a Sixt,
a Sevnt, and an Eigt, ar fo called, becaus dey contein fo
many feverall Sounds. Dat der€for€ wi€ conteinet 4 is called a *Diateffaron* or a Fowrt : and dat wi€ conteinet 5 is
called a *Diapente* or a fift. But de 4 founds of *Diateffaron* ar
but 2 Ton€s and a Semi-ton€ aboov de Ground, as *Fa* is a-
boov *Vt*, or *Sol* aboov *Re* : and de fiv€ founds of *Diapente* ar
3 Ton€s and a Semiton€ aboov his Ground, as *Sol* is to *Vt*,
or *La* to *Re*. Lik€wil€ from *Pa* to *Mi* aboov ar 4 founds, as
in a *Diateffaron* : but dey ar 3 wol€ Ton€s from de Ground,
wer€of dat Interval is called *Tritonus* : and from *Mi* to *Pa* a-
boov ar 5 diftinƈt founds, as in a *Diapente* : but dey ar from de
Ground, but 2 Ton€s and 2 Hemiton€s, wer€of dat Interval
is called * *Semidiapente*. So dat de *Tritonus* is an exceffiv€
Diateffaron, half a Ton€ too mu€ ; and de *Semidiapente* is a
defeƈtiv€ *Diapente*, half a Ton€ too little : wi€ in effeƈt is all
on€ wit *Tritonus*. And der€for€, as in de tru€ *Diateffaron*, de
refpeƈt or relation of *Vt* to *Fa* or of *Re* to *Sol*, and, in a
tru€ *Diapente*, de relation of *Vt* to *Sol*, or of *Re* to *La* (becaus dey ar Concords) is Harmonical ; fo, in de exceffiv€
Diateffaron, de relation of *Pa* to *Mi*, and, in de defeƈtiv€ *Di-*
apente, de relation of *Mi* to *Pa*, (becaus dey ar Difcords)
is called *Relatio non Harmonica*.

But def€ harf Difcords, by de help of Flats and farps,
ar reduced to deir tru€ Concords. For as de *Tritonus*, eider
by flatting de farp, or farping de Fat, is mad€ a tru€ *Diatef-*
faron ; fo de *Semidiapente*, by de fam€ means, is mad€ a tru€
Diapente.

A
Synopsis of
de Concords.

Ut : Eigt.	Re Eigt.
to { La, 3 *imperf.* / Sol, 4. / Fa, 5. / Mi, 6 *imperf.* }	to { Pa, 3 *perf.* / La, 4. / Sol, 5. / Fa, Sixt *perf.* }
La : Sixt perf.	Pa : Sixt imperf.
to { Fa, 3 *perf.* / Mi, 4. }	to { Sol, 3 *imperf.* / Fa, 4. }
Sol : Fift.	La : Fift.
to Mi, 3 *imperf.*	Sol : Fowrt.
Fa : Fowrt.	Fa : Third imperf.
Mi : Third perf.	
	RE :
UT :	

Affiniti of Con-
cords.

Beween de Third and de Sixt, and between de Fift and de Fowrt, is soom affiniti : for a Third to de Bas, is a Sixt to his Eigt ; and a Sixt to de Bas, is a Third to his Eigt. Lik'wis a Fift to de Bas, is a Fowrt to his Eigt ; and a Fowrt to de Bas, is a Fift to his Eigt.

De Sixt and
Third must bee
lik.

A Sixt bæing joined wit a Third, must bæ always sue as de Third is : if eider bæ perfect, de oder must not bæ imperfect : as becaus from Re to Fa ſarp is a perfect Third ; der'for Pa wic is a Sixt, must bæ lik'wis ſarped, dat it may also bæ Perfect : becaus from Sol to Mi is a perfect Sixt : der'for Pa, bæing to Sol a Third, must bæ ſarped, dat it may lik'wis bæ Perfect.

(o) Al-

(o) Aldowg Unifons and Eigts ar good in de Beginnings, and neceffary in de Clozes ; yet in oder places of a
Song, dey ar fparingly to bæ ufed, in few Part's : unles
foom fpecial caus, [as *Fuga, Cadenc*, or *Melodi*] reqir' dem :
but den moft' conveniently, wen dey mæt' in divers † Figur's, and not at de fam' inftant: as

(o)

† *Vid.* (a) *in c.*
2, § 4.

Concords doo' den found moft' fwæt'ly, wen dey ar fet in
deir Natural and proper Places.

(p) De proper places of an Eigt, a Fift, and a Fowrt,
ar in de lower Part's : and of Thirds, bot' Perfect and Imperfect, aboov.

(p)

And der'for' wen de Part's ftay togeder, (fpecially at
Clozes) de Concords ar moft' fitly placed in deir Natural
order. But generally, in de compofing of Melodious Harmoni, dey ar varioufly intermedled, in all Part's, according to de Grounds and Rul's of Art.

¶ *Concerning* de *Proportions of Concords,* fee C. 2, §. 4, & (f)

Difcords ar de Perfect and Imperfect Second, de Perfect and Imperfect Sevnt : and de *Tritonus* or *Semidiapente.*

DISCORDS.

As all Part's muft agræ wit de Baf', fo muft dey not
difagræ among dem felvs : and der'for' if on' Part' bæ a
Fowrt ; an oder may not bæ a Third or a Fift, but a Sixt :
if on' bæ a Fift ; an oder may not bæ a Sixt or a Fowrt,
but a Third : for den woold' dey difagræ among dem felvs
in a Second. Lik'wif' if on' bæ a Sixt, an oder may not bæ
a Twelft : (wi e is a Compound Fift) for fo wil dey difagræ in de Sevnt : &c.

Yet a Difcord, as in Oeconomi, fo in Mufik, is foomtim'
allouable, as making de Concord following de fwæter : but
neider in dat nor in dis is it to bæ held too long : and der'-
for' in fwift Divifion it is beft, and moft ufed : efpecially
in * Gradation, [wi e is a continued order of Not's afcen-

* *V. c.* 2, § 6.

G 2   ding

ding or deſcending :┐ wer˪ de Diſcord doˀt better in de
ævn, dan in de od Placˡ : as in dis Example.

Alſo a Diſcord is good in Binding : (eider in Cadeneˡ or
oderwiſˡ) werˡ it is always de od Notˡ, or de latter Partˡ
of de Syncopated Meſurˡ-notˡ. *V. Sincope in* §4, ¶2.

Likˡwiſˡ de Melodi of a Partˡ and de mainteining of a
Point may excuſˡ a Diſcord.

ANNOT. to §3. ¶ 1 & 2.

(a *Harmonia eſt diverſorum ſonorum unio, reducta ad concentum.
Non enim tantùm ſimplicem, in acutioribus aut remiſſioribus
ſonis, Modulationem* (hoc eſt ſingularis vocis Melodiam) *admittit, &
ab intervallo ad intervallum, vel velociore vel tardiore motu, ſecundùm
Tempus in Figuris Muſicis præſcriptum, procedit ; ſed etiam alias voces,
quæ concentum faciunt, accinentes habet : ex quibus, tanquam ex Partibus, Harmonia componitur.* Sethus Cap. 2.

(b) *Intervallum eſt ſoni acuti graviſq; diſtantia. Conſonantia eſt acuti ſoni graviſq; mixtura ſuaviter auribus accidens. Diſſonantia eſt duorum
ſonorum ſibimet permixtorum ad aurem veniens aſpera atq; injucunda
percuſſio.* Boetius l. 1, c. 8.

(c) Simple Intervalls. *Intervalla Simplicia ſunt Diapaſon, & quæ
in qualibet ejus ſpecie continentur : ut ſunt ſecunda, Tertia, Quarta,
Quinta, Sexta, Septima.* Calviſ. Cap 3.

(d) (d) (d) De Præſes heerˡ of Muſik and of Pyſik doˡ accord : de
Numeralls of bodˡ being underſtood incluſivˡ. For as de Pyſicians doˡ
ſay a Tertian Aguˡ, wie yet commet but every ſecond day, and a Qar-
tan woſˡ acceſ is every tird day ; (becaus dey count de firſt Fit-day
for onˡ) ſo doˡ de Muſicians call a Third, a Fowrt, and a Fift ; (wie
yet ar but 2, 3, and 4 Notˡs from de Ground) becaus dey account de
Ground it ſelf for onˡ.

(e) *Pytagorici Conſonantias Diapente ac Diateſſaron, ſimplices arbi-
trantur : atq; ex his unam Diapaſon Conſonantiam jungunt.* Boetius
Lib. 5, c. 6.

(f) Compound Intervalls. *Compoſita Intervalla ſunt majora quàm
Diapaſon : & ſunt ex quolibet Intervallo ſimplici cum aliqua Diapaſon
ſpecie : ut ſi Tonus ad Diapaſon addatur, vel Tertia, vel Quarta ; oritur
Nona, Decima, Vndecima : & ſic de aliis.*

(g) (h) *Vide* (b) *ſupra.*

(i) An Eigt. De Diapaſon or Eigt (ſayt * Sr. *Francis*) is in Muſik, de ſweeteſt Concord : in ſo mue as it is, in effect, an Uniſon.
And

And *Calviſius* lik'wiſe, *Diapaſon prima eſt omnium Conſonantiarum, & perfectiſſima : Nomen inde duxit, quòd omnia intervalla Simplicia complectatur.*

(k) *A Fowrt.* Þis Concord is one of þe * þree, ſo famous in all Antiqiti : wiþ þe Symponi wer'of þe firſt Muſicians did content þem ſelvs ; and for þe inventing of woſe † Proportions, þat moſte ancient and ſubtil * Philoſoper haþ been ever ſince ſo mue renouned among all Poſteriti. Þe joint-doctrine of þeſe þree Concords, þowg it bee as ancient as Muſik it ſelf, approoved not on'ly by *Pythagoras*, but alſo by *Ariſtotle, Plato Ptolome, Eucl de*; and by *Ariſtoxenus, Boetius, Franchinus, Glareanus,* and all learned Muſicians ; yet ſoom pregnant wits, of later timeſ, hav' made noe bon's to teae þe contrari : and nou, forſoþe, þis *Diateſſaron* wie for þouſands of yeers haþ been a ſpecial Concord; (witout any þe leaſt empeaement or qeſtion) muſt need's uppon þe ſudden bee reckoned among þe Diſcords : and þat, not on'ly by Autoriti, but Reaſon alſo, and þe very iudgment of þe † Ear, reclaiming. For hee þat liſteþ to tri' upon þe Organ or wel-tuned Virginal, ſall find' þat of it ſelf it doo't * wel accord wiþ þe Ground, and better þan either of þe oþer Secundari Concords, [þe Sixt or imperfect Third :] and wiþ a Sixt to yeeld as tru' a Symponi, as a Third wiþ a Fift : and mor' ſweet' þan a Third wiþ a Sixt : and wiþ a Sixt and an Eigt, to ſound fully and Harmoniouſ/, in pleaſing varieti, among oþer ſymphoniſ. So þat, aldowg, beeing no Primari Concord, it bee not ſet to þe Baſe in a Cloze ; (See befor' Primari Concords) yet is it god in oþer Places, even immediatly befor' þe Cloze, and þat in ſlow tim' : as in þis example.

Mor'over, albeit befor' þe Cloze, a † Diſcord either wiþ þe Baſe, or wiþ an oþer Parte, bee ſomtim' alloued ; (þe Not' beeing but of ſort tim', and a ſweetening Concord preſently ſucceeding) yet in þe Cloze, (wer' all Parteſ meet togeþer) in a long-timed Note, nor witout ſoom pauz uppon it, (ſo þat þe ear doo'þ ſpecially attend it) þer' is never any Diſcord at all : but all þe upper Not'ſ ar Concords of one ſort or oþer : and þoſe, as Primari to þe Baſe, ſo Secundari among þemſelvs. For example, wer' þe Cloze-note of þe Baſe is in *Gam-ut*, (and conſeqently þoſe of þe oþer Parteſ in *B-mi, D-ſol-re*, and *G-ſol-re-ut*, or þeir Eigtſ) *B-mi* beeing a perfect Third to þe Baſe, is an imperfect Third to *D-ſol-re*, and a Sixt to *G-ſol-re-ut* : and lik'wiſe *D-ſol-re*, beeing a Fift to *Gam-ut*, is a Third imperfect to *B-mi*, and a Fowrt to *G-ſol-re-ut*. Seeing þen þat in Clozes, wie ar ſimply harmonious, noe Diſcord is admitted, but all Not'ſ concord among þemſelvs ; it followeþ, þat a Fowrt as wel as a Sixt, or an imperfect Third, muſt bee a Concord : and ſeeing þat a Ground

---

Right margin notes:

* [*Diateſſaron, Diapente, and Diapaſon*]
† [*Seſquitertia, Seſquialtera, and Dupla.*]
* *Pythagoras.*

† *As Ptolome* l. 1 c. 5. *expreſly: Conſonantiæ ſenſus quidem percipit: & eam quæ Diateſſaron i. Quarta, dicitur, & eam quæ Diapente i. Quinta.*
* *Vid. infra* III.

† *V. mox* ☞

and his Eigt ar as it wer‘all on‘, (*vid.* ☞ *in c.* 2. § 1.) how can any man ꞷink ꝺat *D-ſol re*, wie is a Fiſt unto *Gam-ut*, and a Fowrꞇ unto *G-ſol re-ut* [his Eigt] ſꝩld‘bœ ꝺe ſwœteſt Concord unto ꝺe on‘, and a Diſcord unto ꝺe oꝺer ; and yet ꝺat *B-mi*, wie is but a Third unto ꝺe Ground, ſꝩld bœ a Concord alſo to ꝺe Eigt ?

† Dè Lord *Verulam*, Cen- tûꞃi 2, and Numb. 110.

And ꝺer‘for‘ ꝺat honourable † Sag‘ (woſ‘ general knowledg and judgment in all kind‘ of literatur‘ is generally applauded by ꝺe learned) rejecting ꝺeir novel fanci ꝺat rejeꝗ ꝺis ancient Concord, profeſſeꞇ himſelf to bœ of an oꝺer mind‘. Ðe Concords in Muſik (ſayꞇ hœ) be- twœn‘ ꝺe *Vniſon* and ꝺe *Diapaſon*, ar ꝺe Fiſt : (wie is ꝺe moſt perfeꝗ) ꝺe *Third* next : and ꝺe *Sixt*, wie is mor‘ harꝼ : and (as ꝺe Ancients eſtœmed, and ſo dꝩ‘my ſelf, and ſꝏm oꝺers) ꝺe *Fowrꞇ*, wie ꝺey call *Diateſſaron*. Among ꝺoſ‘ Oꝺers, ꝺat ſingular Muſician (ꞇo wom‘ ꝺe Students of ꝺis abſtruſ‘ and myſterious Faculti ar moꞇ‘ beholding, ꝺan to all ꝺat ever hav‘ written ꝺer‘of) [*Sethus Calviſius*] is on‘. His wꝏꞃds ar deſ‘: *Rejicitur hodiè à pleriſq; Muſicis, ex numero Conſonantia- rum, Diateſſaron: ſed minùs reꝗè. Nam omnes Muſici veteres, tam Græci quàm Latini, eam inter Conſonantias collocârunt : id quod monumenta ipſorum teſtantur. Deindè quia conjuncta cum aliis Intervallis, parit Con- ſonantiam : ut ſi addatur ad Diapente, ſit Diapaſon : ſi ad Ditonon, vel Triꞇemitonion, ſit Sexta major aut minor. Ꞁihil autem quod in Intervallis plurium proportionum conſonat, per ſe diſſonare poteſt. Tertiò, ſi chordæ in Inſtrumentis Muſicis, exactè juxta proportiones veras intendantur; † nulla diſſonantia in Diateſſaron apparet ; ſed ambo ſoni uniformiter & cum ſua- vitate quadam aures ingrediuntur : ſic in Teſtudinibus chordæ graviores boc intervallo interſe diſtant, & ratione Diateſſaron intenduntur. Quartò nulla cantilena plurium vocum haberi poteſt, quæ careat hac Conſonantia. Nequaquam igitur eſt rejicienda ; ſed, propter uſum, quem in Melopoeia (ſi dextrè adhibeatur) habet maximum, recipienda.* But weiꝺer ꝺis Con- cord bœ Perfect or Imperfect, [*i.* Primari or Secundari] it is a Qeſtion. *Vide infrà* (m) & (n).

*C. 4.

I

II.

III.

† *Vt ſuprà* Pto- lomæus.

IV.

(1) Vniſon. *Vniſonus dicitur quaſi unus ſonus : & definitur, quòd ſit unio duorum aut plurium ſonorum in eadem Clave conſiſtentium. Inter- vallum autem Vniſonus non eſt, nec propriè Conſonantia : idq; vel indè patet, quòd Intervallum diſtantia ſit acuti ſoni graviſq; : Vniſonus autem diſtantiam ſonorum, quoad acumen & gravitatem, non admittat. Adjun- gitur autem Conſonantiis, & quidem perfectis ; propterea quòd nihil ma- gis conſonum aut perfectum eſſe poſſit ; quàm quod reſpectu ſui unum eſt.* Sethus Calviſ. c. 4.

*C.4. † C.5.

(m) Primari Concords *Sethus* calleꞇ * Perfect, and Secundari † Imper- fect : but *Perfect* and *Imperfect* ar differences of ꝺe Intervalls : as a Perfect and Imperfect Second, a Perfect and Imperfect Third, a Per- fect and Imperfect Sixt, a Perfect and Imperfect Sevnꞇ.

Mor‘over hœ makeꞇ ꝺe 4 old‘ Concords [*Diapaſon, Diapente, Dia- teſſaron* and ꝺe *Vniſon*] to bœ of ꝺe firſt ſort ; and ꝺe 4 nu‘ [ꝺe perfect and imperfect Third, ꝺe perfect and imperfect Sixt] to bœ of ꝺe ſe-

cond

cond fort : aldowg *Ditonus*, or a perfect Third, bee found to bee a perfect, *i.* a Primari Concord, as admitted into de Cloz'; and a Fowrt or *Diateſſaron* to bee but a * Secundari, and excluded.   * *Vide* n.

(n) A *Fowrt.* Aldowg *Sethus* joining *Diateſſaron* wit his old' fellows *Diapente* and *Diapaſon*, doo' account it a Perfect [*i.* a Primari] Concord ; yet doo't hee ſeem' to extenuat' its perfection, ſaying † in on' plac', *quæ aliquo modo perfecta cenſetur :* and in an oder plac' of de ſam' Chapter, *quæ vix perfecta exiſtimatur.*   † *c.* 4.

(o) *Non frequenter in paucioribus vocibus collocandæ ſunt Octavæ aut Vniſonus : quæ, cum variationem concentus non admittant, Harmoniam generant aliquanto ſimpliciorem, & quaſi egenam. Non tamen ideò ſunt prorſus vitandæ : Harmonia enim, ut Clauſulas formet, & Modulatio ut elegantiùs & volubiliùs procedat, ſæpe earum præſentiam requirunt. Convenientiùs autem uſurpari poſſunt, ſi ambæ nec paribus Figuris, nec codem temporis momento coincidant : ſed ſi altera vox poſteriorem Notulæ altrius partem occupet.* Seth. c. 9.

(p) *Hæc tria Intervalla verſantur naturaliter in gravibus ſonis : atq; poſt Diſdiapaſon, ſeu Quintam decimam, Ditono ac Semiditono proprius locus attribuitur, qui in gravibus minùs ſonora ſunt. Has eſſe veras & naturales harum Conſonantiarum ſedes, uſus & quotidiana, in Inſtrumentis Muſicis, experientia liquidò oſtendunt.* Sethus Calviſ. c. 10.

---

§ IV. *Of de Ornaments of Melodi and Harmoni.*

¶ I. *Of Confecution.*

Vnto de perfection of Melodi and Harmoni, ar reqired deſ' 4 Graces or Ornaments:[Confecution, Syncope, Fuga, and Formaliti.]

Confecution is de following of Intervalls, Conſonant or Diſſonant, upon Concords. In wiç, skilful Artiſts hav' obſerved divers neceſſary Cautions, dat may bee reduced unto certain brief Rul's or Canons.   *Confecution.*

Confecution of Conſonant Intervalls is eider Simple or Mixt.

Simple Confecution is of Concords upon Concords of deir own kind'. Concerning wiç der' ar deſ' Rul's.

CANON I. *Of Simple Confecution.*

De Confecution of Uniſons upon Uniſons, of Fifts upon Fifts, and of Eigts upon Eigts, or of deir Compounds,   *Simple Confecution of Vniſons, Fifts and Eigts alloued.*

poonds, not canging deir Keyz, is gœd, and der'for' Alloued: as

C A N O N I I.

Simple Confe-
cution of Vni-
fons,&c. Pro-
hibited.
(a)

But de Simple Confecution of def' 3 primari Concords, bot'
in Gradations and Skippings, is (a) irkfom to de ear, and
der'for' prohibited: as

C A N O N I I I.

(b)

(b) Def' prohibited Confecutions ar of dat forc',
dat dey ar not taken away by de interpofition eider of Difcords, or of de fmaller Refts.

Firft, de Confecution of *Vnifons* is not avoided by a *Se-*
cond, nor of *Eigts* by a *Nin't* or a *Sevnt,* nor of *Fifts* by a
Tritonus or *Semidiapente,* interpofed: as

Secondly, neider ar def' Confecutions avoided by in-
terpofing any Reft, les dan a Sembrief: as

But if de Not', anfwering de Reft, bæ of de fam' tim',
and

and ðe Not's fellow bæ mœved into an oðer key ; ðe faulty Confecution by ðat means is avoided.

C A N O N IV.

But ðe continued Confecution of oðer Concords is al- *De Simple Con-*
loœd, as wel afcending and defcending, as immorant in ðe *fecution of*
fam' plac' : efpecially of *Thirds* and *Sixts* in (1) Gradation, *Thirds and*
and (2) fœmtim' in Skipping : boð' wi∈ [bæing, in diffe- *Sixts alloœd.*
rent *Intervalls, (c) Perfect and Imperfect] dœ', wiꞇ ðeir va- ** Vi. § 3, ¶ 1.*
rieti, avoid ðat tedioufnes, wi∈ ðe Confecution of Uni- *(c)*
form primari Concords dœ'ꞇ incur : (*Vide* (a)) as

C A N O N V.

De Confecution of Fowrꞇs bæing uniform, [*i.* all of *Simple Confecu-*
on' Intervall, as ðe primari Concords ar] is not fo good : *tion of Fowrꞇs.*
yeꞇ becaus ðey bæ but fecundari Concords, ðey ar fœmtim'
continued : as ðe † Mufician did obferv : *Vix quidem Quar-* *† Sethus c. 10:*
tæ ita vitari poſſunt, ut duæ vel tres continuæ non admittantur :
tamen id plerumq; variatâ Bafi, & in certa forma Claufularum
fieri confuevit. And again hæ fewet it to bæ ðe practic' of
moft' Muficians, to continu' Fowrꞇs in Sixts : fo ðat ðey
begin wiꞇ a primari Concord, and end' wiꞇ an Eigꞇ. *Ob-*
ferveiur (inquit) *quòd plures Sextæ (fi mediatione, Tertiam*
inferiore loco habeant, & Quartam fuperiore) continuantur a
pleriſq; Muficis : maximè defcendendo : tantùm, modo in per-
fecta Confonantia inchœent, & in Octava finiantur : as in def'
2 examples of 3 Part's.

H   Wer'

Werᶜ de upper Partᶜ of de firſt example, and likᶜwiſᶜ of de ſecond, hat 4 continued Sixts to de Baſᶜ : wiᶜ ar ſo many Fowrᵗs to de Thirds in de Tenor.

And deſᶜ Conſecutions ar Simple: [of de ſeverall kindᶜs of Concords following demſelvs.]

Mixt Conſecu-
tion.

Mixt Conſecution is of all ſorts of Concords, variouſly entermedled, and enter eangᶜably ſuccᵉᵉding onᶜ an oᶜer.

Dis Mixt Conſecution hat deſᶜ Rulᶜs.

CANON I. *Of Mixt Conſecution.*

(d)

(d) De divers ſorts of Concords dooᶜ beſt follow onᶜ an oᶜer in Degrᵉᵉᶜs, and in contrari motion : [onᶜ Partᶜ aſcending, wilᶜ de oᶜer deſcender.]

CANON II.

(e)
Mutual Conſe-
cution of Pri-
mari Concords.

(e) Deſᶜ 3 Primari Concords, Uniſon, Flft, and Eigt, dooᶜ wel follow onᶜ an oᶜer ; if onᶜ Partᶜ procᵉᵉdᶜ by Degrᵉᵉᶜs, and de oᶜer by Skips.

CANON III.

(f)
Conſecution of
oder Concords
upon dem.

(f) De Conſecution of de oder Concords, [as Thirds and Sixts perfeᶜt and imperſeᶜt, wit deir Compounds] upon deſᶜ Primariᶜs, Uniſon, Fift, and Eigt (botᶜ by Degrᵉᵉᶜs and Skips, Aſcending and Deſcending) is facil and familiar.

And deſᶜ Conſecutions ar npon de 3 primᶜ Concords, [Uniſons, Fifts, and Eigts :] dotᶜ dat follow ar upon de reſt : [Thirds, Fowrᵗs, and Sixts.]

CANON. IV.

(g)
Conſecution up-
on de Third.

By Vniſons.

(g) De Third, botᶜ perfeᶜt and imperfeᶜt, is followed by de Uniſon, in (1) Degᵉᵉᶜs wen de Partᶜs moovᶜ contrarily ; and in Skipping, botᶜ upward and dounward, (2) wen

(2) wen on᷄ of dem ſtayet in his plac᷄: alſo (3) wen bod᷄ Part᷄s aſcend togeder, de Superior by Degræ, and de Inferior by Skip. But wen bod᷄ Part᷄s dꝏ᷄ (4) deſcend ; and wen bod᷄ Part᷄s (5) Skip togeder ; de Confecution is not good.

Secondly de Third is followed by a Fift, in Degræ᷄s, (1) wen de Part᷄s mꝏv᷄ contrarily ; and by Skipping bot᷄ upward and dounward, (2) wen on᷄ of dem ſtayet in his plac᷄ : as alſo wen de Part᷄s deſcend or aſcend bod᷄ togeder, (3) de Superior kæping Degræ in Deſcending, and (4) de Inferior in Aſcending : and ſo de Fift may follow a Tent ; (wi᷄ is a Compound Third) aldowg de Tent dꝏ᷄ not aſcend, but deſcend : for a Compound deſcending a Fift, is as his Simple aſcending a Fowrt. Laſtly (5) wen bod᷄ deſcend by Skipping, ſo dat de Superior Fall de diſtanc᷄ of a Third.

By a Fift.

De Confecution in de firſt and laſt of deſ᷄ fiv᷄ ways is excepted againſt, *propter* * *relationem non Harmonicam.* But dis happenet ſeldom : for of all de 7 Relations of de 7 Not᷄s, in bod᷄ deſ᷄ ways, der᷄ is but on᷄ *Non Harmonica* ; and dat, wen it happenet, by flatting de Sharp or ſarping de Flat, may bee corrected.

* *V.* ☞ in §3, ¶ 2.

r.n.h.   r.n.h.

Thirdly,

By an Eigt,

Thirdly de Third is followed by an Eigt in contrary moovings, (1) de Inferior Partᶜ defcending, and de Superior afcending : and (2) fomtimᶜ wen de Inferior Stayeꝛ : efpecially if de Sixt, to wi e de Superior Skippeꝛ, bæ imperfeꝗ, and in de *Arſis* or Elevation : (3) but de afcending of bodᶜ togeder is not good.

I   I   I   I   2   3

By a Fowrꝛ.

Fowrꝛly de Fowrꝛ followeꝛ de Third, wen de Inferior Stayeꝛ, and de Superior afcendeꝛ by Degræᶜ ; or wen de Superior Stayeꝛ, and de Inferior defcendeꝛ. It may alfo follow a Fift, wen de Inferior Stayeꝛ and de Superior defcendeꝛ ; or wen de Superior Stayeꝛ & de Inferior afcendeꝛ. And as de Fowrꝛ followeꝛ a Third and Fift, fo is it followed by dem : and wen it is fet to a Baſᶜ-cadencᶜ, (by reafon dat de

* *Vide Cadencᶜ.*   * Binding-notᶜ is farꝛed) it is followed by a Semediapente.

Notᶜ heerᶜ dat de Fowrꝛ is commonly taken in de *Arſis* or Elevation : if de Notᶜ bæ Syncopated, it is ftil taken in de *Theſis* : and in Simple *Confecution* it is taken bodᶜ ways.

Dis example bæing divided into twifᶜ 7 Minims, befidᶜs de Cloz-notᶜ ; in de fecond Minim of de firft Partᶜ, de Fowrꝛ in † *Arſis* followeꝛ a 3, and is followed by a Fift : and den (a Sixt interpofed) de 4 in *Arſis* followeꝛ a 5, and is followed by

† * *V. c.* 2, § 4, ¶ 1.   a 3. In de oder Partᶜ begun wit an Unifon, a Semidiapente followeꝛ de 4 in * *Theſis* : den de 4 in *Arſis* followeꝛ a 3 : and laftly de 4 in *Theſis* is followed by a 3 : wit de Clozᶜ in an Eigt.

By a Sixt.   De Third is alfo followed by a Sixt, (1) wen de Partᶜs

Part's moov' contrarily : and (2) wen on' of dem kæpet his key.

As de Sixt followet deThird; fo is it followed by deThird: (1) de on' proceeding by Degræ de oder by Skip ; or (2) on' of dem Staying ; or (3) bod' Skipping.

De Sixt by a Third.

De Sixt is lik'wif' followed by a Fift, (1) on' of dem Staying: and by an Eigt (2) in contrary mooving : (3) fel-dom wen dey afcend or defcend togeder, de on' by Degræ, de oder by Skip.

De Sixt by a Fift and an Eigt.

Confecution of Difcords.

And fue is de Confecution of Confonant Intervalls. Der' is alfo a Confecution of de Diffonant : (h) de wie bæing rigtly taken, not on'ly ar tolerable in Harmoni ; but alfo ad a Grac' and Ornament unto it : as wer'by bot † de Concords ar mad' fwæter ; and alfo many Mufical Points (wie coold' not bæ witout dem) ar fwæt'ly mainteined. Yea de moft' harf Difcords *Tritonus* and *Semidiapente*, wie, for deir extrem' jarring aboov oders, ar branded wit * *Rela-tio non Harmonica* , bæing ordered arigt becoom Hermo-nical.

Confecution of Difcords.
(h)

† *V.Difcords in* § 3; ¶ 2.

* *V.* ☞ *in* § 3, ¶ 2.

In dis Confecution def' Rul's ar to bæ obferved.

Firft dat de Not's, becaus dey ar Difcords, bæ of fort tim'

(i)

† *V. C. 2, § 6.*

(k)

* *Vide Syncope.*

tim⁵ [Minims, Croⅽets, Qaveʁs:] for ſo (i) even *Relatio non Harmonica* wil not offend. 2 Đat dey bæ uſed almoſt⁵ altogeder in † Gradation, aſcending or deſcending : in Skipping ſeldom, and not abꝏv a Not⁵ or two at onc⁵ ; wer⁵as in Gradation, dey may paſ tꝏrrow a wol⁵ *Diapaſon*, or furder, if næd⁵ bæ.

3. (k) Đat dey wie ar of de ſam⁵ tim⁵ dꝏ⁵ follow deir leading Concords iu de Ævn Plac⁵ : except in * Binding, wer⁵ dey ar alwais taken in de odⅰor oderwiſ⁵ ſꝏmtim⁵, wen, for de continuing of a Gradation, de Concord and Diſcord bæ forc⁵t to ⅽang⁵ Places: as wer⁵ *Mi fa* anſwer to *Fa* below dem : *Vide* D I S C O R D S *in* § 3.

4. Đat dey begin wel uppon a Pointed Not⁵.

Example of *Tritonus* amd *Semidiapente*.

Hær⁵ de 2 *Pa⁵s*, ſet below, ar 2 *Tritons* to de *Mi⁵s* abꝏv : and de ſam⁵, ſet abꝏv, ar 2 *Semidiapentes* : yet, bæing dus taken, dey mak⁵ gꝏd Harmoni : yea dowg de *Minim-Pa* bæ alſo a Sevnt to de Baſⅽ· But to turn dis diſcordant Minim into a Groⅽet, wit a Point added to de Minim precedent, is mor⁵ uſuall : dus

Đeſⅽ Conſecutions bot of Conſonant and Diſſonant Intervalls, dowg generally dey ar to bæ obſerved in Harmoni ; yet muſt dey ſꝏmtim⁵s giv plac⁵ to de greater Graces, [Report⁵ and Revert, de Melodi & Formaliti of de Part⁵s;] wen

wɛn ðey cannot bɛɛ wel effected witout ſoom violation of
ðe Rul's of Confecution. But hɛɛ ðat wold' bɛɛ torrowly
informed in deſ' Myſteri's, had nɛɛd' firſt to peruſ' de furder
Directions of ðe moſt' Artful Doctors : ſu c as ar *Paduanius*,
Calviſius, and our Countriman Mʳ. *Thom as Morley* : and
ðen to examin ðe Examples of ðe † moſt' skilful *Melopœi-*
ans, for imitation.

† *Vide Epilog.*

ANNOT. *to* §4, ¶1.

(a) **I**S *Irkſom to ðe Ear.* On' caus hɛɛr'of is ðe excelling
ſwɛɛt'nes of deſ' Concords : wer'wit ðe Ear bɛɛing ſatiſ-
fy ed, ðe iterating ðer'of is tedious : for ðe ſwɛɛteſt tings (as ðe Orator obſervet in his own Faculti) dœ' ſoneſt brɛɛd' ſatieti. † *Quæ max-*
imè ſenſus noſtros impellunt voluptate, ab iis celerrimè faſtidio quodam &
ſatietate abalienamur. An oðer caus is ðe want of Varieti in deſ' Concords, to prevent ſatieti. For all *Fifts* hav' but on' Interval, [of 3
Not's and a half :] and all *Eigts* hav' lik'wiſ' but on' Interval, [of 5
Not's and 2 half. not's] wer' as *Thirds* and *Sixts* hav' ðis pleaſing varieti in ðem ſelvs. For on' *Third* conſiſtes of 2 Not's, and an oðer of
a Not' and a half : on' *Sixt* conſiſtes of 4 Not's, and an oðer of 4 and
a half : ſo ðat deſ' dœ' follow on' an oðer * witout ſatieti : wie to
avoid, ðe *Fifts*, *Eigts*, and lik'wiſ' *Vniſons*, had nɛɛd' of ſoom oðer
Concord to cœm betwɛɛn' ðem. And yet in Multitud' of Voices, ðis
fault, as oðers, bɛɛing not eaſily obſerved, may bɛɛ ſuffered. † Els
wer' ðe Stop of Twelfs in Organs (wie is added on'ly for fulnes of ðe
Muſik) inexcuſable ; ſɛɛing ðat ðer'by, ðe Simple Confecution of *Fifts*,
as wel moving as immorant, is perpetuated.

† *Orat. l.* 3.

* *Vide Can.*
IV. *and* V.

†

(b) *Tanta vis eſt hujus Confecutionis, ut neq; Pauſis minoribus, neq;*
Diſſonantiis tolli poſſit. Sethus C. 9.

(c) *Perfect* and *Imperfect.* De ſevn Not's dœ' mak', in Confecution,
7 ſeveral *Thirds* ; werof trɛɛ ar perfect, and fowr imperfect : alſo ſo
many ſeveral *Sixts* ; wer'of fowr ar perfect, and trɛɛ imperfect. For
Vts Third and *Sixt* ar boð' perfect : *Re's Third* and *Sixt* ar boð'
imperfect : *Mi's Third* and *Sixt* ar boð' imperfect : *Fa's Third* and *Sixt*
ar boð' perfect : S O L'S *Third* is imperfect, and his *Sixt* perfect :
La's Third and *Sixt* ar boð' imperfect : and *Pa's Third* and *Sixt* boð'
perfect. Of all deſ' *Thirds*, on'ly two perfect immediatly follow on' an
oðer : nam'ly, Pa Re, and Vt Mi. wie dowg ðey bɛɛ Primari Concords (as wel as *Vniſons*, *Fifts*, and *Eigts*) yet ſɛɛing ðey ar not of ðem
ſelvs ſo ſwɛɛt' ; ðey paſ wel enoug among ðe reſt, witout ſatieti.

(d) *Ex Conſonanti s perfectis ad imperfectas, & contra, tranſimus*
(quantum fieri poteſt) in Gradibus, & in motu vocum contrario : ita ut ſi
altera aſcendat, reliqua deſcendat, Calviſ. C. 10.

(e) *Conſonantiæ perfectæ non ejuſdem generis, ſeſe ſequi poſſunt ; ſi*
altera

altera procedat Gradibus, altera verò Saltu. Sethus C. 9. But *Morley* wil not allou riſing from a Fift to an Eigt, nor from an Eigt to a Fift: wie hæ callet Hitting de Eigt in de fac: as

(f) *Ex perfectis ad imperfectas facilis eſt tranſitus, tam per Gradus, quàm per Saltus: tam aſcendendo, quam deſcendendo. Sic Vniſonus tranſit in Tertiam* * *minorem, ac* † *majorem: & in Sextam minorem, rarius in majorem. Quinta verò in Sextam majorem ac minorem: item in Ditonum ac Semiditonum. Atq; ita de Octavis.* Idem C. 10.

(g) Concerning deſ and de oder Conſecutions uppon *Thirds,* See mor in *Calviſius.*

(h) *Diſſonantiæ, ſi non temere, ſed* * *certis quibuſdam modis Harmoniam ingrediantur; non tantum facilè tolerantur; ſed concentum etiam magnopere exornant.* Calviſius C. 11.

(i) *Tritonus etiam & Semidiapente celeritate obliterantur.* ibidem.

(k) *Quæ unius* † *formæ ſunt, alternatim conſonent: ita ut Conſona inchoet, Diſſona ſequatur. In integro itaq; Tactu conſonare debet ex duabus Minimis prima, quæ Tactum in Depreſſione inchoat: ex quatuor Semiminimis, etiam prima, quæ eſt in Depreſſione Tactus; & tertia quæ eſt in principio Elevationis: & ex octo Fuſis impares quatuor [prima, tertia, quinta, ſeptima.]*

* *ſeu imperfectam.*
† *ſeu perfectam.*

* *Nempe in Conſecutione, & Syncope.*

† *ſeu figura, quæ ſcilicet tempus indicat.*

---

§4 *Of Ornaments,*
¶ 2 *Of Syncope.*

(a) S Yncope is (b) de Diſjoining and Conjoining of (c) a Meſur-not: wen (in reſpect of Tim) it is disjoined into 2 Part's; wer of de former is conjoined wit de precedent half-not in on Tim, and de latter wit his ſubſequent half-not in an oder Tim: (d). De Conjoining of wie latter wit his half-not following, is called by *Sethus Alligatio,* and by *Morley,* Binding. In wie, for diſtinction, de firſt of deſ two conjoined half-not's is called de Bound-not, and de ſecond de Binding-not: unto wie two, der anſweret (eider in de Baſ or in ſom oder Part) on (e) entir Meſur-not, wie is as it wer de Band, dat holdet dem bod togeder: as anſweret to

Dis

(f)

Đis Ornament is (f) very uſ^eful, not on^ely becaus it
graceꞇ and ſwæꞇ^eneꞇ đe following Concords ; but alſo becaus it helpeꞇ mu ꞓ to vari đe Harmøni, and to ſew đe *en-*
ergi and efficaci of đe Ditti.

¶ Đe Not^es dat ar bound in Syncope, ar eider Diſcords,
or ſecundari Concords.

Binding of Concords.

Of ſecundari Concords, đe Fowꞇ is freqently bound
wiꞇ a Third : ſeldom wiꞇ a Diapente, and yet ſœmtim^e wiꞇ
(g) a Semidiapente.

B. of đe Fowrꞇ

(g)

In đe firſt Bar ar 3 Fowrꞇs bound wiꞇ Thirds : in đe ſecond and ꞇird, 2 Fowrꞇs bound wiꞇ Semidiapentes : in đe
Fowrꞇ, a Fowrꞇ bound wiꞇ a Fift.

Đe Third is bound wiꞇ a Fift, or a Fowrꞇ : and đe Sixt
wiꞇ a Fift.

B. of đe Third and of đe Sixt.

In đe firſt Bar is a Third bound wiꞇ a Fift, and a Fowrꞇ
wiꞇ a Third : in đe ſecond two Thirds wiꞇ Fowrꞇs, and a
ſecond wiꞇ a Third : in đe ꞇird two Sixts wiꞇ Fifts.

¶ Su ꞓ is đe vertu^e of Syncope, dat it makeꞇ đe ſecundari
Concords as ſwæꞇ^e as đe Primari : yea and đe very Diſcords
as gœd as any Concords.

Binding of Diſcords.

Of Diſcords đe Second is freqently bound wiꞇ a Third,
and ſœmtim^e wiꞇ an Uniſon : and đe Sevnꞇ freqently wiꞇ a
Sixt, and ſœmtim^e wiꞇ an Eiꞡt.

B. of đe Se-cond and of đe Sevnꞇ.

In đe firſt Bar ar ꞇræ Seconds bound wiꞇ Thirds : in đe

fecond is a Second bound wiŧ a Unifon : in đe ŧird Bar ar ŧræ Sevnŧs bound wiŧ Sixŧs : and in đe Fowrŧ is a Sevnŧ bounđ wiŧ an Eiʒt, and a Ninʿŧ wiŧ an Eiʒt.

De Tritonus is bound wiŧ a Fifŧ : and đe Semidiapenŧe wiŧ a Sixt ; and ſœmtimʿ wiŧ (h) a Third : but ſo, đe Bound and Binding Notʿs wil want * đe entirʿ Band, ꝩiŧ is neceſſari to a perfeĉt Alligation.

B. of Tritonus &
Semidiapente.
(h)
* *Vid.* c. *ſuprà.*

Trit. 5.   4 ½ 6   4 ½ 3. 23.

In đe firſt Bar is a Tritonus bound wiŧ a Fifŧ : in đe ſecond is a Semidiapente wiŧ a Sixŧ:in đe ŧird a Semidiapente wiŧ a Third ; and a Second wiŧ a Third.

Binding ſingle
and continued.
(i)

Alligation or Binding is eiđer Single, or continued.

If đe Binding (i) Concord bæ a Single or lonʿ half-notʿ; đe Alligation is đerʿ ended Single : but if it bæ đe half of an ođer Meſurʿ-notʿ ; đe Alligation is (k) continued : and đat morʿ or les, according to đe number of ſuŧ disjoined Meſurʿ-notʿs, immediatly following onʿ an ođer.

(k)

Example of a Single Alligation you havʿ in đeſʿ Notʿs ꝩerʿ a Fowrŧ is bound wiŧ a Third.

Cadenŧʿ.

Moſtʿ excellent in dis kindʿ is a Cadencʿ : ꝩiŧ is an Alligation, ꝩoſʿ Binding ſemitonʿ falleŧ into đe next key (l) alway ſarp: of ꝩiŧ falling đe Cadencʿ haŧ his namʿ : (m) by ꝩiŧ đe Harmoni & ſœm partʿ of đe Ditti inclineŧ to reſt.   Cadencʿ is eiđer Perfeĉt or Imperfeĉt.

(l)
(m)

c. Perfeĉt.
(n)

(n) A perfeĉt Cadencʿ is đat ꝩiŧ to đe disjoined Meſurʿ-notʿ and đe Binding Concord, addeŧ a ŧird Notʿ in đe key of đe disjoined : ꝩiŧ muſt bæ eiđer an Eiʒt or an Unifon to đe Baſʿ : as

Reſolution of
Cadences.

De two Notʿs of Syncope in dis Cadencʿ (leſt đe often Repetition of đem in đe ſamʿ manner ſœldʿ wax tedious) ar wœnt to bæ diverſly Reſolved into Notʿs of les figurʿs, đus :

Alſo

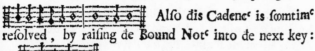 Alſo dis Cadenc͏ᶜ is ſͦͦmtim͏ᶜ
reſolved, by raiſing de Bound Not͏ᶜ into de next key:
as

(o) De Imperfect Cadenc͏ᶜ dͦͦᶜ͏t ſignifi͏ᶜ very little reſt, eider
of Harmoni or of Ditti: but dat dey ar bod͏ᶜ to proͤͤd͏ᶜ
furder: and it differe͏t from de perfect in de tird or laſt Not͏ᶜ:
wi͏ͼ eider it ſilence͏t, as 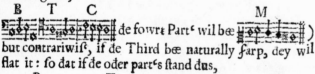, or mͦͦve͏t from de proper key of an Eigt or Uniſon, to ſͦͦm oder: as

Sͦͦmtim͏ᶜ dis ͼang͏ᶜ is mad͏ᶜ in de Baſ͏ᶜ, de Cadenc͏ᶜ re-
maining whol͏ᶜ: wi͏ͼ neverdeles is imperfect; becaus de laſt
Not͏ᶜ, by dis means, is neider Uniſon nor Eigt: as

So proper is a Diſcord to a Cadenc͏ᶜ, dat if der͏ᶜ bͣͣ non͏ᶜ
in de Cadenc͏ᶜ to de Baſ͏ᶜ; yet is a Diſcord wel admitted, in
ſͦͦm oder Part͏ᶜ, to de Cadenc͏ᶜ. Wer͏ᶜ not͏ᶜ dat if de Not͏ᶜ
in a fowr͏t Part͏ᶜ, anſwering de Bound-not͏ᶜ and his Diſcord, bͣͣ a Third to de Baſ͏ᶜ; it is better imperfect dan perfect: aldowg de perfect bͣͣ a Fift to † on͏ᶜ Part͏ᶜ, and de
imperfect bͣͣ neider Fift nor Forwr͏t, but * a Diſcord of a
half-not͏ᶜ betwͣͣn dem bod͏ᶜ. And der͏ᶜfor͏ᶜ if dat Third bͣͣ
naturally flat, dey wil not ſarp it: (ſo dat de oder Part͏ᶜs
ſtanding dus,

B   T   C   M

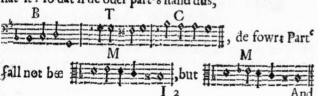 de fowr͏t Part͏ᶜ wil bͣͣ)
but contrariwiſ͏ᶜ, if de Third bͣͣ naturally ſarp, dey wil
flat it: ſo dat if de oder part͏ᶜs ſtand dus,

B   T   C

, de fowr͏t Part͏ᶜ
         M   M

ſall not bͣͣ, but

Margin notes:
C. Imperfect.

Cadences reqir͏ᶜ Diſcords.

† *Counter.*
* *Semidiapente.*

And hederto of Single Alligation. What Continued Binding is, fæ befor^c (i) and (k). Examples der^{c}of, Mr *Morley* upon his Plain-fong, hat def^c two.

1.

2.

In de firft Example ar, firft a Fowrt Bound wit a Third, and 3 Sevnts Bound wit Sixts : den, dis Continued Binding bæing ended wit a fingle half-not^c, de next Continued Binding (caufed by an oder od half-not^c befor^c de disjoined Mefur^c-not^c) is of a Sixt wit a 5, a 4 wit a 3, a 6 wit a 5, a 6 wit a 6. and 2 Sevnts wit Sixts.

In de fecond ar 4 Fowrts Bound wit Thirds, a Nint wit an Eigt, and again 4 Fowrts wit Thirds.

Mor^{c}over de firft example finget every not^c of de plainfong, and den concludet wit a Minim-cadenc^c. And de fecond example ftrang^{c}ly defcendet from de higeft plac^c of de Lin^c to de loweft, concluding wit 2 Croeets to ævn de tim^c, befor^c de Cloz^c-not^c.

And def^c Syncope^{c}s ar of *Sembriefs*.

De Syncopating [or Disjoining and Binding] of *Minims*, hat 4 fpecial ways : wi-e ar wœnt to bæ taugt among de Rudiments of Setting. In de træ firft ways de Binding is Single : and in de fowrt, Continued.

De firft is wen de Binding not^c is a fingle Croeet, making ævn de latter part^c of de *Minim*, disjoined, in Tim^c, by a Croeet precedent : and fo, all træ making up a juft *Sembrief* ar often iterated witout alteration : as in dis example.

De

De fecond is wen to all def 3 Not's often iterated, you prefix on od *Minim*, [in Reft, or Not, or bod :] by means wer of de *Sembrief* wil always end in de middle of de disjoined *Minims* ; and fo wil de Not's never coom ævn, til at de laft you ad to de ♩ ♩ ♩ a *Minim*, [de fellow of de prefixed *Minim*, dat mad de ods :] dus :

De tird way is wen to every fue 3 Not's you prefix a *Minim* : de wie is not disjoined, as every fecond *Minim* is. Def 4 Not's dubbled mak 3 juft *Sembriefs* : dus :

or oderwif wen you fet de *Minim* after dem : but den de form of de Point is altered : dus :

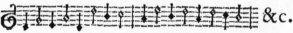 &c.

De fowrt is a continued Binding : wen after an od *Crocet* der follow many Syncopated *Minims*, befor you coom to an oder fingle *Crocet*, to mak de tim ævn. For until den, every *Sembrief-tim*, and every *Minim-tim* end et in de middl of a *Minim* : dus :

Annot. to C. III. §IIII. ¶ II.

ΣυγKοπὴ Conciſio.

(a) **S**yncope. Aldowg συ꜑ in dis Compound may ſeem꜄ to ad noting to ꝺe ſens of ꝺe Simple ; yet, ſeeing ꝺat *Syncope* dœ꜄ heer꜄ ſignifie not on꜄ly ꝺe Disjoining of an Inregrall into two Part꜄s, hut alſo ꝺe Conjoining again of ꝺe Part꜄s into 2 Integralls ; as *κοπη* [*ſectio*] dœ꜄ import꜄ ꝺe on꜄, ſo may συν [*ſimul* or *unà*] intimat꜄ ꝺe oꝺer : and ſo ꝺe * Notation of ꝺe Nam꜄ is a full Definition of ꝺe Thing.

* *Vide Orat. l. 2, c. 2, § 5.*

† *Cap. 12.*

(b) *Disjoining and Conjoining.* Agreeable hœr꜄unto is ꝺe Definition of † *Sethus* : *Syncope eſt irregularis applicatio Notulæ ad Tactum, facta propter minorem Figuram præcedentem.* wie hee dœ꜄t ꝺus explan꜄ : *Semibrevis enim, cum Tactu ſuo abſolvatur, Regulariter in Depreßione Tactus incboatur, & in Elevatione finitur. Quando autem ante Semibrevem Minima in Notulis vel Pauſis collocatur, quæ Tactum incboat in Depreſſione ; neceſſe eſt ut Semibrevis in altera parte Tactus, hoc eſt in Elevatione, incipiatur, & in Depreßione ſequentis Tactus deſinat : atq; ita partibus ſuis ad diverſos Tactus diſtrahatur.*

* *Liſthenius, and Calviſius, c. 12.*

(c) *Meſur꜄-not꜄.* [Sembrief or Minim.] For as anciently * *major Tactus* was of ꝺe Brief, and *Minor* of ꝺe Sembrief ; ſo nou, wee having qit꜄ forgotten to keep꜄ Brief-tim꜄, and learned (in qik Figur꜄s) to keep꜄ ꝺe Tim꜄ of a Minim ; our *major Tactus* muſt bee Sembrief-tim꜄, and our *Minor,* Minim-tim꜄. *Vide C. 2, § 4, &* (b) *in Notis.*

(d) *In an oꝺer tim꜄.* So ꝺat ꝺe Not꜄, wie regularly is Meſured by ꝺe Theſis and Arſis of on꜄ and ꝺe ſam꜄ *Tactus,* beeing Syncopated ha꜄ ꝺe former Part꜄ in ꝺe Arſis of on꜄, and ꝺe latter in ꝺe Theſis of an oꝺer. For wie caus a pointed Sembrief, and a pointed Minim in Arſis (woſ꜄ Points begin ꝺe Theſis of a nu꜄ *Tactus*) ar accounted Syncopata :

as *Semibrevis ac etiam Minima, cum Puncto, ſi Minima in Elevatione Tactus ponatur, Syncopatis annumerantur.* Seꝺus C. 12.

† *Vide* (a) *in c. 2, § 4.*

(e) *Entir꜄ Meſur꜄-not꜄.* Entir꜄ in reſpect of ꝺe *Tactus :* ꝺowg, for ꝺe Ditti´s ſak꜄, it may bee parted into ſundry † Figur꜄s : as

or for

(f) *Plurimum utilitatis habet Syncope, non tantùm quòd magnam ſuavitatem addit ſequentibus Conſonantiis ; ſed etiam quòd multum facit ad variandam Harmoniam, & ad energian Textus demonſtrandam.* Calviſ. C. 9.

(g) *Faciliùs Quarta in Semidiapente reſolvitur, tantùm modò inde in Ditonum perveniatur.* Seth. C. 12.

(h) *Semidiapente, ſi fiat notula Syncopata, hac conditione toleratur, modò in Ditonum perveniat.* Sethus C. 12.

(i) **W**eiꝺer ꝺe Bound-not꜄ bee Concord or Diſcord, ꝺe Binding not꜄ is always a Concord : ſav꜄ on꜄ly ꝺat a Fowr꜄ may bee bound, in a Cadenc꜄, wi꜄ a Semidiapente. *Vide* (g)

(k) *Syncope*

(k) *Syncope aliquando continuatur : & non una tantùm Notula ad Tactum irregulariter applicatur, sed plures : donec redeat ejus potestatis Notula, cujus fuit Figura, quæ Sincopes causam in initio præbuit.* Sethus C. 12.

(l) *Always ſharp.* Yea ðowg ðe Cadenc⁶ bœ in ðe Baſ⁶, and a flat in ſoom upper Part anſwer unto it : as

Wie Example *Morley* doⁱt ðus defend : As for ðe ſarp in ðe Baſ⁶ for ðe Flat in ðe Treble, ðe Baſ⁶ bœing a Cadenc⁶, ðe natur⁶ ðer⁶of reqiret a ſarp : let ðe ear bœ Judg : ſing it, and you wil lik⁶ ðe ſarp mu⁶e better ðan ðe Fiat. Ðis is confirmed by * *Calviſius,* wer⁶ hœ deſcribet ðe natur⁶ of a Cadenc⁶ : *Clauſula omnis, ſive ſit in Acutis ſive in gravibus, conſtat tribus Notulis, quarum penultima deſcendit, ultima aſcendit : & tam deſcenſus quàm aſcenſus per ſemitonium ſit : ſive id ſit in iis Clavibus, quæ ſemitonio naturaliter diſtant; ſive in alijs in quibus per* † *ſignum Chromaticum, intervallum Toni diminui & ad Semitonium redigi poteſt. Natura enim in his locis appetit hoc Intervallum, & elevat quodammodo ſonum, etiam ſigno Chromatico non aſcripto.*

(m) *Clauſulam* [i. *Cadentiam*] *vocamus illum modulationis actum, in quo Harmonia ad quietem inclinat, Parſq; aliqua Textus finitur.*

(n) *Perfectæ cadentiæ ſunt, quæ integræ* [i. *quæ dictis tribus conſtant notulis,*] *& in perfectiſſimis Conſonantiis terminantur : ut in uniſono aut octava,*

(o) *Imperfectæ Clauſulæ ſunt, quæ Harmoniam minùs ad quietem deducunt, ſed eam aliquo modo ſuſpendunt, & ulteriùs modulando progrediendum eſſe deſignant : quod fit cùm ultima notula vel ex propria ſede mota ſit, vel aliàs in imperfectam Conſonantiam incidit.*

* C. 13,

† X.

<hr>

§ 4 *Of Ornaments,*
¶ 3 *Of Fuga.*

FUga is ðe (a) Repeating of ſoom Modulation or Point, in (b) Melodi and Harmoni : an Ornament (c) excœding deligtfull, and wiⁱout ſatieti : and ðer⁶for⁶ Muſicians ðe mor⁶ ðey ar exerciſed in Setting, ðe mor⁶ ſtuddi and pains ðey beſtow in ðis Ornament.

A Point is a certain number and order of obſervable Notⁱs in any on⁶ Part⁶, iterated in ðe ſam⁶ or in divers Part⁶s : witin ðe tim⁶ commonly of two Sembriefs in qik Sonners, and of fowr or Fiv⁶ in graver Muſik.

Ðe Part⁶s of *Fuga* ar (d) two, ðe Principal, wⁱe leadet ; ðe Repli⁶, wⁱe followet. And ðe Sorts lik⁶ wiſ⁶ two, Report⁶ and Revert.

(a)
(b) (c)

A Point.

(d)

Report⁶

Reportᶜ.

Reportᶜ is de Iterating or mainteining of a Point in de likᶜ motion, [*per Arſin aut Theſin* ;] de Principal and Replicᶜ bod Aſcending, or bodᶜ Deſcending.

Reportᶜ is eider Direct, wiɛ iteratez dePoint in de famᶜ Cliefs and Notᶜs [Uniſons or Eigts ;] or Indirect, wiɛ iteratez de Point in oder Cliefs : for it may bæ taken at any diſtancᶜ from de firſt Notᶜ of de Point : but ſpecially at a Fowrz or Fift.

Direct Reportᶜ, or in de famᶜ Cliéfs, is ɵommonly in divers Partᶜs : Indirect, or in divers Clifes, in de famᶜ Partᶜ.

Revert.

Revert is de Iterating of a Point in contrari Motion, [*per Arſin & Theſin* ;] de Replicᶜ mɵoving *per Theſin*, if de Principal Aſcend, and *per Arſin*, if de Principal deſcend. Wiɛ kindᶜ of Fuga is muɛ (e) morᶜ difficult dan Report.

κατ᾽ ἄρσιν,
ᶄ Θῆσιν.
(e)

Obſervations in Fuga.

1. Fugaᶜs, as Cadences, ſɵoldᶜ kæpᶜ witin de Air of de Song ; begining and ending in ɵnᶜ of de Fowr (f) Airnotᶜs : ſpecially in de Tonᶜ it ſelf : Whoſᶜ Cadencᶜ hat de Pɵuer to reducᶜ all wandring modulations to deir Proper Air. *Vid*.(i) *in* ¶ 4.

(f)

(i) *in* ¶ 4.

2. Fuga may cɵom in wel witout a Reſt ; dowg better upon a Reſt, ſo it bæ not abɵov 3 or 4 Sembriefs : but beſt upon ɵnᶜ od Minim-reſt or ɛræ.

3. Aldowg a Sixt may not begin a Song ; yet may it begin a Fuga, dat beginez a Part, after a Reſt.

☞

4. Neider in Reportᶜ nor in Revert, dɵoᶜ Muſicians always ſtrictly tyᶜ dem ſelvs to de juſt Number, Figurᶜ, Interval, or Tactus, of de Notᶜs in de Point : and riſing or falling a Fowrz for a Fift, or a Fift for a Fowrz is uſual : as in deſᶜ 3 examplᶜs of Mr *Morleys*, [ɵnᶜ of Treble-diſcant, and 2 of Baſᶜ-diſcant] upon his Plain-ſong, in de ſecond Partᶜ of his Bɵokᶜ. Werᶜ you may wɵonder to ſæ hou many oder ſeveral Diſcants hæ hat madᶜ for his ſeveral purpoſes upon dat ɵnᶜ Ground.

In

In de firſt Example de Point conſiſtet of 8 Not's, in 4
ſembriefs : wiᴇ is Reverted in a Fift wit 11 nots, in 4 ſembriefs : and den Reported in a Fowrt (for of dat diſtanc'
ar all de Not's, except de firſt wiᴇ is a Fift) in 3 ſembriefs
and a half, befor' de Cloz'-not'.

In de ſecond de Point conſiſtet of 10 Not's, in 4 ſem-
birefs and a half : of wiᴇ der' follow nin' Reverted in a
Fift, in 3 ſembriefs, de laſt Not' bæing omitted : and den
8 Not's reported in a Second, in 3 ſembriefs and a half,
2 Not's, befor' de Cadenc', bæing omitted. For de laſt
qavers and cro-cets ar bnt a breaking of de Cadenc' : de
wiᴇ is a Fowrt to de firſt Cadenc'.

In de tird example de Point conſiſtet of nin' Not's, in
fowr ſembriefs and a half : wiᴇ ar Reverted in a Second in
les den fowr ſembriefs : de laſt Not' wer'of beginnet a
Report of de 4 precedent Not's in a Second : but de laſt of
de Report riſing to *Elami* canget de Interval : de wiᴇ, as
wel as Number and Figur', you may find' not always kept,
in def' and oder Reported and Reverted Points. *Ui.* ☞ *ante.*

5 De fift and laſt obſervation is, dat all ſorts of Fuga's,
[Reports and Reverts, of de ſam' and of divers Points, in de
ſam' and divers Canons, and in de ſam' and divrrs Part's,]
ar ſomtim' moſt' elegantly entermedled : as in dat inimi-
table Leſſon of Mr *Birds,* conteining two Part's in on'
upon a Plain-ſong : wer'in de firſt Part' beginnet wit a   **1 Point.**
Point ; and den Revertet it, Not' for Not', in a Fowrt or
Elevnt : and de ſecond Part' firſt Revertet de Point in de
Fowrt as de firſt did ; and den Reportet it in de Uniſon.

          K   Befor'

Befor^c de end^c wer^c of de firſt Part having reſted 3 Minims after his Revert, ſingeɀ a ſecond Point, and Reverteɀ it in de Eigt : and de ſecond firſt Reverteɀ de Point in a fowrɀ ; and den Reporteɀ it in a Fowrɀ. Laſtly de firſt ſingeɀ a ɀird point, and Reverteɀ it in de Fift ; and den Reporteɀ it in an Uniſon: and ſo clozeɀ wiɀ ſoom annexed Not^cs : and de ſecond firſt Reverteɀ it in a Fift, and den Reporteɀ it in an Uniſon, and ſo clozeɀ wiɀ a ſecond Revert. Wer^c, to mak^c up de ful Harmoni, unto def^c 3 Part^cs is added a Fowrɀ, wiɛ very Muſically touɛeɀ ſtil upon de Points Reported and Reverted. De Leſſon is dis.

Fuga ligata.

Iterating of de (g) wolᶜ modulation of a Song [namᶜly wen two or moᶜ Partᶜs ar madᶜ in onᶜ] is a kindᶜ of Fuga : wiᵉ *Calviſius* calleᵗ *Fuga ligata.*   (g)

Deſᶜ Partᶜs [Principal and Repliᶜ] ſoomtimᶜ dey prik doun ſeverally by demſelvs : as in Mʳ *Morleys* examples of two Partᶜs in onᶜ, in (h) Epidiateſſaron and Epidiapente, botᶜ in Counterpoint and Diſcant.   (h)

In Counterpoint dus.

In Diſcant dus.

Soomtimᶜ dey writᶜ onᶜly de Principal : and prefix a (i) Title, declaring botᶜ de Diſtancᶜ of de Repliᶜ, and de timᶜ wen it coomeᵗ in : (adding afterward, in his duᶜ placᶜ, de markᶜ of his Clozᶜ) wiᵉ Title de Muſicians call *Canon.* As in dis example of *Calviſius.*   (i)

De Canon is *Fuga in Epidiapaſon, ſeu Octava ſuperiore, poſt duo* ∗ *Tempora.*

∗ i. *Brevia, non Semibrevia. Vide* (b) *in Notis ad* C. 2. § 4.

    Werᶜ

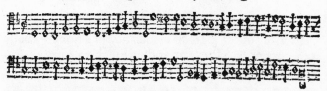

Wer‹, for mor‹ sur‹ti, de Not‹ in ðe Principal, upon wi‹ ðe Repli‹ coomeꞇ in, is marked : ðus ·ꞇ·

But nou ðey hav‹ found a mor‹ eafy and furer way : ſewing ðe Diſtanc‹ of ðe Repli‹, by ðe plac‹ of an oder Signed Clief Prefixed ; and ðe Tim‹ of his cooming in, by ðe Reſt annexed : according to wi‹ Clief ðe Repli‹ is to bæ ſung, as if ðe firſt Clief wer‹ not : as in deſ‹ 2 examples of *Calviſius.*

De Canon of ðe firſt is,
Fuga in Tertia ſuperiore Poſt Tempus.

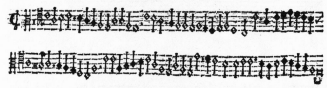

De Canon of ðe ſecond is,
Fuga in Hypodiapente poſt Tempus.

But wer‹ ðe ſecond Clief wiꞇ his Reſt ſeweꞇ ðe Canon, ðe Title wiꞇ ðe Mark of cooming in may ſæm‹ ſuperfluous.

If you mak‹ mo‹ Part‹s [3, 4, or 5,] in on‹ : ðeir Canons alſo may bæ lik‹wiſ‹ ſignifyed by ðeir Cliefs & Reſts, prefixed in order on‹ to an oder : as in ðis example of *Jacobus Gallus* cited by *Calviſius.*

De

De Canon is,
Fuga 5 Vocum in Tertia superiore, post Tempus.

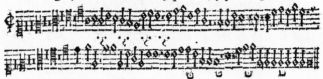

As *Fuga Soluta,* so lik'wis' *Ligata* may bœ Reverted, Ite- *Fuga Ligata per*
rating de Pincipal as wel by Contrari, as by lik' Motion: *Arsin & The-*
as in de Example alleaged by *Calvisius* out of de great *sin.*
Musician *Joseph Zarlinus.* Wos' Canon is,

Fuga in Unisono post duo Tempora, & per
Contrarium Motum.

Resolution of de Repli' prickt as it is sung.

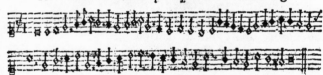

(k) A Cat€ is also a kind' of *Fuga* : wen, upon a cer- (k)
tain Rest, de Part's doo' follow on' an oder round in de
Unison. In wi€ concis' Harmoni, der' is mu€ varieti of
pleasing Conceipts : de Compoders wer'of assum' unto
demselvs a special licenc', of breaking, soomtims', *Priscians*
head : in unlawful taking of Discords, and in special
Conseeution of Unisons and Eigts, wen dey help to de Melodi of a Part.

¶ De knowledg of des' mysteri's is best obteined, by obser-
ving and imitating de (b) best Autors : and de practic'
der'of, as it serve€ to exercis'and sarpen de wit ; so wil it
mu€ avail you to skilful and reddy Composing.

Harmonia

Harmonia Gemina.

Ðerᶜ remaineꞇ yet a kindᶜ of *Fuga,* ꝭ de Italians call
Contrapunto doppio [Dubble Counterpoint :] (belikᶜ becaus it was at firſt praᶜtiſed onᶜly in eꝗal-timed Notᶜs)
& de Engliſh (becaus it is nou madᶜ in qickerFigurᶜs alſo)
dꝏᶜ call it Dubble Diſcant : but *Calviſius* morᶜ fitly termeꞇ
it *Harmonia Gemina :* [a general namᶜ, dat comprehendeꞇ
bodᶜ :] and becaus dey havᵉ gon ſo far in dis ſtrangᶜ Invention, as to invert a ꞇird Part alſo ; hæ addeꞇ *Tergemina.*

Ðis qeint Harmoni hæ dꝏᶜꞇ dus defin͛ : *Harmonia Ge-*
mina aut Tergemina eſt, qua, vocibus inverſis, ſecundâ aut
tertiâ vice cani poteſt : ubi ſemper alius atq; alius concentus ex-
auditur.

Ðat ꝭ Inverteꞇ onᶜly two Partᶜs, hæ deſcribeꞇ dus :
Gemina harmonia fit ex duabus vocibus, ſi Gravis exaltetur,
Acuta verò deprimatur : dat is, ꝭen 2 Partᶜs [ꝭ ar called
de Principal] ar ſo Compoſed, dat bæing bodᶜ mꝏved out
of deir Keys, de Superior dounward, and de Inferior upward, dey dꝏᶜ yet agræ togeder in an oder Harmoni : ꝭ
2 Partᶜs dus inverted ar called de Repliᶜ.

Of *Harmonia Gemino* and *Tergemina,* derᶜ ar many ways,
boꞇᶜ in likᶜ and Contrari motion.

Ðe firſt way of *Harmonia Gemina* is, ꝭen de Superior
falleꞇ a Fift, and de Inferior riſeꞇ an Eigt. As in dis example of *Zarlino* cited by *Calviſius.*

Vox ſuperior,
or de higer Part of de Principal.

Vox inferior,
or de lower Part of de Principal.

(m) *Resolutio Vocis superioris, quæ descendit ad Quintam :*
or de Repli^c, of de higer part, in *Hypodiapente*
or de Fift below.

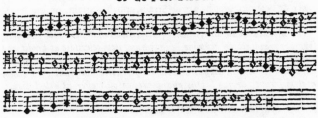

Resolutio Vocis inferioris quæ ascendit ad Octavam :
Or de Repli^c, of de lower Part^c, in Epidiapaſon or de Eigt aboov.

De ſecond way is, wen de Superior fallet a Tent, and de
Inferior riſet an Eigt.

De tird is, wen de Superior fallet an Eigt, and de Inferior riſet a Tent.

De Fowrt is in Contrari motion, wen de Superior de-
ſcendet to de Nin^t, and de inferior aſcendet to de Sevnt.

                                        But

But de fundry ways of *Gemina* and *Tergemina Harmonia*, bot' in lik' and Contrari motion, wit pregnant Examples and deir Refolutions, ar taugt by *Calvifius* in his 20 Cap. and by Mr *Morley* in de end' of his Second Part. Unto wof' fubtil Tractat's, I refer de Curious Reader, dat defiret to tri' and exercif' his wit in def' abftraf' and qeint Conceipts.

Annot. *to* §4, ¶3.

(a) F*Uga eſt certa alicujus modulationis Repetitio.* Calviſius C. 15.

(b) *In Melodi and Harm.* Not only in de Harmoni of Part's, wer' it ha a great Grac'; but alfo in de Melodi of ea' fingle Part' : der' being fcarc' any Tun' (fpecially in de Kromatik and Dorik Mod's) wort de hearing, wer' in a wol' Strain, or half a Strain, or foom Part', is not on' or often repeated.

(c) *Modulationum Repetitiones (disjunctæ tamen intervallo temporis, fonorum gravitate & acumine, numerorum item celeritate ac tarditate) non tantum, quando primum audiuntur, mirum in modum mentes humanas afficiunt, atq; in confiderationem fui fere totas abripiunt ; ſed etiam ætatem ferunt, & quo ſæpius audiuntur, eo plus afferunt delectationis. Mufici itaq;quo funt exercitatiores in condendis Harmoniis, eo magis ſunt in Fugis effingendis occupati.* Calv. Cap. 15.

(d) *Partes Fugæ duæ funt : Prior eſt vox quæ præcedit , altera quæ fequitur : five una ſit, five plures. Quæ præcedit vox, Ducis officio fungitur: Ducis igitur nomine etiam inſignitur: quæ fequuntur, Comites appellantur.* Ibid. De 2 Part's of Fuga wie *Morley* callet Principal and Repli', ar heet' called *Dux* and *Comes.*

(e) *Difficult. Difficilior modus eſt, fi Comes Ducem fuum contrariis paſſibus fequatur, & tantum deſcendit quantum Dux aſcendit, & contrà: quæ Fuga dicitur fieri per contrarium, five κατ' ἄρσιν, ἢ θήσιν. Accidit autem in aliquibus tantùm formis : ut in Semiditono aut Septima.* Calvif. C. 19.

(f) *Air-not's.* Dat is de final Not's of on' of de fowr Cadences proper to de Air. *Vide* (h) *in* ¶ 4.

(g) *Fuga eſt vel per totam Cantilenam, vel in Parte tantum. Quæ eſt per Cantilenam totam, Fuga ligata dicitur : ubi neceſſe eſt, omnia accidentia Cantus quoad Tempus ac Figuras obſervari.* Calv. C. 15.

(h) *Epidiateſſaron.* De Interval of de Repli' from de Principal, is foomtim' abov it, and foomtim' bened' : and is der'for' called fuperiour or Inferiour. But de tree old' Concords, [*Diateſſaron*, *Diapente*, and *Diapaſon*] ar commonly diftingui fed by de Prepofitions; 'επι & ὑπο : as Epidiateſſaron, Epidiapente, and Epidiapaſon, wen de Repli' is in de Diateſſaron, Diapente, or Diapaſon abov de Principal : and Hypodiateſſaron, Hypodiapente, and Hypodiapaſon, wen de Repli' is in de diftanc' bened'.

(i) **A Title.** *Fuga ligata inscribitur certo Titulo, (quem Canonem Musici vocant) quo, & Temporis Intervallum, in quo Comites Ducem sequuntur, & modus canendi indicatur.* (Calvis. C. 12.) as in de examples der following.

(k) **A Cate.** *Fugæ etiam species est, quando voces aliquot, post certum tempus, in Vnisono in orbem canunt, & a fine ad Principium redeunt.* Of dis kind hee has 3 examples : and wee infinit : wer of On has collected, and set fort a great Part.

(l) **Best Autors.** M Morley has givn us many artificial Examples of 2 Part s in on, upon a Plain-song diversly placed, [i. somtim abov de 2 Part s, somtim bened] at all distances of de Repli from de Principal [9, 10, 4, 5, 6, 7, and 8.] bot abov and bened it, and as wel in Contrari, as in Lik motion. M. Iohn Farmer [Autor of de sixteen Madrigals in 4, and de sevnteen in twis 4 Part s,] has mad 40 sue upon on Plain-song (wie is lik wis diversly placed in respect of de 2 Part s, wit oder witti conceipts inserted) in Imitation haply of dos two Famous Musicians [*Bird* and *Alphonso*] wo in a loving contention. (as * M Morley speakes) mad upon de Plain-song of *Miserere*, 40 several ways. But M Georg *Waterhous* has in dis kind far surpassed all : wo, (as M Morley der testifyes) upon de sam Plain-song, has mad abov a tousand : every on different from an oder.

* In de end of de Second Part.

(m) **Resolutio.** Dat wie *Calvisius* calles Resolution of *Vox superior,* and *Vox inferior,* [de two concordant Part s wie ar inverted] M Morley calles de higer and de lower Part of de Repli, to de higer & lower Part of de Principal.

---

§ 4 *Of Ornaments.* ¶ 4 *Of Formaliti.*

DE last and eiefest Ornament is Formaliti : wie is de mainteining of de (a) Air, or Ton of de Song, in his Part s.

(a)

Dis is *Ornamentum Ornamentorum* : de Ornament of Ornaments : wit wie de Part s ar sweet ly conformed on to an oder, and eae of dem to it self : and witout wie, not on ly de oder Ornaments los deir vertu and ceas to bæ Ornaments ; but also bot Melodi and Harmoni demselvs, los deir Grac, and wil bæ neider good Melodi nor good Harmoni : de wol Song bæing noting els, but a Form-les *Chaos* of confused sounds.

De proper Ton of eae Song, is (b) de Cloz-not of de Bas in his Final Key : wie sold ever bæ sue, as best suites wit (c) de Entranc, and Progres of de *Subjectum,* [* *Cantus* or Plain-song ;] and also agræes wit de Cloz-not

Wat de Air or Ton is.
(b)
(c)
* *Vide* ☞ in *Cap.* 3. § 2.

L

not῀ der῀of, in de fam῀ Interval, or at leaſt in ſoom oder Primari Concord. *Vide* (m) *in c.* 3, § 3.

Ton῀s 6.
† *V. c.* 2. § 2. (b)
(d)

Of Ton῀s der῀ ar ſix ſeveral Sort῀s, defined and diſtinguiſed by de ſix † Servil not῀s, [(d) *Ut, Re, Fa, Sol, La,* and *Pa* :] de Sevnt (wi᷄ is de Maſter-not῀) wil not bæ ſubjeᶜt to his Subjeᶜts, nor, in dat low plac῀, agræ wit dem.

Of def῀ Six Airs, de Third, Second, Fowrt, and Firſt [*Fa, Re, Sol,* and *Ut*] ar freqent : *Pa* is rar῀, and *La* mor῀ rar῀.

De Air or Ton῀ bæing dus deduced from de Subjeᶜt, or oderwiſ῀ (witout a Subjeᶜt) eoſen and conſtituted by de Auᵗor, is to bæ mainteined in all places [Entrauc῀, Progreſ, and Cloz῀,] of de Song. De firſt two ar manifeſt.

*A Cloz῀.
Clauſula.*
(e)
† *Vers, or oder
Period.*
(f)

De Cloz῀ is a Formal mæting of all Part῀s in Primari Concords, (commonly wit a Cadenc῀, and not witout ſoom preparation and proluſion unto it) for (e) de concluding eider of de wol῀ Song, or of ſoom † Principal Part der῀of. De wi᷄, as *Epilogus Orationis,* ſœlds bæ (f) ſwæteſt and moſt῀ Paᵗetical : and der῀for῀ reqiret moſt῀ Art.

(g)
* *V. infra.*

Of Clozes ſœm ar Simple, witout any Additament to de Cloz῀-not῀ : ſu᷄ ar fit for Counterpoint. And ſœm ar extended, or augmented wit (g) an Appendix : in wi᷄ de * træ Means of Mainteining de Air, ar or may bæ ſwæt῀ly entermedled : ſu᷄ ar fit for Diſcant : eſpecially in de Lydian Mœd῀. Of bod῀ wi᷄ ſort῀s, many Formal Examples, wit Cadences and witout, bot῀ for grav῀ and ligt Muſik, in 4, 5, and 6 Part῀s, (collected, as I ſuppoſ῀, out of de beſt Auᵗors) ar particularized by Mr *Morley* in de tird Part῀of his Introduction. De wi᷄ ar wœrdy to bæ diligently examined and imitated of all Students and Practicioners.

De Air mainteined by tree Means.

Proper Cadences.

(h)

De Means, wer῀by de Air in def῀ træ Places is mainteined, ar træ : [Cadences, Fuga῀s, and certain ſingle obſervable Not῀s.

Cadences, in reſpeᶜt of de Air, ar eider Proper, or Improper : and Proper, Primari or Secundari.

De Primari Cadenc῀ is formed (h) in de Ton῀ it ſelf [Uniſon or Eigt.]

De

Đe Secundari Cadences ar træ : formed in đe træ Confonant Intervalls of đe Tonᶜ. Đe firſt In đe medieti of đe
Diapaſon : wiᴇ is đe higeſt Notᶜ of đe Diapente : đe ſecond in đe medieti of Diapente, wiᴇ is đe Third : and đe
Third in đe middle betwænᶜ đe Fift and đe Third, wᴌᴇ is
đe Diateſſaron. So đat all đe proper Cadenᴄes [onᶜ Primari,
and træ Secundari,] ar conteined in đe Tonᶜs Diapente.
As if, đe Tonᶜ bæing S O L, đe Diapaſon bæ [♪ notation],
đe primari Cadencᶜ wilbæ [notation] , đe Fift-Ca-
dencᶜ [notation] , đe Fowrt-Cadencᶜ [notation] ,
and đe Third-Cadencᶜ [notation] .

Đe Primari Cadencᶜ onᶜly is uſed in Clozes , dowᴇ not
in đe Clozes onᶜly ; but in all oder paſſages alſo of đe Song :
and đat morᶜ freᴇently, đan any of đe Secundari Cadences,
wiᴇ ar taken in đoſᶜ places onᶜly : in wiᴇ it hat (i) dis
peculiar pouer aboov đe reſt, đat wen træᴇ Improper, eider
Cadences , or Points, or great Figᴜrᶜs, đe Harmoni ſæmet
to digreſ into any oder Ayr, it onᶜly can coover đe Informaliti, and reducᶜ đe Harmoni to its proper Air again.

Of Secundari Cadences đe Fift is ᴄief, as moſtᶜ pleaſing
and beſt mainteining đe Air : đe Third bæing đe medieti
betwænᶜ đe Tonᶜ and his Diapente, is counted next in
uſᶜ, and in affiniti to đe Tonᶜ. But becaus, in truᶜ Cadenᴄes, đe Binding half-notᶜ muſt ever bæ * ſarp ; derᶜforᶜ in đe
firſt and tird Tonᶜ [*Vt* and *Fa*] đe Third is excluded : and
in đe ſecond and fift Tonᶜ [*Re* and *La*] đe Fift is excluded :
becaus đeir Binding half-notᶜs ar (k) neider ſarp, nor apt
to bæ ſarped. But (l) đe Fowrt (woſᶜ Binding half-notᶜ,
in all Airs, eider is or may bæ ſarped) is never excluded :
never đe les it is ᴄiefly uſed in đoſᶜ Ayrs, werᶜ eider đe Third
or Fift is wanting : for werᶜ đey ar, đey ar preferred.

Improper Cadences ar likᶜwiſᶜ træ, [đe Sixt, đe Second,
and đe Sevnt ˙] đe wiᴇ, becaus đey ar ſtrangᶜ and informal to
đe Air, ar derᶜforᶜ (m) ſparingly to bæ uſed : and wen, upon
occaſion, any ſuᴇ ar admitted ; đey ar to bæ ᴄalified by đe
principal Cadencᶜ fitly ſuccæding. *Vide* (i) *ſuprà.*

*Đe Air Main-
teined by Ca-
dences.*

(i)

** V. (1) in Notis
ad ¶ 2.*

(k)
(l)

*Improper Ca-
dences.*

(m)

Fugaᶜs likᶜwiſᶜ and obſervable Notᶜs ar (in reſpeƈt of ðe Air) eider Proper or Improper : and Proper, Primari or Secundari. Ðe Primari (as Primari Cadences) ar formed in ðe Tonᶜ : ðe Secundari in ðe Tonᶜs ꞇræ Concords, [Fiſt, Fowrꞇ, and Third.] And ðe Improper in all oðer Intervals.

By Fugaᶜs.
(n)

Ðe Air is mainteined, in all places, by deſᶜ Proper Fugaᶜs, wen ðe Points begin (n) in ðe Tonᶜ it ſelf [Simple, or Componnd ;] or in any of his ꞇræ Concords : eſpecially doſᶜ ðat ar found in ðe Subjeƈt. It is alſo formally mainteined, wen any Point of ðe Subjeƈt is iterated.

By ſingle Notᶜs.

Ðe Obſervable Notᶜ werᶜby ðe Air is mainteined in ðe Entrancᶜ, is ðe firſt Notᶜ of ðe Baſᶜ or loweſt Part , formed unto ðe firſt Notᶜ of ðe Subjeƈt : after deſᶜ Direƈtions.

(o)

I. (o) In wat Intervall ſoever from ðe Tonᶜ ðe Subjeƈt dœᶜꞇ begin, ðe Baſᶜ may begin in ðe famᶜ key wiꞇ him : but ſo ðat hæ reparᶜ,as ſœnᶜ as may bæ, to ðe Tonᶜ.

(p)

II. (p) If ðe Subjeƈt begin in ðe famᶜ key [Simple or Componnd] wiꞇ ðe Tonᶜ ; (wiε is moſtᶜ Formal, and derᶜforᶜ moſtᶜ uſual) takᶜ nonᶜ but ðe Tonᶜ for ðe Baſᶜ.

(q)

III. (q) If in ðe Fiſt or Third to ðe Tonᶜ ; takᶜ likᶜwiſᶜ ðe Tonᶜ : or to ðe Fiſt, ðe Third.

¶ If ðe Subjeƈt begin in any oðer Intervall ; ðe Baſᶜ may takᶜ any fuε Concord, as is conſonant to ðe Tonᶜ.

(r)

I. (r) As if it begin in ðe Compound Second ; ðe Baſᶜ may takᶜ ðe Tonᶜs Fiſt : wiε wil bæ ðe Seconds Fiſt alſo : and if in a Simple Second ; ðe Baſᶜ muſt takᶜ ðe Hypodiateſſaron, or Fowrꞇ below ðe Tonᶜ : wiε is ðe famᶜ key wiꞇ ðe Fiſt abœv.

(ſ)

II. (ſ) If in ðe Sevnꞇ ; ðe Baſᶜ may takeᶜ ðe Tonᶜs Fiſt, wiε wil bæ ðe Subjeƈts Third : or ðe Tonᶜs Third, wiε wil bæ ðe Subjeƈts Fiſt.

(t)

III. (t) If ðe Subjeƈt begin in ðe Sixt ; takᶜ ðe Fowrꞇ to ðe Tonᶜ : wiε is his Third.

IV. If in ðe Fowrꞇ ; (becauſ neider ðe Tonᶜ nor any of ðe Tonᶜs Concords can bæ ſet unto it) ðe Baſᶜ muſt bæ content to takᶜ his Eigt or Uniſon : (as it may dœᶜ, in wat Intervall ſoever ðe Subjeƈt dœᶜꞇ begin : *Uide* (o) *ſuprà*)

his

his oðer Concords ar not Formal ; as having noᶜ kindᶜ
of Concordancᶜ wiᵵ de Tonᶜ.

Ðe Obſervable Notᶜs mainteining ðe Air in ðe Progreſ
and Clozᶜ, ar likᵉwiſᶜ, firſt ðe Tonᶜ it ſelf, [Simple or Compound:] ðeɴ ðe ᵵræ ſpecial Concords: (wᵉrᶜof ðe Fiſt is
ðe ᶜieſ) namᵉly wen in ðe Baſᶜ, or oðer Partᶜ of ðe Song,
ðey ar inſiſted upon in ſœm Greater Figurᶜ, (or his divided
partᶜs) conteining twiſᶜ, or ᵵriſᶜ, or oftner, ðe timᶜ of ðᵉ
Meſurᶜ-notᶜ.

Unto ſuᴇ a Great Figurᶜ, many qik Notᶜs (wiᴇ ar com-
monly (u) qickeſt towards ðe endᶜ) dœᶜ uſually anſwer : to-   (u)
geðer wiᵵ iterated Points of likᶜ timᶜ. And ſœmtimᶜ after ðe
Simple Clozᶜ, (eſpecially in Motets) ðe Tonᶜ is (x) inſiſt-   (x)
ed upon in oɴᶜ Partᶜ, wilᶜ ðe oðer dœᶜ Diſcant upon it: until
at ðe laſt, ðey mæᵵ all togeðer again in ðe ſamᶜ Clozᶜ final.

Ðeſᶜ Greater Figurᶜs, hærᶜ and ðerᶜ interpoſed, ar uſual and gracᶜful.

In Talliſes † *Abſterge,* ðe Baſᶜ haᵵ ſix Brief-figurᶜs, and a   † Ðe ſecond
Pointed Sembrief in Uniſon : fowr Brief-figurᶜs in Dia-   Motet of *Can-*
pente : onᶜ in Diateſſaron : and oɴᶜ in Semiditonus.   *tiones ſacræ.*

Ðe Tenor haᵵ oɴᶜ Brief-figurᶜ in Diapaſon : and fivᶜ in
Diapente ; wᵉrᶜof ᵵræ ar Pointed, and onᶜ haᵵ a Minim annexed : alſo onᶜ Long wiᵵ a Sembrief.

Ðe Firſt Counter haᵵ ᵵræ Briefs, onᶜ pointed Brief, onᶜ
Brief wiᵵ a Minim, and onᶜ Long in Diapaſon: two pointed
Briefs wiᵵ a pointed Sembrief, and onᶜ Brief, in Diapente :
alſo onᶜ Brief in Semiditonus.

Ðe ſecond Counter haᵵ ᵵræ Briefs, a Minim wiᵵ a Brief,
a Brief wiᵵ a Sembrief, and a Sembrief wiᵵ a Minim, in Diapente : alſo onᶜ Brief in Semiditonus, and onᶜ in Ditonus.

Ðe Mean haᵵ 4 Briefs, and two Pointed Longs, in Diapaſon: two Briefs in Diapente ; and onᶜ in Semiditonus.

Ðeſᶜ Greater Figurᶜs ar Proper to ðe Air. But as Improper Cadences, ſo Improper Figurᶜs [Seconds, Sixts,
and Sevenᵵs] may ſœmtimᶜ, for varieti, bæ inſerted among
ðe Proper : by wiᴇ (as wel as by Proper Cadences) ðey ar
ſuddenly to bæ qalified ; leſt by ðat means ðe Air ſœldᶜ
ſæmᶜ to bæ ᶜanged.

Annot. to § 4, ¶ 4.

(a) Air, or Ton*. In dis word is a larg* *Metalepfis*. Air, of *Aer*, for *Percuffio aeris*, *Metonimia eft Subjecti* : *Percuffio pro Sono*, *Meton. Caufae* : *Sonus pro Tono*, Synecdoche generis : *& Tonus pro finali Tono Baffi*, eadem Synecdoche.

(b) *The Cloz-not* *&c.* According to de general Rul* of Muficians, *In fine videbitur cujus Toni*, Calvif. C 17.

(c) De Entranc* and progr. &c. *In hoc chorali cantu, diligentiffimè confideret huic Arti deditus, quae fint ubiq; Modulationis Progreffus, quod Exordium, & quis Finis : ut cognofcat ad quem Modum referatur. Inde enim tam Primariam illius Modi claufulam, quàm Secundariam, eruere, & convenientibus locis annotare, & inferere poterit.* Calvif. C 17.

† *V*. (e) *in* C. 1.   Not* heer* dat by *Modus* [de proper name* of † a Mood*] Calvif. meanez de de Air or Ton*. In wie fens *Boetius* alfo haz taken it. (*Vide infrà in fine* (d).) But *Boet.* (to avoid de Ambiguiti) do*z der* explan* himfelf by z oder known Term*s [*Tropus* and *Tonus*.] Mor*over by *Claufula* [de proper nam* of a Cloz*] hee heer* meanez a Cadenc* : and yet der* is fo mue differenc* between* dem, dat a Cadenc* may bee witout a Cloz*, and a Cloz* witout a Cadenc*. But it is meet* (for facil and fpeedy inftruction) dat different dings fœld* hav* different nam*s. Bot* des* words in des* acceptions, fee again in (e).

(d) *Vt, Re, Fa, Sol*, &c. De diftinction of de Airs by de Keys, (wie *Calvif.* feemez to allou) is uncertain ; becaus in de fam* Key ar many different Ton*s : as in *D*, may bee *La*, or *Sol*, or *Re* : in *C*, may bee *Sol*, or *Fa*, or *Vt* : &c. So dat, if wee fay de Ton* is in *D la fol re*, *C fol fa ut*, or *G fol re ut*, &c ; wee ar yet to feek* wie of de zree Not*s, in any of des* Keys, to tak* for de Ton*. But de diftinction of de Airs by de Not*s, is certain and conftant, in wat Keys fo ever dey ftand. It is tru*, dat every of de fix Ton*s, haz zree feveral Keys, (according to de num-
* *V*. (i) *in* C. 2.   ber of de * *Mi*-cliefs) in wie it may indifferently bee fet : but wer* fo-
§ 2.   ever it bee fet, all cœmez to on*. For example : If *Re* bee de Ton* or Air*-not* ; weider it ftand in *Are*, (de *Mi*-clief beeing **B**) or in *D fol re*, (de *Mi*-clief beeing *E*) or in *Gamut*, (de *Mi*-clief beeing *A*) der* is no* differenc* at all, eider in de Song, or in any Part* of de Song, or in any Not* of a Part*. Lik*wife, if *Sol* bee de Ton* ; it makez no matter, weider it ftand in *D fol re*, or *Gamut*, or *Cfaut*, *&c*. If you object, dat albeit de order of de Not*s, boz in nam* and Sound, bee ftil de fam* ; yet on* of des* Keys is higer dan an oder ; dat is nor material : tor weider de Key bee hig or low ; it reftez in de Difcretion of de Cantor, to fet de Tun*s, according to de *Ambitus* or Compas of his Voices.
† *l*. 4. *V. infrà*   Dis in effect dœez † *Boetius* teae, wer* hee diftinguifez de Ton*s, not by de Keys, but by de feveral Diapafons : wie ar grounded upon de
* *V*. C. 3 § 3.   feveral Ton*s : every on* wer* of, confifting of his * z Part*s [Diateffa-
and (e) *in* Notis.   ron and Diapente,] conteinez in de Diapente, or lower Part, not on*ly de Ton* it felf; but alfo his zree Proper Concords, [Fift, Fowrz, and
† *l*. 4. C. 14.   Third.] † *Ex Diapafon igitur Confonantiae fpeciebus, exiftunt qui appellantur Modi : quos eofdem Tropos vel Tonos nominant.*

                                             (e) For

(e) For ꝺe concluding eiꝺer, &c. *Primaria Clausula, cum ubiꝗ* *Sethus C. 18.]
quidem [*Principio, medio & fine*] *cujuꞅ bet Harmoniæ locum habeat ;*
(*ne per alias clausulas, in alium atꝗ; alium Modum deducatur, sed ut*
nbiꝗ verus Modus conspicuus sit) tanto tamen cum apparatu, & ajection, ac
conatu nullibi fieri solet ; ac in fine vel totius Cantilenæ, vel Periodorum.

(f) Sweeteꞅt. *Cum ubiꝗ; Tropus Harmoniæ ostendendus sit ; maximè*
tamen in fine : unde omnis ejus bonitas, elegantia, & perfectio judicatur.
Sethus C. 17.

(g) *Appendix.* Vide mox (x) in Notis.

(h) In ꝺe Tonꞇ it self. † *Primariam Clausulam* [i. Cadentiam] † *Vi. suprà* (c)
formant in ipsa Clave finali, quæ eꞅt infima in Diapente. Calv. c. 14.

(i) ꝺis peculiar pouer. *Primariæ Clausulæ usus eꞅt in Principio &*
fine Cantilenarum : tum etiam quando, per assumptas alias Clausulas,
Cantilena ad alium Tropum inclinare & traduci videtur. Per hanc enim
propriam Clausulam revocatur, & in ordinem redigitur. Calv. C. 14.

(k) *Neiꝺer ſarp nor*——*Neverꝺeles ꝺe* La cadencꞇ is ſomtimꞇ
admitted : as in ꝺeꞅ examples.

In ꝺe firꞅt ꝟerꞇof a Sevnꞇ is bound
with a Sixt.
In ꝺe second a Ninꞇꞇ is bound wiꞇ
an Eigt.
In ꝺe ꞇird, a fowꝛꞇ wiꞇ a ꞇird.

Soom, to makꞇ ꝺislikꞇ oꝺer Cadences, takꞇ upon ꝺem to ſarp *Sol* : but
ꝺis is unnatural, and unapt to bæ ſung ; houſoever, by ꝺe help of ꝺe
inordinat half-tonꞇs, it may bæ played.

(l) ꝺe Fowꝛꞇ——ꝺe Fowꝛꞇs, in all Airs, ar abſolutꞇ of ꝺemſelvs :
ſavꞇ onꞇly ꝺe Fowꝛꞇ of Pa, Wieꞇ is a Tritonus : but by flatting ꝺe Ma-
ꞅter-notꞇ, it becoomꞇꞇ a perfeꞇt Diateſſaron.

(m) Sparingly, wiꞇ judgment. *Si præterea,* i. *Præter Proprias,*
[*Primarias & Secundarias*] *alias,* i. *Improprias, aꞅꞅumunt Muſici ; extra*
ordinem hoc faciunt, atꝗ; cum judicio & delectu. Sethus C. 14.

(n) In ꝺe Tonꞇ it ſelf. *Quando exordium Subjecti in finali illius Tro-*
pi clave fuerit ; ſi Fugam ſolutam inſtituere cogitat, infimæ vocis notulam,
cum Subjecto, in Vniſono vel in Octava conſtituat : aut etiam ad Dia-
pente, vel Diateſſaron ; vel Tertiam [*Toni Conſonantias*] *Voces quas ad-*
jungit, vel elevare vel deprimere poterit. Claviſ. C. 17.

(o) *Vide* ☞ *in* (p).

(p) *Cognito Tropo & Clave finali, accedat Melopoeus ad exordium*
Subjecti : id ſi in Propria illius Tropi clave fuerit ; infimæ Vocis notulam
cum Subjecto in Vniſono vel in Octava conſtituat : ne, ſi aliam Clavem
ſub Subjecto ſumpſerit, alium Tropum miſcere videatur : reliquas ſupe-
riores (ſi tantùm conſonent) ubicunꝗ; velit, collocet.

☞ *Quando autem Subjectum in aliena Clave exordium ſumpſerit, ſæpe*
quidem in ea, qua Subjectum inchoat, Clave, reliquæ Voces incipiuntur :
ita tamen ut quàm primùm in Clauſulam ejus Toni Propriam concedat.

⚘ *Quando tamen ad Propriam Clavem Prima Subjecti notula conſonat ;*

in

† *Nempe propriâ Clave.*

in † *illa inferior aliqua Vox addita fundamentum* Subiecto Substruat : *ut ita, statim in principio, Harmoniæ Tropum non obscurè ostendat.*

(q) *Vide* ⚹ *in* (p).

(r) *If it begin in ꝺe Comp. Second.* In *Magnificat*, set by Mr *J. Farmer*, ꝺe Cloz-notᵉ of ꝺe *Cantus* or €yre-tunᶜ, is *Re* in *G sol re ut* ; and ꝺe Tonᶜ answering ꝺerᶜto, is *Re* in *Gamut* : unto wie ꝺe first Notᶜ of ꝺe *Cantus* [*Mi* in *Alamire*] is a Compound Second : And ꝺerᶜ-forᶜ ꝺe first Notᶜ of ꝺe Basᶜ is *La* in *D solre* : wie bœing a Fift unto ꝺe Tonᶜ is alſo a Fift unto ꝺe Compound Second, or first Notᶜ of ꝺe *Cantus.*

*Vi § 2.

(ſ) *If in ꝺe Sevnꞇ.* In ꝺat ancient *Scottiſ tunᶜ, ꝺe laſt Notᶜ of ꝺe *Cantus* is *Sol* in *G sol re ut* ; and ꝺe Tonᶜ answering to it, *Sol* in *Gamut* : unto wie ꝺe first Notᶜ of ꝺe *Cantus* [*Fa* in *F fa ut*] is a Sevnꞇ. And ꝺerᶜſerᶜ ꝺe first Notᶜ of ꝺe Basᶜ is *Re* in *D solre* : wie is a Fift to ꝺe Tonᶜ, and a Third to ꝺe Sevnꞇ.

Ðis Tunᶜ haꞇ bœen set in 4 Partᶜs, onᶜ way by Mr *Tho. Ravenſcroft*, Baꞓeler of Muſik, in ꝺe namᶜ of Oxford-tunᶜ : and an oꝺer way by *J. Douland* B. of Muſik : and an oꝺer way many yœrᶜs ago, [abøv 60. in my memori] all kœping ꝺe samᶜ *Cantus* and ꝺe samᶜ Tonᶜ. During wie timᶜ, and I know not how long beforᶜ, it haꞇ bœen freꝗented in our €yrees, wiꞇ approbation. And ꝺerᶜforᶜit may sœmᶜ ſtrangᶜ, ꝺat any man (eſpecially a profeſt Muſician) ſøldᶜ adventurᶜ, wiꞇout any Ground, to ꞓargᶜ ꝺe truᶜ Muſik of it wiꞇ Informaliti, and ꝺe skilful Artiſts, ꞉orrow woſᶜ handsit haꞇ paſſed, wiꞇ negleꞓt or ignoranᶜ.

(t) *If in ꝺe Sixt.* In *Da pacem* set by M. *Ravenſcroft*, ꝺe laſt Notᶜ of ꝺe *Cantus* or €yre-tunᶜ, is *Vt* in *G sol re ut* ; and ꝺe Tonᶜ answering to it, is *Vt* in *Gamut* : unto wie ꝺe first Notᶜof ꝺe *Cantus* [*La* in *Elami*] is a Sixt : and ꝺereforᶜ ꝺe first Notᶜ of ꝺe Basᶜ is *Fa* in *C fa ut* : wie bœing a Fowrꞇ to ꝺe Tonᶜ, is a Third unto ꝺe Sixt.

† C. 17.

(u) *Ꝗickeſt toward ꝺe endᶜ.* Ðis practicᶜ is obſerved by † *Calviſius*, werᶜ hœ sayꞇ, *Circa finem motus Harmoniæ sit aliquo modo concitatior, quàm in principio ; ut ita quàm maximè Naturalem imitetur motum, qui similiter in principio tardior, in fine velocior eſt.*

(x) *Is inſiſted upon.* Ðis Gracᶜ of extending ꝺe Clozᶜ, is likᶜwiſᶜ remembred by *Calviſ.* in ꝺe samᶜ placᶜ. *Poſt Clauſulam illam propriam & finalem, brevis Appendix annecti solet : sed hac ratione, ut vox quæ eſt in Clave Primaria (sive fiat in mediis, sive in acutus sonis) ꝺ́ꞃ́ιveꞇoꝺ, i. immobilis relinquatur : & Baſſus tandem, vel in eandem elevetur, vel in ejus Diapaſon, aut Diſdiapaſon deprimatur.*

CAP. IV.

CAP IV. Of ꝺe two ways of Setting.

§ I. *Of Setting in Counterpoint.*

SEtting is eiꝺer in (a) Counterpoint or Diſcant. Counterpoint is ꝡen ꝺe Not's of all ꝺe Part's, bæing of eqal tim' and number, go' jointly toge-ꝺer. If ſoomtim', by reaſon of Binding and Diſ-joyning, ꝺe Not's dœ' happen to bæ od ; ꝺey ar preſently maꝺ' ævn again : and if, for ꝺe Muſiks ſak', a Not' bæ ſoom-tim' divided ; ꝺe Part's bæing in divers places, ar tyed by ligatur' unto on' ſyllable, as if ꝺey wer' one Not'.

Counterpoint is uſed in Rhyꞇmical vers, as Pſalms in Mæter, and oꝺer Tun's, meſured by a ſet number of ſylla-bles : unto ꝡic ꝺe lik' number of Not's dœ't anſwer.

Setting in Counterpoint is after ꝺis manner. Having reddy ꝺe *Melodious Part, of your own or of an oꝺers in-vention, firſt draw ſo many (b) lin's, [or rews of Rul's] as you mean to mak' Part's : (fowr in ꝺis kind is beſt) ꝺen, if ꝺis certain Part' ſall bæ a Mean, prick it doun in ꝺe fowrꞇ lin' : if a Tenor, in ꝺe ſecond : and diviꝺ' every Strain wiꞇ a dubble Croſ-bar drawn ſtraigꞇ ꞇorrow all ꝺe fowr lin's ; and ſubdiviꝺ' dem in ꝺe midle wiꞇ a ſingle bar : then accor-ding to ꝺe rul's of Art, ſtuddi to ſet a formal Baſ' unto ꝺe Mean or Tenor : and after ꝺat, mak' ꝺe oꝺer two Parts as formal lik'wiſ' and melodious as you may : and conſider ſtil how ꝺey all agræ, not on'ly to ꝺe Baſ', but alſo among demſelvs. Ꝺe Bars wil direct you to a preſent ſynopſis of all ꝺe Not's anſwering one an oꝺer ; ꝺat you may ꝺe ſooner and ſurer eſpi ꝺe faults, if any bæ, as in ꝺis example.

Tr.

M.

Te.

B.

M   ANNOT.

Annot. to Cap. 4, § 1.

(a) **C**ounterpoint. In Latin *Contrapunctum :* ſo called, be-caus, in ðe beginning, (wen ðer' was no varieti of Tim's and Figur's of Not's) ðey marked out ðeir Songs by Pricks or Points ; wie, in framing ðe Part's, ðey ſet on' againſt an oðer : ſo ðat *Contrapunctum*, or Counterpoint, is ðe proper Term for Setting of Plain-ſong ; as Diſcant (wie ſignifyet Diviſion in ſinging) is of Fi-gured Muſik.

† *Sethus Calvi-ſius. Cap. 1.*

† *Cum ob pares quantitates, diverſitas Figurarum neceſſaria non eſſet, per Puncta tantùm libuit Cantum componere : & cum Punctum ita Puncto opponeretur ; Contrapunctum hæc ars vocata eſt.* De moſt ancient Latin Songs wer' plain, of eqal-tim'd Not's in Counterpoint : ðe curious ſundry-tim'd Diſcant, is ðe invention of later days : ðat ſort is called by Muſicians, *Muſica plana, vetus, Gregoriana :* ðis, *Fi-gurata, nova, Ambroſiana.* But nou, as ðe eqal-tim'd Not's of ðe Plain-ſong ar ſoomtim' uſed in Figured Muſik ; (*Vide* ☞ in § 2) ſo ar ðe ſundry-tim'd Not's of Figured Muſik ſoomtim' inſerted into Plain-ſong. But a little communiti doo't not confound ðe *Species*, wie hav' ðeir Denomination from ðe greater Part'.

* *Inſtruments, wie reaȝa greater compas, reqir' more. V.(b) in c.2. § 1.* † *Oðerwiſ' a Stanȝe or Staf.*

(b) A Muſik-lin' is * ʒ parallel Rul's, wiȝ ðeir Spaces : deviſed for ðe diſtinguiſing of Ton's, drawn out to ðe lengȝ of a Ditti-lin', wer'of it is ſo called. For as *Song* is a nam' common boȝ' to ðe Muſik and Ditti ; ſo ar ðe Part's of Song : ſo muȝ Muſik as anſweret to a †Vers, a Strain, a Lin' of ðe Ditti, is lik'wiſ' called a Vers, a Strain, a Lin'.

Cap. IV. § II.

Of Setting in Diſcant.

Diſcant.

DIſcant is, wen unto Integral Not's of longer tim' in on' Part', ar ſung eqivalent Particles, or Not's of ſorter tim', in an oðer : (as to on' Sembrief, 2 Minims, 4 Croeets, or 8 Qavers) ðe Parts following on' an oðer in Melodious Points, Reported, or Reverted, or bod' ; (wiȝ oðer Harmoni interpoſed) until at ðe laſt ðey meet' all togeðer in ðe Cloz'.

☞

Hær' not' ðat ſlow-tim'd Muſik, nou and ðen interpo-ſed, doo'ȝ grac' ðe qik : and ðat ðe moſt artificial runing Diſcant, if it bæ continued too long ; wil at ðe laſt wax te-dious, even to ðe vulgar : as *Tulli* did wel obſerv : *Quantò*

Orat. l. 3,

molliores ſunt & delicatiores in Cantu flexiones, & falſæ voculæ, quàm certæ & ſeveræ ? quibus tamen, ſi ſæpius ſunt, non modò auſteri, ſed multitudo ipſa reclamat.

Soomtim'

Soomtim' on' Part singet Plain-song, and de rest doo discant upon it : as in D. *Bulls* Ground : de wie upon but 4 Plain Sembriefs [de first in *C-fa-ut*, de 2 in *F-fa-ut*, de 3 in *G-sol-re-ut*, and de 4 in *C-fa-ut*,] hat 21 several Discants, all conjoined in on' sweet' Lesson : and in de excellent Musik of de *In-nomine's* of *Parsons*, *Taverner*, D. *Ty*, &c.

But commonly all Part's doo' sing Plain-song : soomtim' on', soomtim' an oder, soomtim' mor', soomtim' les : and all doo' lik'wis' discant upon de plain Not's, in deir turn's, as sall seem' good to de Composer.

In Discant soomtim' de Parts begin togeder as in Counterpoint: Example de 8th Motet of Mr *Tallis* : but most' commonly on' after an oder : and den de first beginnet wit a Point, wie it self and oders doo' maintain (as afterward dey doo' oder Points) enter-cang'ably : Example de 2 Motet of Mr *Tallis*.

In setting of Discant, (weider it bee upon a Plain-song or oderwis')first, at every 2 or 3 Sembriefs, draw de Bars torrow all de Lin's, or Parts of your Song : dat you may de mor' easily see, in tru' Musik, to contriv' your Points togeder, and afterward espi' and correct your errours, if any bee in de Points, or Concords : den consider wat Point to begin wit, and hou it may bee best mainteined : and so proceed' from Point to Point, til you conclud' all wit a ful Harmonious Cloz'.

Example de for'-cited Motet.

EPILOGVS.

ÐE foundation of deſᶜ Rudiments bæing layd, you may begin to build your Practicᶜ derᶜon. But hæ ðat affeᵏtet perfeᶜtion in dis rarᶜ faculti, and ðe honour of a good COMPOSER, let him firſt ſæ ðat hæ bæ furniſhed wit Naturᶜs gifts : [aptnes, and abiliti of wit and memori :] ðen let him torrowly peruſᶜ & ſtuddi ðe learned and exqiſitᶜ Preceps of ðat primᶜ Doᵏtor Mʳ *Thomas Morley*, (concerning ðe Setting of 2, 3, 4, 5, and 6 Partᶜs) in ðe ſecond and tird Partᶜs of his Introduᵏtion : and laſtly, let him hædᶜfully examin, obſerv, and imitatᶜ ðe Artificial woorks of ðe beſt Autors : ſuᴄ as ar *Clemens Non-Papa, Horatio Vecchi, Orlando di Laſſo, Olphonſo Faraboſco, Luca Marenzo, I.Croche, D.Farfax, D. Tyᶜ, Mʳ Taverner, Mʳ Parſons, D. Bull, Mʳ Douland, Mʳ Tallis, Mʳ BIRD, Mʳ Whitᶜ, Mʳ Morley,* and now excelling Mʳ *Tho.* and *I. Tomkins* [ðat *Aureum par Muſicorum*] wit many oðer of admirable, divinᶜ, unſeareable skil in dis myſteri. For as in * Oratori, ſo in Muſik, ar neceſſarily reqired to perfeᵏtion ; 1 Naturᶜ, 2 Art, and 3 Exercitation according to Art and Examples.

And yet wen all is doon, ſo full of difficultiᶜs and hidden myſteriᶜs is dis faculti of Setting ; ðat all ðeſᶜ helps concurring, wil not ſufficᶜ to ðe framing of a good Leſſon ; (eſpecially in ðe Lydian Moodᶜ) unles ðe Autor, at ðe timᶜ of Compoſing, bæ tranſported as it werᶜ wit ſoom Muſical furi ; ſo ðat himſelf ſcarcᶜ knowet wat hæ dooᶜt, nor can preſently giv a reaſon of his dooing : even ſo as it is wit doſᶜ ðat play voluntari : of womᶜ derᶜforᶜ ðe *French-man* ſayt, *Lear eſprite eſt en le boute des doits* : Ðeir ſowl is in ðeir fingers ends.

* Vid. Orat. Epilog.

ÐE
SECOND BOOKᶜ,
OF ÐE
USES OF Musik.

C. 1. § 1. Of Inſtruments.

TO Ðe eſſencᶜ of an Art † 2 tings ar requiſitᶜ [a *Syſtema* or conſtitution of Rulᶜs and Precepts; and ſoom profitable Uſes or Ends, werᶜ unto ðey ar referred.]

Ð Principles and Precepts of ðis Art, in Singing and Setting, bæing declared; coom wee nou to ðe profitable Uſes derᶜof : wiє, dowg ðey bæ many, may bæ all reduced unto * two : [onᶜ Eccleſiaſtical, for ðe Servicᶜ of God; ðe oðer Civil, for ðe Solacᶜ of Men.]

Deſᶜ 2 Uſes ar diverſly performed : [by Voicᶜ, or by Inſtrument, or by bodᶜ :] werᶜof, Muſik is divided into Vocal, Inſtrumental, and Mixt.

Inſtruments ar of 2 ſorts : [(a) *Entata*, and (b) *Empneuſta*: String- and Windᶜ-Inſtruments.

Of bodᶜ deſᶜ ſorts, ðe pregnant wits of induſtrious Artiſts havᶜ deviſed (c) many different kindᶜs : as (of *Entata*) *Harp*, *Lutᶜ*, *Bandora*, *Orparion*, *Cittern*, *Gittern*, *Cymbal*, *Pſalteri*, *Dulcimer*, *Viol*, *Virginal*, &c. and (of *Empneuſta*) *Pipᶜ*, (d) *Organ*, *Shalm*, *Sagbut*, *Cornet*, *Recorder*, *Flut*, *Waits* or † *Hobois*, *Trumpet*, &c. And deſᶜ latter curious timᶜs havᶜ conjoined two or moᶜ in onᶜ : making ðe *Organ* and ðe *Virginal* to goᶜ bodᶜ togeðer wit ðe ſamᶜ keys : yea and wit ðe

M 3

† Ars eſt comprehenſio preceptionum coexercitatarum.; ad aliquem in vita Finem utilem. Lucian in Paraſito.

* *Two general Vſes of Muſik.*

Inſtruments.
(a) (b)

(c)
(d)
† So alſo dœᶜ ðe French ſound it, dowg ðey writᶜ it Haultbois [big or loud ſounding woden laſtruments.]

ðe ſamᶜ keys to ſound divers Pipᶜs of ðe *Organ* [gravᶜ and acutᶜ] by reaſon of ðe Nuᶜ-invented divers Stops.

Conſort.   Ðe ſeveral kindᶜs of Inſtruments ar commonly uſed ſeverally by dem ſelvs : as a Set of Viols, a Set of Waits, or ðe likᶜ : but ſoomtimᶜ, upon ſoom ſpecial occaſion, many of bodᶜ Sortᶜs ar moſtᶜ ſweetly joined in Conſort.

ANNOT. to § I.

(a) ENtata of 'εντείνο, *intendo : quia, intentis nervis ſeu fidibus ſonant* : ðey ar alſo called *Pſelapeta* of ✦ψᾱλλω and ἁψάω : *utrunꝗ; idem ſignificat,* [*tango, leniter percutio :*] *niſi quòd* ✦ψᾱλλω *magis proprie de chordarum tactu & pulſatione dicitur.* In Hebruᶜ ðey ar called *Neginoth.*

(b) *Empneuſta* of 'εμπνέω, *inſpiro inflo : quia, ſpiritu tibiis immiſſo, ſonant.* In Hebruᶜ *Nehiloth.*

* Dipnoſoph.
14. *Sub perſona*
Ariſtoxeni.
† *Synecd. ſpeciei.*
* *Gen. 4. 21.*
† *1 Cor. 14. 7.*
* *In vita Periclis.*
† *Qui præmium certaminis ſtatuit.*
* *Met. 12.*
Sympona and
Aſympona.

(a) (b) Ðeſᶜ two general ſorts of Inſtruments dooᶜt * *Athenæus* obſerv : ðe wie *Tremelius* ſewet to bæ underſtœd by 2 of ðeir ſpecial kindᶜs, [† *Organ* and *Harp*] in ðat placᶜ, werᶜ * *Iubal* is ſaid to bæ ðe Autor and Inventer of ðem bodᶜ.

In an oðer placᶜ † ðe *Pipᶜ* and *Harp* ar named as ðe 2-cief ſpecies : wie ar ſo uſed in Profanᶜ Autors : as in *Plutarch* : * *Tunc primùm ingenti ſtudio Pericles tulit, ut certamen Muſicorum Panathenæo celebraretur : digeſſitꝗ; id ipſe, creatus* † *Athlothetes, quemadmodum certantes, Tibiâ, vel Voce, vel Ciharâ, canerent :* and in *Ovid:*

     * *Non illos Citharæ, non illos carmina vocum,*
       Longaꝗ; multiſori delectat tibia buxi.

In wie examples, ðe Vocal Muſik is joined wiþ ðe Inſtrumental of bodᶜ ſorts. Of boþ ſorts ſoom ar *Symphona*, ðat havᶜ a *Symphoni* or *Harmoni* of Partᶜs in ðem ſelvs, (as *Organ, Harp, Lutᶜ* :) ſoom ar *Aſymphona,* ðat play but onᶜ Part : as ðe *Cornet.*

(c) Ðe many different kindᶜs of all Inſtruments, boþ ᶜ *Entata* and *Empneuſta,* ar copiouſly declared, and curiouſly deſcribed by *Merſennus* in his exact Treatis *De Harmonicis inſtrumentis. Vide C. 2. § 4. Pag. 33.*

Synecdoche generis.

(d) *Organ.* Of ðe Grœkᶜ Ο᾿ργανον, *Proprie Inſtrumentum :* and Synecdochicè *Inſtrumentum Muſicum :* (as *Plut.* Sympoſ. 9. Ο᾿ργάνων καίρωσι τοῖς εμπερπῆς ηκῶσι : and *1 Chron. 23. 5.* 4000 praiſed ðe Lord wiþ ðe Inſtruments wie *David* madᶜ : wie, becaus ðey werᶜ uſed in ðe ſervicᶜ of God, ar † elſwerᶜ called ðe Inſtruments of God) and, by a Metalepſis of ðe ſamᶜ Synecdoche, ðis *Polyaulon organon,* ðis grand windᶜ-Inſtrument is ſignifyed : (as *Iob 21. 12.* and *Pſal. 150. 4.*) bæing ſo colled κατε᾿ξοχῶν [*per excellentiam*] becaus it is ðe moſt excellent Muſical Inſtrument of all.

† *1. Kr. 16. 42.*

                                   Cap.

C. I. § 2. *Of ðe Voicᵉ.*

Ut ðe Voicᵉ, wiᵉ is ðe woork of Naturᵉ, dooᵗ far ex-
Bceedᵉ all deſᵉ woorks of Art.

De Voicᵉ.

Good Voices alonᵉ, ſounding onᶜly ðe Notᵉs, ar ſufficient, by ðeir Melodi and Harmoni, to deligᵗ ðe ear : but bœœ-
ing furniſhed wiᵗ ſoom laudable *Ditti,* ðey becoom yet morᵉ
excellent. *Cantus, etſi per ſe hominum animos oblectet ; atta-*
men cum illi oratio ſubjicitur, quæ ſit Numeroſa, & pedibus qui-
buſdam alligetur, (ut Verſus eſſe cernimus) ſuavior multò red-
ditur. P. M. Loc. com. Claſſis 3, Paragr. 25. And *Calviſ.* C.
18. *Etſi Harmonia nuda (ut videre eſt in Inſtrumentis Muſicis,*
ſcienter & peritè ab Artificibus tractatis)propter Numerorum ac
Proportionum rationem, quibus ſeſe humanis mentibus inſinuat,
plurimam in Affectibus excitandis exercet potentiam; tamen ſi ac-
ceſſerit humana vox, quæ ſententiam inſignem numeris Harmoni-
cis expreſſam, ſimul accinat ; propter duplicem, quam & Harmonia
& Sententia aliqua præclara gignit, dele&rationem, Muſica multò
eſt mirabilior, auguſtior, auribuſq; pariter atq; animo acceptabilior:
Ðis numerous *Ditti,* or Rhymᵉ applyed to ðe Notᵉ, ðe Piloſoper eqalizeᵗ to ðe *Melodi* it ſelf, for Reſembling and
Mooving manners and affections. *Sunt autem in Ryhthmis*
& Melodiis ſimilitudines, maximè penes veras naturas iræ, &
manſuetudinis, ac fortitudinis, & temperantiæ, & contrariorum
his, & aliorum omnium quæ ad mores pertinent. Patet id ex ef-
fectu : Mutamus enim animum talia audientes. And afterward hæ makeᵗ it a Partᵉ of Muſik : ſhewing ðat Muſik is
madᵉ as wel by *Poeſi* as by *Melodi.* † *Quoniam videmus Mu-*
ſicam eſſe per Melodiam, & Rhythmos ; horum utrunq; latére non
debet q:am vim habeat ad Doctrinam : utrùm præferenda ſit ea
Pars quæ in Melodiis conſiſtit, an ea quæ in Rhythmis. And
ðer ʻforᵉ it is, ðat ðe moſtᵉ pouerful Muſicians (ſuᵉ as werᵉ
Orpheus and *Arion* : yea ſuᵉ as was ðat *Divinᵉ Pſalmiſt*) werᵉ
alſo Poets. And ſuᵉ ſooldᵉ our Muſicians bœ, if ðey wil bœ
completᵉ : For hæ ðat knoweᵗ bodᵉ, can beſt fit his Poeſi
to his own Muſik, and his Muſik to his own Poeſi. And
mor·over hæ is enabled to judg of ſuᵉ verſes as ar browgᵗ

De Voicᵉ.

Ditti-Muſik.

* *Polit. l 8. c.7.*

† *Ibid. C. 7.*

Poeſi and Har-
moni, eqall
partᶜs of Muſik:
Boðᶜ profeſt by
ðe ancient Mu-
ſicians.

unto

unto him, and, for a need, soomwat to alter dem ; dat de woords may bæ de mor consonant to his present vein. To dis effect speaket *Calvisius: Etsi hodie Melopœiis liberum relinquitur ut Textum Harmoniæ exornandum vel ipsi singant & forment, vel ab aliis sumant ; tamen necesse est ut convenientem cuilibet Textui Harmoniam condant. Poetæ autem veteres simul materiam, quam tractandam susceperunt, verborum Metro comprehensorum elegantia, ac figurarum sententiarumq; splendore illustraverunt ; & Harmoniam proposito argumento accommodatam addiderunt.* In fine Capitis 1.

Observations in Ditti song.

Concerning Setters.

De tings to bæ obsérved in a Ditti-song, doo eider concern de Setter, or de Singer. Concerning de Setter, hæ must hav a special car dat de Not agræ to de natur of de Ditti. Plain and slow Musik is fit for grav and sad matter : qik Not's or Triple tim, for Mirt and rejoicing. A manly, hard, angry, or cruel matter is to bæ exprest by hard and harss sort ton's, qik Bindings, and concording Cadences ; and dat wit de ordinari or unaltered Not's of de Scal : but woords of effeminat lamentations, sorrowful passions, and complaints, ar fitly exprest by de inordinat half-not's, (suc as ar de smal keys of de Virginals) wit cang de direct order of de Scal ; flatting de Not's naturally sarp, and sarping dem wit ar naturally flat : and dos in longer tim ; wit slow Bindings and discording *Cadences. Also woords importing de circumstances of Tim and Plac, ar to bæ fitted wit Not's agræable : as dos dat signifi runing, or speedy motions, also de sort syllables of any woords, wit sort Not's ; and de contrari wit de contrari. Lik'wis dos dat signifi higt and ascending, wit hig not's ; and dept or descending, wit low. Wi e tings may bæ dœn in Discant, by many Part's : to wit, in a Point successiv'ly iterated : but in Counterpoint (wer all de Part's sing de sam woords of de Ditti togeder) it is enoug dat dey bæ dœn in de *Cantus* or Tun, [de most Melodious and observable Part.] *Franchinus* direction is dis : *Studeat insuper cantilenæ Compositor, Cantus suavitatem Cantilenæ verbis congruere : ut cum de mortis petitione, aut quævis lamentatione fuerint verba, flebiles pro posse sonos pronunciet : cùm vero verba indignationem & increpationem dicunt,*

* *V. Syncope.*

dicunt, aſperos decet ſonos & duriores emittere : verùm laudis & modeſtiæ verba medios quodammodo ſonos expetunt. But Calviſtus is morᶜ punᶜtual. *Vegetior erit Harmonia, ſi abſint* † *ſigna Chromatica : & contrà pronior ad miſericordiam, amorem, preces, &c. ſi crebrò miſceantur. Violentior erit ex pedum celeritate, manſuetior ex tarditate.* And again, *Res profunda, difficilis, ſilentium, deſcenſus, timor, planctus, ſuſpiria, materia funebris, amaritudo, &c. Harmoniam in ſonis Gravibus conſiſtentem requirunt : in Acutioribus contra, ſi lætitia, riſus, aſcenſus, altitudo, clamor, &c. fuerint exprimenda. In interitu aut ſilentio, interdum omnes Voces ſilent.* Cap. 18.

† *Signa Chromatica ar doſᶜ dat betoken de inordinatᶜ Hemitonᶜs.*

Reportᶜs reqirᶜ Repetᶜs : dat if de Points Ditti bee not apprehended at de firſt ; yet, in de iterating derᶜof, it may.

2

Sucᴇ Repetᶜs ſooldᶜ bee Empatical, importing ſoom ſpecial matter : and wiᴇ, in Divinᶜ uſes, may help botᶜ to excitᶜ and to expreſ daᶜ zelᶜ and Devotion.

Ligaturᶜs obſcurᶜ de Ditti : and derᶜforᶜ ar to bee avoided as mucᴇ as may bee ; and ſoom partᶜ of de Ditti rader to bee iterated, if it may bee conveniently doon.

3

As de Ditti is diſtinguiſed wit Points, [Period, Colon, Semicolon, and Comma ;] ſo is de Harmoni, anſwering unto it, wit Pauſes, and Cadences.

Directions bot for Ditti and Harmoni.

Sembrief-reſts onᶜ or moᶜ anſwer to a Period, or to a Colon : wiᴇ alſo is of Perfect ſens. (*V.Gram.C.*4. §3. ¶1.) Minim- and Crocet-reſts, to Semicolons, Commaᶜs, Breadings, and Sigs.

So likᶜwiſᶜ, Primari Cadences Perfect, wiᴇ clozᶜ de Harmoni, anſwer fitly to Periods ending de Ditti ; or ſoom principal partᶜ of it : and Secundari, to Colons or Interrogations. But Improper, and Imperfect Cadences, anſwer to Points of Imperfect ſens, [Commaᶜs, and Semicolons.]

Deſᶜ Directions bæing obſerved (wit diſcretion) in de Harmoni, help not a little to de manifeſting and underſtanding of de Ditti.

✦ Concerning de Singers, deir firſt carᶜ ſooldᶜ bee to ſit wit a decent erect poſturᶜ of de Bodi, witout all ridiculous and uncoomly geſticulations, of Hed, or Hands, or any oder

Obſervations Concerning Singers. 1

N   Partᶜ :

2

3

†*V. Rhet. L.* 2.
C. 2.
† *Franchinus.*
l. 3. *C.* 15.

Parte : den ((dat de Ditti (wie is half de grace of de Song)
may bee known and underſtood)) to ſing as plainly as dey
woolde ſpeak : pronouncing every Syllable and letter (ſpecially de Vouels) diſtinctly and treatably. And in deir
great varieti of † Tones, to kæpe ſtil an eqal * Sound :
(except in a Point) dat one voice droun not an oder. Dus
dooe dat † expert Muſician adviſe : *Poſtremò novis Cantoribus, inſtitutionis admonitioniſq; cauſâ, duximus proponen-
dum, ne inſolito & inhoneſto oris hiatu, aut ridiculo forte cachin-
no, voces proferant modulando : rejiciant voces tremebundas, atq;
perſtrepentes. Decet autem alterum alteri vocem accommodare, ne
alter alterius clamoris exceſſu confundatur. Inſolens quoq; &
indecorus capitis manuumve motus Cantorem declarat inſanum.*

Cap. 1. § 3. Of mixt Muſik.

*Voic̄ and In-
ſtruments con-
joined.
* Quint. l. 5.
C. 10. in fine.

† Ezekiel 33.
v. 32.

DE Voice, dus fitted wit Ditti (eider in Partes, or
ſingle) is deligtful of it ſelf : but Inſtruments added
make de Muſik more acceptable. * *Cantum Vocis plurimùm
juvat ſociata Nervorum concordia.* And derefore de Lord himſelf comparet de ſwete ſpæce of an Eloqent Preaeer unto
de Muſik of Voice and Inſtrument togeder : †And loe, (ſayt
hee) don art unto dem as a very loovly Song, of one dat hat
a ſwete Voice, and can play wel on an Inſtrument.

☞   In Ditti-mixt-Muſik is alway to bæ obſerved, dat de
Inſtruments dooe eider ſound Submiſly, or by Turns ; dat de
Ditti bæ not obſcured. For dowg de Singers can ſoomtime
content demſelvs wit de Muſik of de Note ; yet de Hearers ar not ſo wel ſatisfyed witout de Ditti, if it bæ good.

❧❧❧❧❧❧❧❧❧❧❧❧❧❧❧❧❧❧❧❧❧❧❧❧❧❧

Cap. II. § I. Of de Divine Uſe of Muſik,
in general.

*De firſt general
Uſe of Muſik.*

DHe firſt Uſe uf Muſik is in Divine ſervice and woorſip of God : werunto de holy Propet, mooved by
de ſpirit of God, dooe often invite and exhort
Gods People.

Sœmtim⁶ to de ſingle Muſik of de Voic : as *Pſal.* 95.

1. *O cœm let us ſing unto de Lord : let us mak⁶ a joyful noiz to de Rok of our Salvation.*

2. *Let us cœm befor⁶ his preſenc⁶ wit tanks-giving, and mak⁶ a joyfull noiz unto him wit Pſalms.*   And *Pſal.* 96.

1. *O ſing unto de Lord a nu⁶ Song : ſing unto de Lord all de Fart.*

2. *Sing unto de Lord, bleſ his nam⁶ : ſew fœrt his ſalvation from day to day.* Su∈ was †this Song, wher⁶in hæ praiſed God for his particular deliveranc⁶ out of de hand of *Saul,* and of all his enimi⁶s. Su∈ alſo ſæmet to bæ de *Eukariſt of *Moſes* and de people, for deir deliveranc⁶ from de *Ægyptians.* And de † *Epinicium* of *Debora* and *Barak* for de overtrow of *Siſera* ; (dowg de benefit wer⁶ publik⁶) becaus, de *Iſraelit⁶s* bæing not yet cœm to de land of deir Reſt, deir Muſik cœld⁶ not den bæ ſo complet⁶.

And ſœmtim⁶ de Propet incitet to de (a) mixt Muſik of Voic⁶ and (b) Inſtruments conjoined : wen as any ſpecial occaſion dœ⁶t reqir⁶ ſu∈ ſolemniti : as *Pſal.* 33. wer⁶ de Propet exhortet de righteous to prais God for his gœdnes, for his tru⁶t, for his juſtic⁶ and mercy, and for his pouer in creating and governing de world.

2. *Prais de Lord wit Harp : ſing unto him wit de Pſalteri, and inſtrument of ten ſtrings.*

3. *Sing unto him a nu⁶ Song : play ſkilfully wit a loud noiz.* And *Pſal.* 98. wi∈ is a ſingular Propeci of de Kingdom of Kriſt⁶, (*U.* 1.) de Saviour (*U.* 2. *&* 3.) and Judg (*U.* 9.) of all de world : wer⁶in de Kingly Propet exhortet all people [bot⁶ Ju⁶s and Gentil⁶s] to prais de Lord, bot⁶ wit voic⁶ and inſtruments, *U.* 1, 4, 5, and 6. Su∈ ſæmet to bæ dat moſt excellent * *Epithalamium* of Kriſt⁶ and his €yr∈, conteining a glorious *Encomion* bot⁶ of de Brid⁶grœm⁶ and of de Brid⁶.

But de moſt⁶ ſolemn Muſik, and ful Harmoni of Voices and loud Inſtruments in Conſort, is moſt⁶ fit for de moſt⁶ ſolemn Congregations, at ſolemn Tim⁶s, & in ſolemn Places ; wen, upon ſœm extraordinari occaſion, de €yr∈ is aſſembled to prais and pray God for his gœdnes : as *Pſal.* 81. di-

† 2 Sam. 22.

* Exod. 15.

† Iudges 5.

(a)
Mixt Muſik·
(b)

* Pſal. 45.

Moſt⁶ ſolemn Muſik·

rected to de cief Muſician upon *Gittith* : in wie de Propet exhortet de people to dis ſolemn ſervic⁶, for deir mighty Deliveranc⁶ out of *Ægypt.*

1. *Sing aloud unto God our ſtrengt, mak⁶ a joiful noiz. unto de God of Jacob.*

2. *Tak⁶ a Pſalm and bring beder de Timbrel, de pleaſant Harp wit de Pſalteri.*

3. *Blow up de Trumpet in de nu⁶ Moon⁶, in de tim⁶ appointed, on de ſolemn feaſt days.*

And lik⁶wiſ⁶ at de 3 ſolemn Remoovings of de Ark of God : firſt by *David,* from de hous of *Abinadab* in *Kiriat-jearim* to *Obed Edoms* hous : and den again, by him, from de hous of *Obed Edom* to de Tabernacle in de Citti of *David :* and laſtly, by *Solomon,* from de Tabernacle in *Sion* to de O-racle of de nu⁶-built Temple in *Jeruſalem.*

De ſolemn Muſik at de 3 Remoovals of de Ark.

I.

De ſolemniti of de firſt Remooval is deſcribed 1 Kron. 13. 6. And *David* went up, and all *Iſrael* to *Baalat,* [i. to *Kiriat-jearim*] to bring up denc⁶ de Ark of God de Lord, dat dwellet betwæn⁶ de Cerubims, woſ⁶ nam⁶ is called on in it. 7. And dey carryed de Ark of God, in a nu⁶ Cart, out of de hous of *Abinadab.* 8. And *David* and all *Iſrael* played befor⁶ God wit all deir migt, and wit Singing, and wit Harps, and wit Pſalteri⁶s, and wit Timbrels, and wit Cymbals, and wit Trumpets.

II.

Of de ſecond Remooval, 1 Kron. 15. V. 25. So *David* and de Elders of *Iſrael,* and de Captaines over touſands, went to bring up de Ark of de Covenant of de Lord, out of de hous of *Obed Edom* wit joy. 27. And *David* was cloded wit a rob⁶ of fin⁶ linnen, and all de *Levits* dat bar⁶ de Ark, and de Singers, and *Kenaniah* de Maſter of de Song wit de Singers : *David* alſo had upon him an Epod of linnen. 28. Dus all *Iſrael* browgt up de Ark of de Covenant of de Lord wit ſouting, and wit ſound of de Cornet, and wit Trumpets, and wit Cymbals, mak⁶ing a noiz wit Pſalteri⁶s, and Harps.

III.

And de ſolemniti of de tird Remooval, 2 Kron. C. 5. V. 2. Den *Solomon* aſſembled de Elders of *Iſrael* and all de Heda of

of ðe Tribes, ðe eief of ðe Faðers of ðe children of *Ifrael* unto *Jerufalem*, to bring up ðe Ark of ðe Covenant of ðe
Lord, out of ðe Citti of *David*, wie is *Zion*.

7. And ðe Priefts browgt in ðe Ark into his place, [into
ðe Oracle of ðe hous, into ðe mofte holy place, even under
ðe wings of ðe Cerubims.]

12. Alfo ðe Levites wie were ðe Singers, [all of ðem of
Afap, of *Heman*, of *Jedutun*] wiɫ ðeir foons and ðeir bre-
dren, bæing arrayed in wite linnen, having Cymbals, and
Pfalteries, and Harps, ftood at ðe Eaft end of ðe Altar, and
wiɫ ðem an hundred and twenty Priefts, founding wiɫ
Trumpets.

Wie folemn zelous fervice hou acceptable it was to
Almighty God, was ðerupon miraculoufly fignifyed, in ðe
place were it was performed.

V. 13. It came to paf as ðe Trumpeters and Singers
were as one, to make one found to bæ heard in praifing and
ɫanking ðe Lord ; and wen ðey lift up ðeir voice, wiɫ ðe
Trumpets, and Cymbals, and Inftruments of Mufik, and
praifed ðe Lord, faying (e) For Hee Is Good,
For His Mercy Endureth For Ever;
ðat ðen ðe hous was filled wiɫ a Cloud, [even ðe hous of
ðe Lord.]

14. So ðat ðe Priefts coolde not ftand to minifter, by reafon of ðe Cloud : for ðe Glori of ðe Lord had filled ðe
hous of God.

Sue a folemn *Synodi* was appointed by good *Ezekiah*,
2 *Kron. c.* 29. at his renuing of ðe Covenant, and reftoring
of Religion.

V. 25. And hæ fet ðe *Levits* in ðe hous of ðe Lord wiɫ
Cymbals, and wiɫ Pfalteries, and wiɫ Harps, according to
ðe commandement of *David*, and of *Gad* ðe Kings Sæer,
and *Natan* ðe Propet : for fo was ðe commandement of ðe
Lord by his Propets. 26. And ðe *Levits* ftood wiɫ ðe Inftruments of *David*, and ðe Priefts wiɫ ðe Trumpets. *V.* 27.
And *Hezekiah* commanded to offer ðe burnt-offering upon
ðe Altar : and wen ðe burnt-offering began ; ðe Song of ðe
Lord began alfo, wiɫ ðe Trumpets, and wiɫ ðe Inftruments

(c)

De firft folemn
Mufik of Eze-
kiah.

of *David*, [King of *Iſrael.*] 28. And all de Congregation woo ſiped, and de Singers ſang, and de Trumpeters foundod. And all dis continued, untill de burnt-offering was finiſed.

De ſecond.
* 2 Kr 30 21.

And likᶜwiſᶜ at de Paſſover, wie hœ proclaimed not long after : for den de * Levitᶜs and de Prieſts praiſed de Lord day by day, ſinging wit loud Inſtruments unto de Lord.

De likᶜ by Ze-
rubbabel.

And after de Captiviti de likᶜ ſolemniti was appointed by *Zerubbabel* and *Ieſhua. Ezra* 3. at de nuᶜ-building of de Temple. *V.* 10. And wen de builders layd de foundation of de Temple of de Lord ; dey ſet de Prieſts in deir apparrell wit Trumpets, and de *Levitᶜs* de ſoons of *Aſap* wit Cymbals, to prais de Lord, after de ordinancᶜ of *David* [King of *Iſrael.*] *V.* 11. And dey ſung togeder by coorſᶜ in praiſing and giving tanks unto de LORD : BECAUS HEE IS GOOD, FOR HIS MERCY ENDURETH FOR EVER.

And by Nehe-
miah.

And again, by *Nehemia, C.* 12. *V.* 27. &c.

ANNOT. to Cap. 2, §1.

(a) HENCᶜ de muſical Propet entitles his 7ᵗʰ Pſalm *Shiggaion* [*Ode mixta*, a Conſort-ſong] † *quæ omnibus rationibus Muſicæ decantabatur ſimul. Tullius Græca voce dixit Synodiam.*

† Tremel. in
locum.

De eief Autors of dis ſacred *Symponiᶜ*, in de days of *David*, werᶜ tree : [* *Aſap*, *Heman*, and *Etan*, or † *Iedutun*] *lineally deſcended from de tree ſoons of *Levi⁶* [*Gerſom*, *Kohat*, and *Merari*] wie bœing expert in all de Points and Myſteries of deir Art, werᶜ called *Magiſtri ſymponiæ*, [de eief Singers :] unto womᶜ de Poetical Propet directed his Pſalms ; (dat dey ſœldᶜ fit deir heavenly Muſik to his heavenly Mœters) bœing eoſen beforᶜ by de Levitᶜs out of all deir Tribᶜ, for de ſamᶜ purpoſᶜ, at de appointment of de King : dey had alſo dᶜs extraordinary prerogativᶜ, dat dey werᶜ Propets, and, *Elizeus*-likᶜ, did propeci⁶ upon deir Inſtruments : and morᶜover dey had, for Aſſiſtants, deir 24 ſoons, † wie werᶜ under deir faders, for Song and for Inſtruments. So dat qeſtionles deir Muſik was den moſtᶜ exqiſitᶜ : compoſed and ordered wit all de Eleganciᶜs and Graces of Melodi and Harmoni, dat eider Art, or Naturᶜ, or practicᶜ, or honour, or *Muſikentuſiaſm*, cœldᶜ ſuggeſt. And leſt defect in de Singers ſœldᶜ obſcurᶜ de perfection of de Setters ; *many of deir bredren were diligently inſtructed in de practicᶜ of Singing : in wie officᶜ † *Kenaniah* was ſpecially imploied. By wie means all confuſion in de multitudᶜ of voices and Inſtruments,

* 1 Kron. 15. 17
†C.9, 16. C. 25, 1
by wie namᶜ de
Propet direct-
ef his Pſalms
unto him: as 39.
and 62.
* 1 Kron. 6. v. 16.
39. 33. & 44.
† 1 Kron. 25. 6.
* 1 Kron. 25. 7.
De number of
dem wit deir
bredren dat
werᶜ inſtructed
in de ſongs of de
Lord [all dat
werᶜ cunning] was 288. † 1 *Kron.* 15. 22. *And Kenaniah [eief of de Levitᶜs] inſtructed about*
de Song ; becaus hœ was skilful.

Inſtruments, tedious diſcordances, breaking of Timᶜ, ill governing of ðe Voicᶜ, rudᶜ geſturᶜ, or any oðer *Indecorum* was avoided.

(b) Ðe Vſᶜ of Inſtruments in ðe ſeivicᶜ of God, ðe Propᵉt moſtᶜ expreſly reqiret Pſalm. 150 : werᶜ ar mentioned as wel *Entata* or *Neginot*, as *Empneuſta* or *Nehilot* : wiᵉ 2 ſortᶜs werᶜ ſeverally taugt and ordered by ſeveral Maſters, and Profeſſors : as appearet by ðe Inſcriptions of divers Pſalms : namᶜly *Pſ.* 4. To ðe ᶜief Mnſician on *Neginot*, [*Magiſtro ſyponiæ fidium:*] and *Pſ.* 5. To ðe ᶜief Muſician upon *Nehilot* [*Magiſtro Symponiæ ad* † *pneumatica.*] But becaus *Entata* at often out of tun ; (wiᵉ ſomtimᵉ happenet in ðe mids of ðe Muſik, wen it is neiðer gᵒd to continuᶜ, nor to correᶜt ðe fault) ðerᶜforᶜ, to avoid all offeneᶜ, (werᶜ ðe leaſt ſᵒldᶜ not bæ givn) in our *Eyre*-ſolemnitiᶜs onᶜly ðe Windᶜ-inſtruments (woſᶜ Notᶜs ar conſtant) bæ in uſᶜ.

Deſᶜ 2 ſortᶜs for morᶜ deligtful varieti werᶜ madᶜ of divers Piᶜees : *onᶜ higer, [*acutæ ſymponiæ*] wiᵉ ðey called *Alamot* ; ðe oðer of an Eigt lower, [*gravis ſymponiæ*] wiᵉ ðey called *Sheminit*.

And for furðer varieti in mixt Muſik, ſomtimᶜs ðe Inſtruments did goᶜ beforᶜ ðe voicᶜ, and ðen ðe ſong was called †*Pſalmus-canticum* : (as *Pſal.* 68. 76. and 92. wiᵉ was for ðe *Sabbat*) ſomtimᶜ ðe Voiᶜe did goᶜ beforᶜ ðe Inſtruments, and ðen ðe ſong was called *Canticum-pſalmus* : (as *Pſal.* 83. 88. and 108. Ðis is obſerved by *Tremellius* upon ðe 48 Pſalm. *Canticum-pſalmum incipiebat vox Cantorum modulari ; & præcuntem ſequebantur inſtrumenta : ac pſalmum-canticum incipiebant Pſaltæ ; ſequebatur vox.*

(c) Ðeſᶜ words ar found in ðe beginnings of 4 Pſalms [106, 107, 118, and 136] In ðe 2 laſt ðey makᶜ a paᵉtical *Epiſtropᵉ*; bæing iteratet 4 timᶜs in ðe onᶜ, and in ðe oðer 26 timᶜs : [even at ðe end of every vers.] Ðe uſᶜ ðat is hærᶜmadᶜ of ðe words of ðe Pſalmiſt, in ðe timᶜ of *Solomon*, is to bæ madᶜ of all ðe Pſalms, in all timᶜs, as ſeveral occaſions ſall reqirᶜ : and ðer forᶜ *Ezekiah* alſo, in his ſolemn ſervicᶜ, commanded ðe Levitᶜs to ſing praiſᶜ unto ðe Lord in ðe words of *David*. For ðe wolᶜ Bᵒkᶜ of Pſalms is obſerved by ðe learned, to bæ, boᵗᶜ for *Matter* and *Form*, incomparable.

For ðe *Matter*, wat is it but a ſweetᶜ Epitome of all ðe Scripturᶜ ? of wiᵉ St. *Baſil*, and from him St. *Auguſtinᶜ*, in a largᶜ commendation of ðis Bᵒkᶜ, haᵗ ðeſᶜ words : †*In ſcriptura quidem ſunt alia quæ Prophetæ tradunt; alia quæ Hiſtorici; alia item quæ Lex ; alia quæ in Proverbiis, monitorum formâ : Pſalmorum verò liber quæcunq; utilia ſunt, ex omnibus comprehendit : futura prædicit ; veterum biſtorias commemorat; legem fert viventibus ; gerendorum ſtatuit modum ; deniq; publicum bonorum documentorum eſt promptuarium quoddam, ea quæ ſingulis conferunt, pro ſtudio ipſorum exhibens. &c.* Ðeᶜ havᶜ you many ſpecial expreſſions of Gods mercy towards man; as in ðe woᵣk of Creation, Redemption, Preſervation and Glorification : his Providencᶜ, Promiſes, Comforts, Deliverances, Humiliations, Exaltations, &c. And likᶜwiſᶜ of mans duty unto God : as Prayers, Praiſes, Thankſ-givings, Repentancᶜ, Conᶜfeſſion,

*Vid. C. 1. §. 1.

† *or Empneuſta.*

* 1 Kro. 15. 20, 21.

† *For Pſalmus coms of Pſallo wiᵉ ſignifyet to tone or ſtrikᶜ: as* χόρδας ψάλλειν *or ſimpliciter* ψάλλειν *to play on a ſtring-inſtrument.*

* 2 Kr. 29. 30.

† *Baſil. in Præfat. ad Pſal.*

feſſion, Obedienc', Complaints, Lamentations, Rejoicings : Medi-
tations on Kriſt's Incarnation, Paſſion, Reſurreƈtion, Aſcenſion, his
Sitting on ðe riȝt hand of God, and his cœming again to judg ðe world.
Alſo of mutual Exhortations, Dehortations, Conſolations, Inſtruƈti-
ons, Reprehenſions, &c : Wic you ſall find' obſerved by our divin'

G. W.

Poet in ðe Arguments of ðe Pſalms. Woſ' Tranſlation, for divere
reſpeƈts, (wer'of you hav' a toue in his Prefac') I cannot but honour
and admir'.

In ðe Tropeis.

And for ðe *Form,* tak' ðe teſtimoni of ðat ſweet' *Bard Dubartas*:

† i. ðe heavenly
Muſ': of ἄ ρανος
cœlum.

Wo, in a Direƈt Proſopopci of † *Vrania,* ſpeaket ðus.

> Never elſ-wer' did plenteous Eloqenc'
> In every part, wiȝ ſue magnificenc',
> Set-forȝ hir Beauti's, in ſue ſundry Faſions
> Of Rob's and Juels, ſuiting ſundry Paſſions;
> As in ðy Songs : Now, lik' a Qœn' for Coſt
> In ſmelling Tiſſu's, rar'ly-riȝ emboſt
> Wiȝ Precious Ston's : Neat, Citty-lik', anon,
> Fin' Cloȝ, or Silk, or Camlet puts ſœ on :
> Anon, mor' lik' ſœm handſœm Shepherdes,
> In cœrſer Cloð's ſœ dœȝ her clenly dreſ :
> Wat e'r ſœ wear, Wol, Silk, or Gold, or Gems,
> Or Cœrſ', or Fin' ; ſtill lik' her ſelf ſœ ſœm's :
> [Fair, Modeſt, Cœr'ful, ſitting tim' and plac',
> Illuſtring all ev'n wiȝ a Heav'n-lik' Grac'.]
> Lik' proud loud *Tigru,* euer ſwiftly roul'd,
> Now, ȝ'rœw ðe Plains ðou pour'ſt a Flœd of gold' :
> Now, lik' ðy *Jordan,* or *Meander*-lik'.
> Round-winding nimbly wiȝ a many Crœk',
> Ðou run'ſt to mœt' ðy ſelf's pur' ſtreams behind' ðœ,
> Mazing ðe Meads wer' ðou dœ'ſt turn and wind' ðœ.
> Anon, lik' *Cedron* ȝ'rœw a ſtraiter Qiȝ,
> Ðou ſtraineſt out a little Brœk or Ril ;
> But yet ſo ſweet', ðat it ſall ever bœ
> Ð'immortal *Neƈtar* to Poſteriti.

And anon (for ðe excellenci as well of Matter as of Form) ðe
heavenly Muſ' ðus propecyeȝ ðe eterniti of ðis ſacred Bœk' :

> Ðou ſalt ſurviv' ȝ'rœw-out all Generations :
> And, plyant, learn ðe languag' of all Nations :
> Now-ȝt but ðin' Airs ȝ'rœw, Ai'r and Sea ſall ſound :
> In hiȝ-buiȝ Temples ſall ðy ſongs reſound :
> Ðy ſacred vers ſall clœr' Gods cloudy fac',
> And in ðy ſteps ðe nobleſt wiȝs ſall trac'.

CAP.

C A P. II. § II.

Of ðe Continuanc of *Eyre-Mufik.*

Ðis folemn Mufik fo pleafing unto God, hað ever finc* (ꝏen ðe tim*s permitted) in one degræ or oðer, bæn obferved in his *Eyre.* Befor* ðe *Ifraelit*s & ðe Krifti-ans had Reft, [ðey from ðeir warz and wandrings, and def* from ðeir poverti and perfecution;] ðeir Mufik cꝏld* not bæ fo complet*, as afterward, in tim*s of peac* and profperiti. Wat Mufik was ufed in ðe Apoftles days, (ꝏeiðer vocal on*ly, or inftrumentall alfo ꝏit it) is not apparent: aldoꝏg ðe Apoftles exhortation fæmeð to reqir* as wel ðe Melodi of Inftruments, as ðe concent of voices : † *Bæ ye filled wit ðe fpirit: fpeaking to your felvs in Pfalms, and Hymns, and fpiri-tual Songs ; Singing and (a) makïng Melodi in your harts to ðe Lord.* And ðe holy goft, alluding to ðis mixt Mufik of ðe *Eyre* militant, dꝏ*ð dus expref ðe heavenly Harmoni of ðe *Eyre* triumpant : * *I heard ðe voie* of Harpers, harping wit ðeir Harps. And ðey fung as it wer* a nu* Song befor* ðe tron* &c.*

† *Epef.5.18,19.*

(a)

* *Revel.14.2,3.*

But houfoever ðis ordinanc* of God migt for a tim* bæ interrupted ; yet fo fꝏn* as ðe *Eyre* obteined reft, and, der*by, means and opportuniti ; ðey ftraigtway renued ðis religious duty, and rejoyced der*wit to prais ðe Lord, in ðeir great Congregations.

† *Ifidor* Ar*bifhop of *Hifpalis,* fpeakeð generally : ðat of ðe ancient cuftom of Singers in ðe old* *Eyre* of ðe Ju*s, ðe Primitiv* *Eyre* tꝏk* example to nurrif Singers : by ꝏof* Songs ðe minds of ðe hearers migt be ftirred up to ðe lꝏv of God. &c. *Pfalmos cantabant filii Afaph continui ̈n diebus, candidis induti ftolis, ad vocem unius refpondente (b) Choro. Ex hoc vetere more, Ecclefia fumpfit exemplum nutriendi Pfalmi-ftas : quorum cantibus ad affeÐum Dei mentes audientium exci-tentur.*

† *De officiis ec-clefiafticis l. 2. c. 12.*

(b)

S*t *Hierom in an Epiftle ꝏi*e hee wrot*, for oðers, from *Hierufalem* to Rꝏm*, fewet ðat der* wer* divers Nations abiding der*, ꝏi*e had every on* of ðem ðeir feveral Qir*s.

* *Epift. Paulæ & Euftochii, ad Marcellam.*

O   *Hic*

Hìc vox quidem diſſona, ſed una religio : tot Pſallentium chori, quot gentium diverſitates.

Athanaſius, [ðat good ortodox Biſhop of *Alexandria*] in his Treatic͟ of ðe interpretation of ðe *Pſalms,* ſayꞇ : *Propheta Pſalmos, ut modulis canerentur, inſtituit, & cum hujuſmodi harmonia recitari voluit. &c.* And a little after, *Modulatim recitare Pſalmos. &c.* To ſing *Pſalms* artificially, is not to mak͞a ſew of cunning Muſik; but an argument ðat ðe cogitations of our minds do aptly agreͤ wiꞇ our Muſik: and ðat Reading wiͼ obſerveꞇ ðe law of Fætͼ & Numbers, is a ſignͼ of a ſober and qiët affection of ðe mindͼ. For to prais God upon ðe wel-tuned Cymbals, upon ðe Harp, and Pſalteri of ten ſtrings, is a notͼ and ſignification ðat ðerͼ is ſuͼ a concent betweͤnͼ ðe partͼs of ðe body, as ðerͼ is among ðe ſtrings.

* *Eccleſ. hiſt. l.2. c. 16.*

   * *Euſebius* ſayꞇ out of *Philo,* ðat ðe Єyr-ees of Ægypt did mak͞ Songs and Hymns, wiꞇ moſt exact qalitiͼs and meſurͼs of verſes, wiͼ ðey ſang in ðe honour and prais of God.

(c) Hymns.

   Đe ͼiefeſt Songs ſung in ðe Servicͼ of G o d, werͼ (c) *Hymns :* wiͼ *Moſes* and *David* in ðe oldͼ Єyre of ðe *Juꞇs* firſt madͼ and ſung : and in ðe Primitivͼ Єyre of *Kriſtians,* Stͼ *Hilari* and St *Ambroſt* did exel in ðat kindͼ: as † St *Iſidorͼ* witneſſeꞇ : *Hilarius Gallus Epiſcopus, Eloquentiâ conſpicuus, Hymnorum carmine floruit. Poſt quem Ambroſius copioſiùs in hujuſmodi carmine claruit : & inde Hymni Ambroſiani vocantur.* And ðeſͼ wiꞇ oðer ſpiritual Songs werͼ ſung in ðe Єyre, ſoomtimͼ by way of (d) *Reſponſoriꞇ,* and ſoomtimͼ by (e) *Antiphonaͼs.*

† *L. 1. C. 6.*

(d)
(e)

Reſponſoriꞇ.
* *Iſidor. l.1.c.8.*

   Đe uſͼ of *Reſponſoriꞇ* is moſtͼ ancient : as bæing found in *Itali* long beforͼ ðe Hymns of St *Ambroſt.* * *Reſponſoria ab Italiâ longo antè tempore ſunt reperta : & vocata hoc nomine, quòd, Uno canente, Chorus conſonando Reſpondeat : interdum duo vel tres canunt communiter, Choro in plurimis reſpondente.* Yea *Iſidorus,* in ðe placͼ aboov-cited, makeꞇ it morͼ ancient : teſtifying it to havͼ been derived unto *Khriſtians* from de oldͼ Єyre : ðe wiͼ (as ðe † Eccleſiaſtical Hiſtorian writͼ-cꞇ) was afterward confirmed to *Ignatius* by a Viſion of Angels,

† *Socrates lib.6. c. 8.*

Angels, praifing ðe holy Triniti, by *Reſponſori* Hymns. *Ig-*
natius Antiochiæ tertius ab Apoſtolo Petro Epiſcopus, unà cum
Apoſtolis aliquando verſatus, viſionem Angelorum per Reſponſo-
rios Hymnos ſanctam Triadem laudantium vidit : & modum vi-
ſionis Antiochenæ Eccleſiæ tradidit : unde & ad omnes Eccleſias
iſta Traditio promanavit.

And concerning *Antiphona^s*, ðe Antiqiti of ðem alſo   *Antiphona^s.*
in Gods Eyrε appœrεt, by *Theodorεt, Sozomεn, Iſidor^c*, and
Baſil ðe Great.   Theodorεtus.

*Theodoret ſewεt ðat in ðe Eyrε of *Antioch*, (wer^c ðe Diſ- * *Eccleſ. hiſt.*
ciples wer^c firſt called † Kriſtians) ðoſ^c devout Bifhops, *lib. 2. c. 24.*
[*Flavianus* and *Diodorus*] ordeined, ðat ðe *Pſalms* of *David* † Act. 11. 16.
ſould^c bœ ſung in Cœrſ^c by a Qir^c of Singing-men, divided
into two part^s. Ðe wiε order onc^c begun at *Antioch*, was
ðenc^c derived farðer and farðer, even unto ðe utmoſt part^s
of ðe world. *Flavianus & Diodorus cum populo verſabantur :*
diéq; ac noctu inſtigabant omnes ad pietatis fervorem. Hi primi,
in duas partes diviſis cortibus, Pſalmos accinentium inſtituerunt
alternis Davidicam Melodiam decantare : quod Antiochiæ fieri
cœptum, pervagatum uſquequaq; eſt : & ad fines orbis terrarum
pervenit.

† *Sozomen* lik^c wiſ^c relatεt, ðat ðe Clergi and People of   Sozomεnus.
Antioch, dividing ðemſelvs into two part^s; did (according † *L. 3. c. 29.*
to ðeir accuſtomed manner) prais God wit Hymns and
Songs.

And * *Iſidorus* affirmεt, ðat ðe Grœk^s accordingly did   Iſidorus.
firſt compoſ^c ðeſ^c *Antiphons* : [two Qir^s finging, by Cœrſ^c, * *L. 1. c. 7.*
lik^c ðe † two Serapims anſwering on^c an oðer in ðeir *Alle-* † Eſai. 6, 3.
luia :] and afterward ðe Latin^s, among wom^c *St Ambroſ^c* was
ðe firſt. *Antiphonas Græci primum compoſuere, duobus choris al-*
ternatim concinentibus, quaſi 2 Seraphim. Apud Latinos autem
primus beatiſſimus Ambroſius Antiphonas conſtituit. Ðe ſam^c * *L. 8. c. 8.*
Cuſtom (ſayt * *Sozomen*) did Kryſoſtom ordein in ðe Eyrε
of *Conſtantinople.*

S^t *Baſil* mentionεt ðe uſ^c of (f) bod^c, not on^c ly in his own, Baſilius Mag-
but generally in all ðe Eaſtern Eyrεes. † *De nocte populus*   nus.
conſurgens, antelucano tempore, domum Precationis petiit : inq;   † *Epiſt. 63. ad*
labore, & tribulatione, ac lachrymis indeſinentibus, facta ad Deum Neocæſarianos.

Confeſſione,

*Reſponſori,
†Antiphona.*

Confeſſione, tandem ab Oratione ſurgentes, ad Pſalmodiam inſtituuntur. Et nunc quidem*in duas partes diviſi, alternis ſuccinentes pſallunt: deinde †uni ex ipſis hoc muneris datur, ut quod canendum eſt prior ordiatur ; reliqui ſuccinant. &c. But neverdeles it ſeemet der wanted not den ſom contentious Cavillers againſt deſ holy Exerciſes : to wom, hæ maket dis ſober Anſwer : *Horum gratiâ ſi nos fugitis ; fugietis ſimul & Ægyptios : fugietis Lybiam utranq; , Thebæos, Paleſtinos, Arabes, Phoenicas, Syros, & qui ad Euphraten habitant. &c.*

Sinc deſ Tims dis ſacred Muſik hat ever been uſed by de godly in de hous of God, for his Divin Servic and woorſip, unto dis day. And if at any tim it hav been abuſed, it is a poor Reaſon, dat der for it ſould not bee reſtored to its ancient rigt uſ again.

ANNOTATIONS to C. 2. §. 2.

(a) **M**Aking *Melodi.* De woord in de Original is ψάλλοντις i. [*citharam pulſantes, fidibus canentes:*] of ψάλλω, wie, ſoomtim alon, and ſoomtim wit *chordas,* ſignifyet to play on a ſtring-inſtrument : as *Plutarch .n Pericl.* ψηθς τὸν ὑἱὸν επιτερπῶς ἐν τ̣ῆ πότε ψήλαρτι. And *Ariſt. Probl. ſect.* 15 *queſt.* 40. *Sub poſtremam cantilenam Pſallunt : & ibid. queſt.* 43. *Si quis, cum Neten pulſaverit, &c.* Of dis woord is derived ψαλμὸς, [*fidium cantus, vel carmen fidibus cantatum* :] also ψάλτης & ψαλτρία, *qui & quæ fidibus ſcit :* and ψαλτήριον *Pſalterium, qnod pſallitur. Athenæus l.* 14.

** Qui ſuaviter
in Compotatione
fides tetigit.*

(b) *Chorus eſt propriè multitudo Canentium. Iſid. l.* 1. *c.* 3.

(c) *Carmina quæcunq; in laudem Dei dicuntur, Hymni vocantur.* I *ſid. l.* 1 *c.* 6.

(d) (e) *Inter Reſponſorias & Antiphonas hoc differt ; quod in Reſponſoriis unus verſum dicit : in Antiphonis autem verſibus alternant Chori. Iſidorus, Originum lib.* 6 *c.* 19.

(f) Deſ *Reſponſori*s and *Antiphona*s, dœ by demſelvs ſeverally mak a Solemn Harmoni : but Boad uſed *alternatim* in de ſam Hymn, or oder Spiritual Song, ar mer Solenn ; and fit for de moſt Solemn Servic, upon de moſt Solemn Feſtivals, or oder eztraordinari Solemn Occaſions.

CAP. 2. § 3. *Of Objections* againſt *Solemn* Єyrє-*Muſik.*

DIs holy Ordinanc of God, inſtituted for his divin ſervic and woorſhip, having de ſam foundation wit oder points of Kriſtian Religion, [de Evidenc of Gods
Woord,

Wœrd, and de Practic' of his Eyre,] I ſœld' marveil dat any
reaſonable man wœld' diſallow ; wer' it not dat a ſetled pre-
judic', (dow'g againſt a cleer' tru'd) grounded on'ly upon
probable *Objections*, is yet hardly remœved. For I am out of
doubt, it is not obſtinat' malic', but zelous ignoranc', dat
dœ'd oppoſ' it.

It is objected, dat exqiſit' Muſik dœ'd not furder but
hinder de Servic' of God ; wil' de people liſtening to de
pleaſantnes of de *Not'*, regard not de matter of de *Ditti* :
and ſo go' away no wit edifyed by de Pſalm dat is ſo tuned.
† St. *Auguſtin'* was of an oder mind' : wer' ſpeaking of his
Baptizing at *Millain*, hee ſai' to God, *O how I wept at dy
Hymns and Songs, bæing vehemently mœved wit de voices of dy ſwæt'-ſounding Eyre. Doſ' Voices did perc'
min' ear's, and dy tru'd diſtilled into min' heart : and der'-
by was inflamed in mæ a lœv of Pieti : de tears trickled
doun, and wit dem I was in a happy caſ'.

bant auribus meis, & eliquabatur veritas tua in cor meum : & ex eâ æſtuabat in me
affectus pietatis, & currebant lachrymæ, & bene mihi erat cum eis-

† In an oder plac' indæd', (aldow'g hæ acknowledg dat
our mind's ar mor' religiouſly & mor' fervently mœved wit
holy wœrds wen dey ar ſung wit ſwæt' & artificial Voices,
dan wen dey ar not ſo ſung) finding himſelf ſœmtim'

dum ipſis ſanctis dictis religioſius & ardentius ſentio moveri animos noſtros in flammam
pietatis, cum ita (i. ſuavi & artificioſa voce : ut ſupra) cantantur ; quam ſi non ita can-
tarentur ; & omnes affectus ſpiritus noſtri, pro ſuavi diverſitote, habere proprios modos
in voce atq; cantu, quorum neſcio qua occulta familiaritate excitentur. Sed delectatio carnis
meæ ſæpe me fallit. &c. Aliquando hanc fallaciam immoderatius cavens, erro nimiâ ſeve-
ritate, ut melos omne cantilenarum ſuavium, quibus Davidicum Pſalterium frequentatur,
ab auribus meis removeri velim, atq; ipſius eccleſiæ. (& quæ ſequuntur de more Alex-
andrino) Verumtamen cum reminiſcor lachrymas meas, quas ſudi ad cantus Eccleſiæ
tuæ, in primordiis recuperatæ fidei meæ ; & nunc ipſe commoveor, non cantu ſed rebus
quæ cantantur. Cum liquida voce & convenientiſſima modulatione cantantur ; magnam
inſtituti hujus utilitatem rurſus agnoſco : magiſq; adducor Cantandi conſuetudinem appro-
bare in Eccleſia : ut per oblectamenta aurium infirmior animus in affectum pietatis aſſurgat.
Our Eyre der'for' knowing de uſ' of bod', dœ'd in deir du' tim' uſ' dem bod'.
De daily portions of de Pſalms ar ſung after de plain manner of *Alexandria* ; and
de ſingle ſelected Hymns, Pſalms, and Songs, after de mor' exqiſit' manner of
Millain.

too muc deligted wit ðe ſweet diverſiti of ðe Muſik, hæ
falleꝫ into a diſput wit himſelf : and at firſt hee ſeemeꝫ to
affeꝫt ðe manner of *Alexandria :* werc ðe Pſalms werc tuned
wit ſo litle altering of ðe Voicc, ðat ðey ſæmed raðer to
bæ red ðan ſung : but recollecting himſelf, hæ conſeſſeꝫ
as beforc : But wen I remember ðe tears wtc I poured
foort at ðe Songs of ðy Ꞓyrc, I am now alſo mooved wit
ðem: and am morc induced to approovc ðe cuſtom of Singing
in ðe Ꞓyrc ; ðat by ðe deligt of ðe ears, ðe weaker ſpirit
may bæ raiſed up to ðe loov of pieti.

* In Præfat. ad
Pſalmos.

To ðis purpoſc, but morc reſolutcly, ſpeakeꝫ * St. *Baſil* :
Delectabiles cantionum modulos documentis ſuis permiſcuit ſpiritus ſanctus ; ut dum ſuavitate & gratiâ mulcetur auditus, utilitatem illam percipiamus clàm, quæ ex ſermonibus iſtis enaſcitur.

Yea and St. *Auguſtine* likcwiſc in his Prolog unto ðe
Pſalms, conſenting wit St. *Baſil* (as his Interpreter) docc
likcwiſc abſolutcly determin : *Spiritus ſanctus delectabilibus
modulis cantilenæ, vim ſuæ doctrinæ permiſcuit ; ut dum ſuavitate carminis mulcetur auditus, divini ſermonis utilitas pariter inſeratur.*

Object. 2.
† John 4. 24.
Reſp.

Yea, but ðe truc woorſip of God docꝫ not conſiſt in ðeſc
outward Graces and ornaments : † *God is a Spirit : and ðey
ðat woorſip him muſt woorſip him in ſpirit and in truc:* Truc :
& ðercforc ðey ðat woorſiped God wit ðis outward ſervicc,
and not wit ðe Spirit, ðeir ſervicc was not accpeted of him:

* C. 5. 23.

as himſelf profeſſeꝫ by ðe Propet * *Amos, Takc ðou away
from mee ðe noiz of ðy ſongs, for I will not hear ðe melodi of ðy
viols.* But ſall wæ ſay, or can wæ ꞇink, ðat ðoſc holy men
of God [*David, Solomon, Ezekiah, Nehemiah,* and ðeir devout companics] wic werc moſt exqiſit in ðeir Muſik, did
not worſip God in Spirit ? *Abſit.* Yea raðer, becaus ðey
woorſiped in Spirit, ðercforc ðey added ðis outward ſervicc : becaus *Davids* hart was reddy, ðercforc his tung and

† Pſal. 108.

his inſtruments werc reddy alſo, to prais ðe Lord. † *O Cod
my hart is reddy, my hart is reddy :* it followeꝫ, *I will ſing
and giv prais wit ðe beſt member ðat I havc. Awokc Pſalteri and
Harp : J my ſelf will awakc rigt ercly.*

Wel :

Wel: bææ it ſo, ꝺat ꝺey wie ſerv God wiꞇ ꝺis outward woorſip, may neverꝺeles woorſip him in Spirit: ꝺe Apoſtle, wer hææ ſpeakeꞇ againſt ꝺe ſervic of God in an unknown tung, not on'ly requireꞇ ꝺe Spirit, but wil hav ꝺe Underſtanding to go wiꞇ it. * *I will ſing* (ſayꞇ he) *wiꞇ ꝺe Spirit, and I wil ſing wiꞇ ꝺe Underſtanding alſo.* Nou our own moꝺer tung ſung in ꝺis exqiſit Muſik, of Diſcant and Inſtruments, is unto us an unknown tung: wee doo not underſtand it. If you doo not; conſider wer ꝺe fault is. Ꝺe Princes, ꝺe Levit's, and ꝺe People of God in ꝺeir great aſſembli's, amid ꝺe ful Symponi, and loud noiꞁ of many Inſtruments, did ſing wiꞇ underſtanding: els woolꝺ not ꝺeir Servic hav been ſo acceptable to ꝺe Lord, as it was. And if ꝺis coolꝺ not bææ; in vain did ꝺe Auꞇor of ꝺis heavenly harmoni reqir ꝺe people to ſing wiꞇ underſtanding: wer hee ſayꞇ, † *God in ꝺe King of all ꝺe earꞇ: ſing yee praiſes wiꞇ underſtanding.* Ꝺe fault ꝺen muſt bææ in your ſelvs. For all ꝺoſ *Anſwers* in ꝺe *Decalog* and *Litani*, wiꞇ oꝺers, (lik ꝺat moſt ſolemn * *Hymnidion* wie drew doun ꝺe glorious preſenc of God) ar known and familiar: and ſo ar ꝺe ordinary Anꞇems, as *Te Deum, Magnificat,* &c. And for ꝺe reſt, ſoomtim on part ſingeꞇ ſingle, wie is eaſily underſtood: and wen ꝺe Qir ſingeꞇ, you hav ꝺe help of ſoom ſpecial treatable voic, (wer unto you may attend) and of ꝺe Repeꞇ's, wie at ꝺe ſecond or ꞇird tim, mak ꝺat plain, wie at ꝺe firſt was not obſerved. And if ꝺeſ helps doo not ſuffic for ꝺe underſtanding of ꝺem; ꝺey ꝺat can read may know them by book, and ꝺey ꝺat cannot, may learn ꝺem by harꞇ: and ſo go along wiꞇ ꝺe Qir ꝺat ſingeꞇ ꝺem. And indæꝺ, wiꞇout ſue help's, neiꝺer can our plain Mæꞇerpſalms bææ underſtood, wen ꝺey ar ſung in ꝺe Ꞇyrꬲ: ꝺe multitud of voices ſo confounding ꝺe woords, ꝺat a good ear liſtening attentiv'ly can ſeldom apprehend ꝺem.

I, but ꝺowg ꝺe Congregation, by ꝺis means, may underſtand waꞇ is ſung, and ſo go along in harꞇ wiꞇ ꝺe Qir; yet can ꝺey not join wiꞇ ꝺem in ꝺeir exqiſit Muſik. No mor can ꝺe wol Congregation join wiꞇ ꝺe Singers of ꝺis plainſong. For ſoom ꝺat hav good mind's, hav not good voices, and

and ſoom dat hav͛ voices, cannot read : ſoom dat can read, cannot ſing, and ſoom can neider read nor ſing. All wi є ar de greateſt part of moſt͛ Congregations. And wy ſoold͛ it bæ mor͛ reqiſit͛, dat all de aſſembly ſoold͛ joyn wit de Qir͛ in de artificial ſinging of deir Hymns and Antems ; dan wit de Prieſt in plain reading or ſaying of de Leſſons, Prayers, and oder part͛s of de *Liturgi* ; or de prayer of de Prea-er befor͛ and after de Sermon? Or wy ſoold͛ not wæ tink dat de Pſalms and Hymns and ſpirituall Songs, ſung by a Kriſtian Qir͛ (de devout harts of de people concurring) bæ nou as acceptable to de Lord, as wen dey wer͛ ſung by de Prieſts and Levits, wit de harty devotion of deir Congregation? For it cannot bæ dat de common people (dowg dey wer͛ to join wit de Prieſts and Levits in ſpirit, and underſtanding of de matter) coold͛ join wit dem in de artificial tuning of deir Songs: except it wer͛ only of ſoom ſort Verſicles, wi є migt eaſily bæ learned by hart: as that iterated Epiſtrope *Pſ.136.*(ſung wit miraculous effeċt 2 Kr.5.13.)and dat Reſpons of de Propetes *Miriam* and hir company, unto de ſong of *Moſes* and de eildren of Iſrael. *Exod.* 15. 21.

But if you wil need͛s partak͛ wit de Muſical Qir͛, in de Ton͛s alſo of deir harmonious Melodi͛s ; den learn to Sing: wi є is an ingenuous Qaliti, fit, in * divers reſpeċts, for all ſu є as ar capable of it.

* *Vid. c. 3. § 2.*

Wer͛for͛ (de premiſſes conſidered) dey wi є wil hav͛, for deir own ſolac͛, de moſt curious Muſik bot͛ of voic, and inſtruments ; and wil allou for de ſervic͛ of God, on͛ly a litle poor͛ plain-ſong, and dat oftim͛s corrupted and diſgraced wit harſ diſcords, untun͛able voices, and oder lik͛ Muſik-ſolœciſms, (wi є cannot but bæ tedious and offenſiv͛, even to de meaneſt and ſimpleſt of de multitud͛) ar lik͛ (mæ tinks)doſ͛ irreligious Sacrificers, dat offered to God de † halt and de blind͛ ; and kept de faireſt and de fatteſt of de cattail for demſelvs.

† *Deut.* 15. 21.

Object. 5.
Reſp.

But you wil ſay dis artificial Muſik, ſo mu є commended, cannot bæ had in all Cyr ees. Tru͛ : and der͛for͛ as in ſoom tim͛s, every wer͛; ſo at all tim͛s, ſoom wer͛, men muſt bæ content wit plain-ſong, eider in Part͛s, or (wi є is mor͛ defeċtiv͛,)

defeᶜtivᶜ) all in onᶜ tunᶜ : and yet, no doubt, if ðey ſing wiꞇ
ðe ſpirit, and wiꞇ ðe underſtanding, hæ ðat accepted of ðe
poorᶜ widdowᶜs miꞇᶜ, wil accept of ðeir good endevours,
according to ðat ðey havᶜ, and not according to ðat ðey
havᶜ not. But it behooveꞇ us hærᶜin to avoid all Indecenciᶜ
and Diſorder, and to aim at Perfeᶜtion in ðis kindᶜ alſo : be-
caus, as St. *Auguſtinᶜ* noteꞇ, * *In choro cantantium quiſquis*   * In Pſal. 149.
voce diſcrepaverit, offendit auditum, & perturbat chorum. For   ☜
wiᶜ purpoſᶜ it werᶜ to bæ wiſed, ðat every Єyrє had onᶜ
skilful Levitᶜ at ðe leaſt, to inſtruᶜt and direᶜt ðe moſtᶜ Muſical and beſt Capacitiᶜs, in ðe ſeveral partᶜs of Song, according to ðe ſeveral piꞇees of ðeir voices : ðe wiᶜ may bæ
Guidᶜs unto ðe reſt : ðat ſo, even in ðeſᶜ plain Dorik tunᶜs,
ðey may ſing wiꞇ a gracᶜ to ðe Lord in ðeir harts ; as
becomeꞇ Saints in ðe hous of God, †werᶜ all ꞇings foldᶜ   † 1 Cor. 14. 40.
bæ doon decently and in order.

C. 2 § 4.   *Of ðe special Uſes of Divinᶜ Muſik.*

DE Special Uſes of Divinᶜ Muſik ar many : as in Ac-
knowledging of Gods woonderful woorks, and in
Praiſing his holy Namᶜ : in declaring his Merciᶜs towards
us, and in Thankſgiving to him for ðem ; in Confeſſion,
in Prayer, in Complaint, in Exhortation, Inſtruᶜtion,
and Conſolation. Of * all wiᶜ, wiꞇ oðers, you havᶜ ſun-   * *Vide* ☞ §1.
dry Precedents in ðe devout *Pſalms* of *David.* As *Pſal.*
10. wiᶜ is an earneſt Complaint of ðe Pridᶜ, Subtilti,
and Preſumption of ðe ungodly Oppreſſor : wiꞇ a Prayer
for Deliveranc. *Pſal.* 1, 11, and 15. wiᶜ ar mærᶜly In-
ſtruᶜtions. *Pſal.* 17. wiᶜ is a Prayer for ðe Rigꞇ, for Con-
ſtanci, and for Mercy : alſo a Complaint of ðe Crueltı ‘and
Proſperiti of his enimiᶜs, wiꞇ Prayer to diſapoint ðem,
and wiꞇ Comfort. *Pſal.* 27. wiᶜ is a confident Conſolation, wiꞇ Prayer. *Pſal.* 37. wiᶜ is ful of Comforting In-
ſtruᶜtions, and Exhortations, variouſly entermedled.
Pſal. 49. wiᶜ is an earneſt Reproofᶜ of ðe Covetous, and
Proud, ſewing ðeir vaniti and deſtruᶜtion : wiꞇ a Comfort
to ðe godly. *Pſal.* 51. wiᶜ is a Prayer, Confeſſion, Com-

fort, Profeſſion of Repentancᶜ, and Amendment of life.
Pſal. 86. wie is a Prayer for Comfort and Mercy, wit
Prais and Thankſ-giving to God for his Greatnes and
Goodnes. *Pſal.* 94. wie is a Complaint againſt ðe wic-
ked for ðeir Tyranny, and a Reprooᶠ of ðeir folli, wit a
Comfort to ðe Righteous. *Pſal.* 103. wie is a Prais of
God for many benefits, an Acknowledgment of his Mercy,
Mans frailti, Gods eterniti, and an Exhortation to his ſervants to Prais him. *Pſal.* 104. wie is a Prais of God for his
Mercy and Wiſdom in Creating and Governing ðe world,
wit an orderly Deſcription of his cief woorks. *Pſal.* 107.
wie is an excellent Exhortation unto ðe people to Prais
God: grounded upon træ points [ðeir Miſeri, ðeir Repentancᶜ, and ðeir Deliverancᶜ:] wie træ ar ſucceſſivly iterated: and ðat wit two *Epiſtropeᶜs Sententiæ,* (alternly re-
petᶜed 4 timᶜs) onᶜ including ðeir Repentancᶜ and Deliverancᶜ, and ðe oðer a Paƭetical *Exponeſis* inciting to prais
God for his goodnes. All wie is concluded wit ðe recital
of divers oðer Bleſſings, as furder Motivᶜs to prais God.
And *Pſal.* 136. wie is an Exhortation to tank God for his
woorks, [general, and ſpecial:] wie ar ðerᶜ recited, wit
ðat perpetuated Epiſtrope of Gods perpetual Mercy, [ðe
ſolᶜ fountain boᵗ ᶜof his woorks, and of our tankſ-giving.]

Extraordinari
uſes of divinᵗ
Muſik.

Beſidᶜs ðeſᶜ Ordinari ſpecial Uſes of Divinᶜ Muſik, wee
read of certain Extraordinari: werby ſtrangᶜ tings werᶜ
browgt to paſ, boᵗᶜ toucing ðe Evil and ðe Good Spirit.
Toucing ðe Evil Spirit, in ðat it was uſed for ðe qiéting
of Men poſſeſſed, and for ðe expulſing of ðe foul fiend:

* 1 Sam.16.23.

wie ting * *David* wrowgt wit his Harp, wen ðe evil Spirit
trubbled *Saul.* And ðat ðis was noᶜ ſtrangᶜ ting in ðoſᶜ
days, appæret by ðe ſuddain unanimous adviſᶜ of *Sauls*

† V. 16.

ſervants. † *Let our Lord* (ſay ðey) *non command ðy ſervants
wie ar beforᶜ ðee, to ſeekᶜ out a man wo is a cunning Player on an
Harp: and it ſall coom to paſ (* wen ðe evil Spirit from God is

(a)

upon ðee,) ðat hæ ſall play wit his hand, and ƭou ſalt bæ wel (a).
And for ðe Good Spirit, ðe likᶜ Muſik was uſed by ðe Propets, ðerᶜby (as it ſæmet) to excitᶜ a ſpecial *Entuſiaſm,*

* 2 Kings 6. 3.
2. &c.

or divinᶜ Rapturᶜ for ſoom preſent Oracle. * So wen *Eliſa*
was

was besowgt to propeciᶜ unto de tree Kings, wat ſooldᶜ bee de ſucceſ of deir battail againſt *Moab* ; beforᶜ hee coldᶜ giv dem any anſwer, hee called for a Minſtrel : and wilᶜ de Minſtrel play'd; (ſayt deText) de hand of de Lord camᶜ upon him : and bee propecyed victori unto dem ; and witall, glad tidings of plenty of water, wiє den dey wanted. So did de Propets wiє *Saul* met, according to de prediction of *Samuel.* † It ſall ecom to paſ, wen dou art ecom to de Citti, dat dou ſalt meetᶜ a coompani of Propets, cooming down from de big placᶜ ; wit a Pſalteri, and a Tabret, and a Pipᶜ, and a Harp beforᶜ dem, and dey ſall propeci. And de Spirit of de Lord will ecom upon dee, and dou ſalt propeci wit dem, and ſalt bee turned into an oder man. And dat oder Propets afterward, did makᶜ de likᶜ uſᶜ of Inſtruments, appæret in de endᶜ of *Habakkuk* : werᶜ hee directet his Propeci unto de cief Muſician on his * Neginot.

† 1 *Sam.* 10. 5.

* Or *String Inſtruments.*

(a) Dis pouer of Muſik againſt evil ſpirits, † *Luter* ſeemet to tink dat it doєt ſtil remain. *Scimus* (ſayt hee) *Muſicam Dæmonibus etiam inviſam & intolerabilem eſſe :* and derupon concludet, *Plane judico, nec pudet aſſerere, poſt Theologiam eſſe nullam Artem, quæ poſſit Muſice æquari.* I verily tink, and am not aſamed to ſay, dat after Diviniti, derᶜ is no Art dat can bee compared unto Muſik.

† In an Epiſtle to *Senfelius Muſicus,* cited by *Sethus Calviſius.*

LIB. II. CAP. II. §V.

An *Apoſtrophe* to our Levitᶜs.

UNto de perfecting of a Cyrє-ſong, de perfection of tree pious Artiſts is neceſſari : [de † Poet, de Compoſer, and de Singer :] de Poet for making de Ditti : de Compoſer, for fitting de Notᶜ unto it : and de Singers for uttering dem bodᶜ togeder in de Aſſembly.

In de oldᶜ Cyrє of de Juᶜs, de cief Poet (at ſuchᶜ timᶜ as Divinᶜ Muſik did floorifᶜ moſt) was dat holy Propet and King, de beloved of God : de Compoſers werᶜ de cief Muſicians [*Aſap, Heman,* and *Jedutun*] filled, as doſᶜ curious woorkmen [*Bezaleel* and *Aholiab*] wit de ſpirit of God: de Singers werᶜ * *Kenaniah* [Maſter of de Song,] and his bredren de Levitᶜs, † inſtructed and * ſanctifyed to de woork.

† *Poeta* of ποιειν [*facere*] to makᶜ: & derᶜforᶜ de Nort callet him a *Maker,* becaus hee maket Verſes.

* 1 *Kro.* 15. 27.
† 1 *Kron* 25. 7.
* 2 *Kron.* 29. 34

All wie concurring in deir perfection, mad⁶ up dat heavenly Harmoni, so pleasing unto almigty God.

In our Eyre, de holy Poet is de sam⁶ : wee hav⁶ also de Psalms of David, wit oder spiritual Songs, endited by Saints and holy men of God : our Composers [eief Musicians bot⁶ on *Nehiloth* and *Neginoth*] troog deir rar⁶ wit, Art, and Practic⁶, ar nou grown to dat perfection, dat, if it wer⁶ possible, dey migt exceed⁶ even *Asaph, Heman*, or *Jeduthun* : and for our Canters and Singing-men, deir skil in all sorts of Musik is most⁶ complet⁶ : deir Voices and Instruments (fitting all Part⁶s) as good as Natur⁶ and Art can mak⁶ : dat noting is nou wanting in our Qir⁶s ; if, witall, dey bee adorned wit sue outward and inward Graces, as becoom dos⁶ dat sing de Lords Songs in his holy Temple. De wie wil⁶ I reqir⁶, I woold⁶ not hav⁶ dem tink, dat I doo⁶ so mue exhort dem to dat dey doo⁶ not ; as commend dem for dat dey doo⁶: according to dat of de Poet,

Ovid Trist. l. 5. in fine. *Qui monet ut facias quod jam facis, ipse monendo*
                                     Laudat, & hortatu comprobat acta suo.

First der⁶for⁶ let de wol⁶ Qir⁶ endevour so to moderat⁶ deir Voices, dat deir woords may bee plainly heard and understood of de Congregation : so dat, if not in Art, yet in Hart dey may go⁶ along wit dem in lik⁶ devotion. Too mue qeint Division, too mue faking and qavering of de Not⁶s, all harf straining of de Voices beyond deir naturall pite, as dey ar odious and offensiv⁶ to de ear ; so doo⁶ dey droun de rigt sound of de woords, and der⁶by depriv⁶ de Hearers of de sens and meaning der⁶of. De rud⁶nes and vaniti of dos⁶ *Stentorian* Vociferations, by soom too mue affected, de *Poet dus taxet in de Singers of his ag⁶.

     Cur tantis, delubra, boum mugitibus imples ?
     Tune Deum tali credis placare tumultu ?

To de discreet⁶ moderating of deir Voices, dey foold⁶ ad all oder outward Decenci. For all idle and car⁶les gestur⁶, all ilfavoured distorting and disfiguring of de countenanc⁶, all foul, fantastik, and uncoomly attir⁶, and watsoever

ever dœ͗t not beſæm͗ grav͗ and ſober Miniſters of God in
his Hous, is but a diſgrac͗ to de Divin͗ Servic͗, and a
ſcandal to de Congregation. But, abœv all ꞇings, let dem bæ
adorned wiꞇ de inward beawti of holines : wer͗ unto de
Pſalmiſt earneſtly exhorteꞇ. †O wœſip de Lord in de beawti of †Pſal. 96.
Holines. For *Holines beœmeꞇ his hous for ever.* Dis counſel of * Pſal. 93.
dat gœd King [de ſacred Singers Lord and Maſter] did your
Predeceſſors [de old͗ Levit͗s] religiouſly obſerv: Wo wen
dey cam͗ to appær͗ befor͗ de Lord, and to perform deir ſo-
lemn ſervic͗ in his Sanctuari ; † de Text ſayꞇ, dat dey wer͗ † 2 Kron. 29. 34.
ſanctifyed to de wœrk : and dat dey wer͗ mor͗ holy dan de
Prieſts, * wom dey ſerved : wiꞇ mad͗ deir ſwæt͗ Singing *1 Kron. 23. 28.
to bæ as a ſwæt͗-ſmelling Sacrific͗ unto de Lord.

And der͗for͗ (dat de Pſalmodi of Kriſtians, in de Goſ-
pel, migt bæ no les acceptable unto God ; dan de devout
Songs of de Ju͗s, in de Law) de Ꞓyr͗ of Kriſt͗ haꞇ ever
bæn car͗ful, dat all ꞇings in dis Divin͗ duti migt bæ dœn,
not on͗ly decently and in order, as befor͗ men ; but alſo religiouſly, and piouſly, as in de ſigt of God. † Iſidor͗, for † Lib. 2. c. 12.
de better performanc͗ of dis excellent Servic͗, reqireꞇ, in
de Singers, excellenci boꞇ͗ of Voic͗ and Art. *Pſalmiſtam*
& voce & Arte præclarum illuſtremq; eſſe oportet : ita ut ad ob-
lectamenta dulcedinis animos incitet Auditorum. Vox autem
ejus non aſpera, non rauca, vel diſſonans ; ſed canora erit, ſuavis,
atq; liquida : habens ſonum & melodiam ſanctæ religioni congru-
entem. *De ſixt Council of *Conſtantinople* ſpeakeꞇ to dis * Canon 75.
purpoſ͗ : reqiring mor͗over zelous attention, and com-
punction of Hart. *Eos qui in Eccleſia ad Pſallendum acce-*
dunt, volumus nec inordinatis Vociferationibus uti, & naturam
ad clamorem urgere ; nec aliquid eorum quæ Eccleſiæ non conveni-
unt, & apta non ſunt, adſciſcere : ſed cum magna attentione &
compunctione, Pſalmodias Deo, qui eſt occultorum inſpector, of-
ferre. And de † Councel of *Aquiſgran* commandeꞇ all Sing- † Canon 137.
ers not to pollut͗ de Skil, givn dem by God, wiꞇ vicious
living ; but to adorn it wiꞇ vertu͗ and holines. *Studendum*
ſummopere Cantoribus eſt, ne donum ſibi Divinitus collatum vi-
tiis fœdent, ſed potius illud humilitate, caſtitate, ſobrietate, &
cæteris ſanctarum virtutum ornamentis exornent : quorum Melo-
dia

dia animos populi circumſtantis, ad memoriam amoremq; cœleſti-
um, non ſolùm ſublimitate Verborum, ſed etiam ſuavitate Sono-
rum, quæ dicuntur, erigat. And St. *Hierom* upon deſᶜ woords

* C.5, 19.

of đe Epiſtle to đe *Epheſ.* [* *Cantantes & Pſallentes in Cordi-*
bus veſtris Domino, Singing and making Melodi to đe Lord
in your Harts] exhortet đus : *Audiant hæc adoleſcentes : au-*
diant bi, quibus in Eccleſia eſt Pſallendi officium, Deo non voce

† Decret. Diſ-
tinct. 92.

tintium, ſed corde cantandum. Wiᴇ woords werᶜ ſincᶜ taken
into đe † *Canon : werᶜ* đey ar expreſſed in đe *Gloſ* by dis
oldᶜ Diſtich :

> *Non Vox ſed Votum, non Muſica Chordula ſed Cor,*
> 　*Non Clamans ſed Amans, cantat in aure Dei.*

Not Voicᶜ but Vou, Harts zelᶜ not Muſiks String;
Loov not loud criᶜ, in đ'ear of G o d dooᶜᴇ ſing.

And đerforᶜ it is not meetᶜ đat any vulgar profanᶜ Pi-
pers (watſoever đeir skil bæ) ſooldᶜ bæ ſuffered, in
đeir diſcordant and irregular Habit, to barᶜ a Partᶜ in dis
holy Action ; nor, *Uzza*-likᶜ, to put đeir hands to dis Ark
of God. But if, for Art and Vertuᶜ, đey ſall bæ towgt meetᶜ
for đe woork ; let đem firſt forgoᶜ đeir profanᶜ Profeſſion,
and bæ ordeined and alloued by Autoriti, beforᶜ đey preſumᶜ
to ſet a footᶜ in đe Qirᶜ : as is reqired by đat ancient *Canon :*

Decret. Diſt. 92.
* Cap. 15.

Non liceat in Pulpito Pſallere aut legere, niſi qui ab Epiſcopo ſunt
ordinati Lectores. Đe * Counſel of *Laodicea* commandet đe
ſamᶜ. *Quòd non oportet ampliùs præter eos qui regulariter Can-*
tores exiſtunt, qui & de codice canunt, alios in pulpitum conſcen-
dere, & in Eccleſia pſallere.

Đe *Simile* wiᴇ good *Tulli* borrowed from skilful Muſicians, Muſicians ſooldᶜ callengᶜ as đeir own, and apply it un-

* Offic. l. 1. ad
finem.

to đemſelvs. * *Ut in Fidibus aut in Tibijs, quamvis paululum*
diſcrepent, tamen id a Sciente animadverti ſolet ; ſic videndum
eſt in vita ne quid diſcrepet : vel multò etiam magis, quo major
& melior Actionum, quam Sonorum conceatus eſt. Đey đat đooᴇ
ſo eaſily obſerv, and abhor đe leaſt Diſcordancᶜ in Muſik
ſooldᶜ as wel diſcern and deteſt all Diſcordancᶜ in Lifᶜ : and
đat ſo muᴇ đe morᶜ, by hou muᴇ đe concent of Actions is
greater

greater and better, đan đe concent of Sounds: lest đat bee justly objected against đem; † *Dis people draweŧ nig unto mee wiŧ đeir Mouŧ, and honoureŧ mee wiŧ đeir Lips; but đeir Hart is far from mee.* † *Mat.* 15. 8.

Đes' fair Beawti's of body and mind', đes' outward and inward Graces, ar your ɛief Ɛyrɛ-ornaments: wiŧout wiɛ your most exqisit' and solemn Servic', wil pleas neiđer God nor godly men: and wiŧ wiɛ, I know not wy your solemn Devotions, assisted wiŧ đe Pieti of a zelous Congregation, ʃoold' not bee as acceptable to almigti God in his holy Ɛyrɛ, as đat of đe Priests, and Levit's, and People of đe Ju's was in đe Temple, * wen đe glori of đe Lord' filled đe hous of God. Put đem on đer'for' (beloved) wiŧ fear and reverenc': and, being onc' put on, let đem never bee put off again; until you ɛang' đem for đos' † wit' rob's, wer'-wiŧ đe great multitud' of đem đat praised God is clođed, (having Palms in đeir hands) befor' đe Thron' and befor' đe Lam. Đen ʃall your Prayers ascend as đe Incens, and your Songs perc' đe higest heavens: đen ʃall you ty' đe ears of đe people to your tungs, and đeir harts and affections to your holy harmoni's: đen ʃall God and đe King bless you, and you hav' caus to bless God and đe King: đen ʃall you mak' your selvs fit to sing, wiŧ đe Saints and Angels in heaven, * *Alleluja's* unto đe Lord God omnipotent: and † to hear đe voic' of đe Harpers harping wiŧ đeir Harps; wos' Song no man can learn, but đey đat ar redeemed from đe earŧ.

* 2 *Kron.* 5. 13. & 14.

† *Revel.* 7. 9.

* *Revel. c.* 19. 6.

† *Ibid. c.* 14. *v.* 2. & 3.

CAP. III. § I.

Of đe allouanc' of Civil Musik, and đe Us' đer'of in general.

And suɛ is đe first and ɛief Us' of Musik in đe Servic' of God. Đe second and civil Us' is for đe Solac' of Men. Đe wiɛ as it is agreeable unto Natur'; so is it allowed by God, as a temporal blessing, to his people.

To

I.

* Ariſtotle.
Polit. l. 8. c. 5.

To ðe firſt point concerning Natur⁴, no man can giv better teſtimoni, ðan ðat * grand Secretari of Natur⁴ : *Habet Muſica naturalem voluptatem, per quam illius uſus cunctis ætatibus, cunctiſq; moribus eſt acceptus.* And again,

† *Ibidem.*

† *Congruit autem Naturæ hujuſmodi diſciplina. Muſica enim ex his eſt, quæ ſunt jucunda ſecundùm Naturam. Et videtur cognatio quædam eſſe nobis cum harmoniis & rhythmis. Quapropter multi ſapientum dixere, alii quidem animum eſſe harmoniam; alii vero habere harmoniam.* And in * an oðer plac⁴, *Quòd motibus*

* Problem. Sectione 19. quæſt. 38.

Naturalibus oblectari, a Natura omnibus datum eſt; numeris, modulis, canticis, deniq; omnibus concinendi generibus, oblectari omnes conſuevere. To ðis purpoſ⁴ ſpeaket † *Boetius : Nihil*

† *Lib. 1. c. 1.*

eſt tam proprium humanitati, quàm remitti dulcibus modis, aſtringiq; contrariis : idq; non modò ſeſe in ſingulis, vel ſtudiis vel ætatibus, tenet; verùm etiam per cuncta diffunditur ſtudia : & infantes, juvenes, nec non etiam ſenes, ita naturaliter affectu quodam ſpontaneo modie Muſicis adjunguntur; ut nulla omnino ſit ætas, quæ à cantilenæ dulcis delectatione ſejuncta ſit. And in ðe Concluding of ðe ſam⁴ Capter, *Ex his perſpicuè appareat, ita nobis Muſicam naturaliter eſſe conjunctam: ut eâ, ne, ſi velimus, carere poſſimus. Quocirca intendenda vis mentis eſt, ut id quod Naturâ eſt inſitum, Scientiâ quoq; poſſit comprehenſum tueri.* Muſik ðen bæing natural unto Mankind⁴, Not to bæ *animal Muſicum,* is Not to bæ *animal rationale.*

II.

To ðe ſecond point, [ðat Muſik is a ſpecial gift of God, wi⁴, among oðer worldly bleſſings, it hat pleaſed him in his wiſdom and mercy to ordein, for ðe Solac⁴ and deligt of ðe ſoons of men,] wæ hav⁴ ðe expreſ teſtimoni of his Word : wer⁴ hæ promiſet ðe fruition ðer⁴of to ðe godly, as a token of his favour, and a reward of ðeir weldoing; and treatenet ðe taking of ðe ſam⁴ away, from ðe ungodly, as a token of his diſpleaſur⁴, and a puniſment of ðeir revolting and diſobedienc⁴. Unto ðe Cyr⁴ of ðe Ju⁴s (wen ðey

* Oſe. 2. 15.

wer⁴ reconciled) hæ promiſet ðis token of his loov : *[Shæ ſall Sing as in ðe days of hir yut⁴, and as in ðe day wen ſæ cam⁴ up out of ðe land of Egypt :]* wer⁴as befor⁴, for ðeir Idolatri,

† *Ibid. V. 11.*

hæ treatenet, † *I wil caus all hir Mirt to ceas : hir Feaſt-days, hir Nu⁴-moon⁴s, and hir Sabbats, and all hir ſolemn Feaſts :* as
lik⁴wiſ⁴

likᶜwisᶜ for ðeir oppreſſing of ðe poorᶜ. * *I will turn your* * Amos 8. 10.
feaſts into mœrning ; and all your ſongs into lamentation. And
again, † *Becaus* ðey bavᶜ *transgreſſed* ðe *laws,* ᴄanged ðe *ordi-* † Iſai 24. 5.
nances, broken ðe *everlaſting covenant ; v. 6.* ðerᶜforᶜ haᵗ ðe *cᴕrs*
devoured ðe earᵗ, &c. v. 8. ðe mirᵗ of ðe *tabrets ceaſeᵗ,* ðe *noiz of*
ðem ðat *rejoyc* endeᵗ, ðe *joy of* ðe *harp ceaſeᵗ:* * aſ it waſ in ðe
timᶜ of *Judaſ Maccabæus,* ᴡᴇn, ðe *ſtori* ſayᵗ ðat * *Joy waſ* * 1 Mac. 6. 3.
v. 45.
taken frᴕm Jacob, and ðe *pipᶜ wit* ðe *harp ceaſed.* Werᶜaſ,
(ᴡen ðeir ſinz had browᵍt ðem into ſorrowful captiviti)
becauſ ðey repented, and praiſed ðe Lord, and. ſaid, † *O* † Jerem. 31. 7
* v. 11.
Lord ſavᶜ ðy *people* ðe *remnant of Iſrael* ; * ðerᶜforᶜ did hæ re-
dæmᶜ ðem from ðe hand of him ðat waſ ſtronger ðan ðey :
and alſo promiſed ðem, (togeðer wiᵗ oðer tokens of his
favour and gᴕdneſ) ðe ſolacᶜ of mirᵗ and Muſik again.
† ðerᶜforᶜ (ſayᵗ hæ) ðey *fall cᴕm and ſing in* ðe *heigt of Zion;* † v. 12.
and fall flow togeðer to ðe *gᴕdneſ of* ðe *Lord, for weat, and for*
Winᶜ, and for Oil ; &c. *and* ðey *fall not ſorrow avy morᶜ.*

It iſ truᶜ, ðat ðe wicked dᴕᶜ ſᴕmtimᶜ enjoy ðiſ deligt, aſ
ðey dᴕᶜ oðer temporal benefits : but it iſ to ðeir greater
condemnation : for a Woᶜ followeᵗ: *Woᶜ unto* ðem (*ſayᵗ* ðe * Eſai c. 5. 11.
Propet) ðat *riſᶜ up early in* ðe *morning,* ðat ðey *may follow ſtrong*
drink ; ðat *continuᶜ untilnigt, til winᶜ inflamᶜ* ðem : v.12. *And*
ðe *harp and* ðe *viol,* ðe *tabret and pipᶜ, and winᶜ, ar in* ðeir *feaſts :*
but ðey *regard not* ðe *wᴕrk of* ðe *Lord.* It followeᵗ, v. 13. ðerᶜforᶜ *my people ar gᴕn into captiviti.* &c. And again, † *Woᶜ to* ðem † Amos c. 6. 4.
ðat *lyᶜ upon beds of Ivori, and* ſtretᴄ ðemſelvſ *upon* ðeir *cou-ees :*
and eat ðe *Lams out of* ðe *flock, and* ðe *Calvſ out of* ðe *mids of* ðe
ſtall : v.5. ðat ᴄant *it to* ðe *ſound of* ðe *Viol, and invent to* ðemſelvſ
inſtruments of Muſik, likᶜ David : &c. v. 6. *but* ðey *ar not griev-*
ed for ðe *affliction of* Joſeph. It followeᵗ, v. 7. ðerᶜforᶜ *now*
fall ðey *gᴕᶜ captivᶜ,* &c.

Heerᶜunto agrœeᵗ ðe Complaint of *Job.* * ðey *ſend fœrᵗᶜ* * Iob 21. 11.
ðeir *litle onᶜs likᶜ a flock, and* ðeir ᴄildren *dancᶜ :* v.12. ðey
takᶜ ðe *Timbrel and Harp, and rejoicᶜ at* ðe *ſound of* ðe *Or-*
gan. It followeᵗ, v. 18. ðey *ar aſ ſtubbk beforᶜ* ðe *windᶜ, and*
aſ ᴄaf ðat ðe *ſtorm* ᴄarryeᵗ *away.*

CAP.

Q

Cap. III. §II.

Of ðe divers special Uses of Civil Musik.

ÐE divers forts of Musik ar hœrᶜ used, as ðe circumſtances of Timᶜ, Placᶜ, and Perſons, ſall reqirᶜ : ſœmtimᶜ ðe Vocal alonᶜ ; [eider Single, or in Set :] ſœmtimᶜ ðe Inſtrumental alonᶜ, [eider † Single, or in Set, or in Conſort :] and ſœmtimᶜ boðᶜ Vocal and Inſtrumental togeder. And all of ðem for divers ſpecial Uſes, according to ðe divers occaſions of ðe Muſik.

† *Eſpecially if ðe Inſtrument bee Sym̄ponon: Vide* (a) (b) *in notis ad c.* I. § I.

I

Onᶜ ſpecial Uſe is to eœrᶜ and comfort men, wilᶜ ðey ar buſy in ðeir painful Vocations ; ſo to deceiv ðeir tedious timᶜ : as ðe * Rhetorician obſerved : *Muſicam Natura ipſa videtur ad tolerandos faciliùs labores, velut muneri, nobis dediſſe.* Naturᶜ ſœmes to beſtow Muſik upon us as a favour, for ðe eaſier enduring of our labours. Ðis uſᶜ did dat Husbandman makᶜ of his Singing, at his wœrk abroad in ðe field.

* *Quintil. l.* I. *c.* 10.

† *Altà ſub rupe canit Frondator ad auras.*

And ðe Gœdwifᶜ at homᶜ about hir huſwifri.

† *Virg. Eclog.* I.

* *Interea longum cantu ſolata laborem,*
Arguto Conjux percurrit Pectine telas.

* *Georg.* I.

Ðis Uſᶜ dœᶻ ðe Poet copiouſly expreſ in ðe † field of *Achilles,* wrowᵹt by ðe Skil and Hand of *Vulcan :* wʰerᶜin, after ðe Uſᶜ of Muſik in Nuptial Ritᶜs, (*V. l.* I. *C.* I. (k) *in Notis*) ar expreſſed oðer Uſes ðerᶜof, in mens ſundry Vocations and Labours : as in Shepherding, Harveſting, Grapᶜgadering, &c. ——— Δύω δ' ἅμα ἕποντε Νομῆες

† *In fine Iliad* Σ.

Τερπόμενοι συερύξι. ———

Duo ſimul ſequebantur Paſtores, oblectantes ſeſe fiſtulis. & ibid.

Γαρθενικαὶ δὲ χ̓ ἠίθεοι ατιλὰ φρονέοντες, &c.

Virgines autem & Juvenes innupti, puerìliter ſapientes,
Textis in calathris portabant dulcem fructum.
Hos autem inter medios, puer cithara ſonora
Suaviter eitharizabat : chorda autem belle reſonabas
Tenellæ voci : hi autem pulſantes ſimul
Cantuq; ſibiloq; pedibus tripudiantes ſequebantur.

And

And ðus dœ' nou many mekanik Artificers; wiє, Single, (having good voices) yæld' sweet' Melodi, as wel to oðers, as to ðemselvs. But, in soom places, (wer' ar many woorkmen togeder) ðey mak' good Harmoni also, of 2, 3 or 4 voices: wiє sur'ly is pleasant enoug to ðe hearers.

Ðis Us' of Singing hat an oder benefit; causing, witall, healt of bodi: it bæing a special means to cleer' & strengten ðe Lungs: so ðat (wer' it not for on' ting) a Singing-man need' never fear ðe *Asma, Peripneumonia*, or *Consumption*: or any oder lik' affections of ðat vital part: wiє ar ðe deat of many Students. If unto ðis inward exercis' of ðe Lungs, wer' added ðe outward exercis' of ðe Lims; ðey sœld' find' it a means to increas ðeir healt and to cleer' ðeir wits, and so (as † *Plato* speaket) to mak' ðem perfect Musicians. *Eum igitur qui Gymnasticam cum Musica pulchrè miscet, & moderatè hæc animo adhibet, rectissimè perfectum quendam Musicum diceremus.* Ðe example of his most' wis' Master confirmet ðe sam': * wo to his Musik, for his exercis', added Dancing. *Socrati exercitatio corporis non injucunda erat Saltatio.*

An oder Special us' of Musik is to recreat' ðe mind's of industrious men, wen ðey ar nou wearyed wit labour, car', or studdi: as ðe Pilosoper advises: † *Musica Medicina est molestiæ illius, quæ per labores suscipitur.*

* Ðus, in old tim', wit singing and wit playing upon string-instruments, did ðe wis' and learned Pytagoreans, after intentiv' studdi's, reviv' ðeir spirits: *Pythagorei mentes suas à cogitationum intentione, cantu fidibusq; ad tranquillitatem traducere sunt soliti.* According to wiє example, many of our hard Students dœ' nou soomtim' ingenuously solac' and refres ðemselvs, eider wit Instrument [† symponon] alon', or wit Voic' and Instrument, or wit a Set of Instruments, or wit a Consort, or (wer' ðer' is a ful Qir') wit complet' Vocal Musik, artificially set, and artificially sung in Part's; (wiє dœ't far exceed' all Instrumental, even ðat wiє is most excellent in his kind') and ðat eider alon'; or wit Instruments too: wiє must næd's bæ best; unles ðe Instruments droun ðe Voices, or ðeir Ditti. *Vide C.1.§3.*

† *De Repub.l.3.*

* *Plutarch. de sanitate tuenda.*

II.

† *Polit.l.8. c.5*

* *Tusc. q. l.4. in initio.*

† *Vide* (a) (b) *in Notis ad c.1.§1.*

But dis uſ of Muſik is moſt ſeaſonable in de tim of
Feaſting : * ᵬen men meet togeder to bœ merry, and to
enjoy de fruit of deir labours : wiꞔ is de gift of Goᴅ.
And der for ſay de † Princ of Phyſicians, not to havꞔa
Harp or oder likꞔ Inſtrument at a Feaſt, was accounted a
very baſ ting. *Abeſſe à convivio lyram, vel id genus aliud,
turpiſſimum cenſebatur.* To him agreeꞔ de * Princ of Poets,

Μολπη ορχηςυϛε τα ῥδ τ' αναθηματα δαιτος
Cantuſq; & choreæ dulcis donaria cœnæ.

and again;

†Ου ῥδ εγωγε τι φημι τελος χαριεϛερον ειναι,
'Η, οταν ευφροσυνη μ εχη κτι δημον απαντα :
Δαιτυμονες, δ'ανα δοματ' ακυαζωντα αοιδ͂ε
'Ημενοι εξειης. —— ——

*Non enim ego quippiam puto magis gratum eſſe,
Quàm, quando letitia habet populum univerſum :
Convivantes autem per domum audiunt Cantorem,
Sedentes ordine.*

So kind is Muſik at a Feaſt ; dat it is compared to a
riꞔe Juel : and is preferred, at dat tim, even befor wiſ ſpeaking. As de * ſoon of Siraꞔe teaꞔeꞔt at de ordering of a Feaſt.

4. *Pour not out words* (ſay he) ᵬer der iꞔ a Muſician,
and few not ſꞔort wiſdom out of tim.

5. *A Conſort of Muſik in a banqet of Win, iꞔ aꞔ a Signet of a
Carbuncle ſet in gold.*

Der for was dis Cuſtom anciently uſed in doſ Civil
and Learned Nations : [Hebru s, Grœk s, Romans.]
Of de Romans ſayꞔ *Quintil.* †*Veterum Romanorum epulis fides
ac tibias adhibere moris fuit.* And *Tulli* : * *Epulis magiſtratuum
fides præcinunt.* And again, † *Graviſſimus author in Originibus*
dixit *Cato,* *morem apud Majores hunc epularum fuiſſe, ut deinceps qui accubarent, canerent ad tibiam clarorum virorum laudes.*
Of de Grœk s, teſtifyeꞔ * *Ariſt.* from *Ulyſſes* in *Hom. Optimam
eſſe degendi rationem, quando letiꞔ omnibus, Convivæ audiunt
citharædum, ſedentes per ordinem.* And *Tulli* of dat Grœcian
Captain, dat hœ was accounted to bœ unlearned, becaus hœ
refuſed de Harp at a Feaſt. † *Themiſtocles cùm in epulis recu-
ſâſſet*

saſſet Lyram, habitus eſt indoctior. Plato in *Gorgia* ſpeakes to dis purpos: wer€ hee mentione€ dat Epithalamium, [*Formoſam eſſe, & divitem & benevalere,*] woont tobee ſung at Brideal€s, or marriag€-feaſts. And for de Hebru€s, wee read dat * wen *Zorobabel* had obteined leav and means of *Darius*, to reedifi€ *Jeruſalem* and de Temple; hee and his bredren feaſted wit Inſtruments of Muſik 7 days. *Vid. Modum Ionicum.*

* 1 Eſdras 4. 63.

An oder U€ is to lament de deats, and to ſolemni€ de funerals of honourable Perſonages: and ſweet€ly to €er€ de ſad and drooping ſpirits of de Moorners. Dis ſpecial U€ did *David* mak€ of it; wen hee lamented de deats of *Saul* and *Jonatan*, in dat moornful Dittĭ: 2 *Sam.* 1.

III.

V. 19. De beawty of *Iſrael* is ſlain upon de big places: how ar de migty fallen?

20. *O tel it not in Gat: publiſ it not in de ſtreet€s of Aſcalon. &c.* Wer€ de Valour and Vertu€s of deſe two woordi€s is woordily honoured, by de Heroik ſtat€ly Vers of dis Princ€ly Poet. * Dus did de Singing-men and Singing-weomen ſpeak of good *Joſia* in deir Lamentations, wen *Jeremiah* and all *Juda* moorned for his untim€ly deat. Dus did *Andromake*, wit de Singers, lament de deat of hir dear *Hector*.

* 2 Kron. 35. 24, 25.

— — Θρᾷ δ᾽ εἷσαν ἀοιδὺς
Θρήνων ἐξάρχυς. — — &c. *Juxta vero collocabant Cantores,*
[*Luctus principes;*] *insuperq; gemebant mulieres:*
Inter illas autem Andromache albiulna cœpit luctum.
Mi vir ætate Juvenis periiſti, &c.

Iliad ω.

Agreeable unto dis practic€ was de old€ Law of de Romans. † *Honoratorum virorum laudes in Funere memorantor: easq; etiam ad Cantum Tibicines proſequuntur, cui nomen* Nænia: *quo vocabulo etiam, Græci cantus lugubres nominant.* De wie Solemniti€s, wit oders, ar lik€wiſ€ uſed at our €ief Funeralls.

† Tulli. de Legibus l. 2. in fine.

An oder U€ of dis Muſik is, upon a contrari occaſion, [ſoom extraordinari proſperous event] to increas and expreſ de extraordinari joy and gladnes conceived der€of.

IV.

* Dis uſ€ did dat Glad-ſad daugter of *Jepta* mak€; wen ſee went foort€ wit Timbrels and wit Dances, to meet€ hir

* Iudg. 11. 34.

Q 3   victorious

victorious Faðer returning from ðe slaugter of ðe *Ammonit's*.

† 1 *Sam.* 18. 6.   † Ðis Us did ðe weomen mak of ðeir Musik, wen ðey cam out of all Citti's, Singing and Dancing, to meet King *Saul*, wit *Tabrets*, wit *Joy, and wit Instruments of Musik*.

Ðus did ðe people expres ðeir joy, at ðe proclaiming of
* 1 *Kings* c. 1. King *Solomon* : * *And all ðe people cam up after him : and ðe*
v. 40.   *people piped wit pipes , and rejoiced wit great joy , so ðat ðe*
                 eart rent wit ðe sound of ðem. So did *Simon*, wen hee had
† 1 *Macca.* c. 13. recovered ðe Tour of *Jerusalem* from ðe enimi ; † *And en-*
v. 51.   *tred into it wit tanks-giving, and branches of Palm-trees ; and*
                 wit Harps, and Cymbals, and wit Viols, and Hymns, and Songs.
* C. 15. v. 13.   Ðus did *Judit* triump wen see had slain *Holophernes*. * Ðe
                 weomen of Israel put a garland of Oliv upon her, and hir maid ðat
                 was wit her : and see went befor ðe people in ðe Danc, leading
‡ C. 16. v. 1, 2. *ðe weomen : and ðe men followed in ðeir armour.* † Ðen *Judit*
                 began to sing (and all ðe people sang after her) ðis song of prais.
                 Begin unto my God wit Timbrils : sing unto my Lord wit Cym-
                 bals : tun unto him a nu Psalm : exalt him, and call upon his
                 Nam.

V   An oðer Us of ðis Musik is to direct and order ðe Danc :
                a ting of it self so harmles and usful, ðat, wer it not for ðe
                concomitant abuses, I suppos ðe strictest Stoïks, and se-
                verest Censors woold raðer giv it applaus, ðan opposition.
                Aristotle, out of *Euripides*, recitet 3 tings ðat moov Deligt,
* *Polit.* l. 8. c. 5. and remoov Car's : [Sleep, Drink, and Musik :] * *Som-*
                nus, Potus, Musica, sunt per se jocunda, & simul cessare Cu-
                ras faciunt. Quapropter instituunt in hac : & utuntur cunctis
                istis similiter, [Somno, & Potu, & Musica.] Unto ðes tree
                (sayt hee) ðey ad Dancing for a fowrt. *In his quoq; Saltati-*
                onem posuerunt. And sur'ly not witout caus. For even ðe stif
                Countri-Hin's wil leav any deligt for ðis : and ðowg ðey
                hav wrougt or travelled hard all day ; yet coom ðey as fres
                unto it, and bestur ðemselvs as nimbly at it, as if ðey had
                doon noting in a week befor : and of ðis you need not
                doubt ; ðat, all ðe wil ðey ar ðus employed, ðeir mind's
                ar never trubbled wit any Car, or grief, or ðe least towgt
                of ðeir own, or ðeir Masters busines. And mor'over, wis
                                                                    ðis

dis joiful recreating of de mind^c, by privation of Car^c, and fruition of Deligt, is joined a healtful Exercis^c of de body: wi-e kæpet men in breat, causing and increasing Nimblenes, Strengt, and Activiti : wer^{c}by dey ar enabled for any servic^c, in peac^c or in war. Der^{c}for^c did dat warlik^c people, de *Persians*, learn as wel to Danc^c, as to Rid^c : supposing dis mesured Motiô of de Body to avail mu-e unto Strengt. †*Verùm sicuti Equitare, ita & Saltare discunt Persæ : modulatam id genus motionem, corporis robori conferre plurimum arbitrati.* Dis practic^c is approoved by *Socrates* himself : wo in his Poems sayt, * *Eos qui optimè saltant, ad bellicas res esse idoneos :* dat dey wo Danc^c wel, ar fit for warlik^c exploits. Neider ar des^c [Healt, Strengt, and Activiti] de on^{c}ly good Effects of dis laudable Exercis* ; it causing mor^{c}over a Concin, and coomly Comportment of de bodi. For wi-e, †*Plato* in his laws reqiret, dat de yut^c of bod^c sexes soold^c bæ taugt to Danc^c. *Pueros & Puellas consentaneum est Tripudium Gymnasticamq; discere. Ideoq; pueris Saltandi magistri, ac puellis ejusdem Artis magistræ tribuantur ; ut in illis exercitationibus aptam quandam corporis conformationem consequantur.* Wi-e Law was accordingly obferved by dat wis^c and warlik^c Nation : as by *Homer* (after oder memorable sings) is expressed in *Achilles* Shield.

'Εϊϑα ιᾠ ἠίϑϵοι ἀ πάρϑϵνοι ἀλφϵσίβοιαι. &c.

Ibi quidem adolescentes & virgines formosissimæ Tripudiabant, invicem in volis manus tenentes. Horum autem, hæ quidè tenues vestes gerebant: illi vero tunicas Induti erant bene textas, sensim splendentes tanquam oleo : Et hæ quidem pulcbras coronas habebant :illi autem gladios Gestabant aureos, ab argenteis cingulis.

Hi verò quandoq; in orbem curfitabant doctis pedibus Agiliter admodum ; sicut quum quis rotam aptatam manibus Sedens figulus tentaverit si currat. Quandoq; autem rursus curfitabant per ordines inter se : Plurima verò delectabilem choream circumstabat multitudo, Oblectantes sese. Duo autem Saltatores inter ipsos, Cantum incipientes, verfabant se per eos medios.

In

† *Cælius Rhodeginus l.18.c.18.*

* *Athenæus lib. 14.*

† *De Legibus lib. 7.*

In fine Iliad. Σ.

In respect of all wie Benefits it is, dat our Indulgent Heavenly Fader, out of his wisdom and looving kind'nes, Permittet and Promiset dis Boon' to his Obedient Children; and, for deir Disobedienc', in his displeasur' Taket it from dem. De first appæret in ðe Propeci of *Jeremi* : wer' de *C. 31. v. 4.* Lord layt unto Israel, * *Dou falt again bæ adorned wit dy Tabrets ; and falt go' foort' in ðe Dances wit dem dat mak' mer-* †*v. 13.* *ry.* And again, † *Den fall ðe Virgin rejoyc' in ðe Danc' : bot' yung men and old' togeðer : for I wil turn deir moorning into joy,* *C. 5. v. 14.* *and wil comfort dem.* &c. De oder in de Lamentations. * *De Elders hæ' ceased from ðe gat' ; ðe yung men from deir Musik :* †*v. 15.* † *De joy of our hart is ceased ; our Danc' is turned into Moorning.* And der'for' wer' des' comfortable deligts cannot bæ had ; ðe want must bæ suffered wit patienc', as a punishment of our ungodlines : but wer' God givet leav' ; it is no fault for men to tak' it, and wit tankfulnes to mak' us' *See de Places* of it. * As *Judit* and de *Ju's* did at ðe deat of *Holophernes :* *for' cited : [Ju-* and as was dœn upon ðe victori of *Saul* and *David* against *dit 15. 13.* de *Philistin's :* and of *Jephtah* against ðe *Ammonit's.* And *1 Sam. 18. 6.* dat dis kind' of rejoicing was used among de Ju's, in de *Judg. 11. 34.]* days of our Saviour ; appæret in de Parable of ðe † Pro- †*Luc. 15. 25.* digal sœn. De wie dat dey migt perform wit mor' deeenci, wen dey wer' men ; it sæmet dey wer' inured to it, wil' *Luc. 7. 32.* dey wer' * cildren. And lik'wis' after dat tim', † *Theodoret* †*l. 3 c. 27.* speaket of Banqets and Dancings wie Kristians used after deliverances : nam'ly dos' of de men of Antioch, wo, for deir peac' and saf'ti by de deat of dat bloodi Apostata *Julian,* mad' publik Feasts and Dancings. His woords ar des' : *Antiocheni cognitâ cæde Juliani, epulis & festis indulgebant, & Choreas agebant. Qui impius Ecclesiæ Persecutor & Apostata, Mortali vulnere sancius, sanguinem in aerem sparsit, & exclamat,* Vicisti Galilæe.

Oðer Civil Uses of Musik sæ in ðe fur' Mood's, *l.* 1. *t.* 1.

CAP.

CAP. III. §III.
Of Objections against ƥe Vſes of Civil Muſik.

SEing derᶜforᶜ dat Civil Muſik, wiƭ hir ſeverall Uſes, ar uſᶜful for men, alloued by God, agræable to Naturᶜ, and praᶜtiſed by ƌe godly for ƌeir comfort ; hou cœmeƭ it to paſ, dat dey ar altogeder diſalloued by ſœm, and accounted unmæᶜ to bæ uſed at all ? Becaus (*ſay* dey) dey ar but Vanitiᶜs, wiᶜ ar commonly ſo abuſed, ƌat dey dœᶜ unto many, morᶜ harm, dan gœd.

Object. I.

Dat dey ar vanitiᶜs, it cannot bæ denyed : for all dat wæ dœᶜ, and all dat wæ havᶜ, and wæ our ſelvs, ar Vanitiᶜs. * De building of gœdly houſes, † de making of fnᶜ gardens and orᶜards, ar Vanitiᶜs : * de ſilver and gold, wiᶜ wæ poſſeſ, yea and all our † worldly wiſdœm, ar Vanitiᶜs : and yet, I ſuppoſᶜ, derᶜ is no man ᶜf dem ſo vain ; dat hæ had rader bæ wiƭout deſᶜ Vanitiᶜs, dan havᶜ dem. Nay our Muſical Propeƭ telleƭ us morᶜ, dat not onᶜly our aᶜtions and poſſeſſions ar Vaniti, but even de Autors and Owners of dem alſo. * *Verily every man living is altogeder Vaniti.*

Reſp. I.

**Eccleſ.* 2. 4. † 5.
* *v.* 8.
† 15.

And, for de abuſᶜ of deſᶜ Vanitiᶜs, ſurᶜly de fault is no les in our oldᶜ Sages dat ſuffer it, dan in fond yunglings dat dœᶜ it. *Temeritⁱⁱ eſt videlicet florentis etatis, prudentia ſeneⱸtis.* Wæ know dat yuᶜ knoweƭ not to moderatᶜ and govern it ſelf : Reaſon and Judgment in dat agᶜ ar weak ; Appetitᶜ and Affeᶜtions ſtrong : ſo dat dey can hardly kæpᶜ or findᶜ de Mean ; but ar apt, wiƭ de leaſt temptation, to fall from gœd to evil, from evil to wœrs, and by degræᶜs (if dey bæ not reſtrained) from wœrs to wœrſt of all. It behœveƭ derᶜforᶜ, de gravᶜ Elders and ᶜief men of eaᶜ placᶜ, to endevour, by all means, de preventing and reforming of Abuſes : firſt by † *bringing up ƌeir children in de nurturᶜ and admonition of de Lord :* dat in ƌeir harts dey may abhor de ƭing dat is evilᶜ ; den, by bæing preſent at ƌeir ſet mætings, to ſæ dat dey demean demſelvs civilly and modeſtly in ƌeir Sportᶜs, wiƭout all rudᶜ ſpæᶜ & behaviour : and dat dey takᶜ timᶜs alloued and convenient for ſuᶜ exerciſᶜ : (for aldowg derᶜ bæ ˮa timᶜ

Reſp. II.

† *Epheſ.* 6. 4.

* *Eccleſ.* 3. 4.

R   to

to Danc^e, as wel as a tim^e to Moorn^e; yet all tim^es ar not fit for it) and in des^e convenient tim^es, to leav of in tim^e convenient, dat de Sun may bæ witnes of ðeir Conversation and Parting: and dos^e dat dey find^e incorrigible or refractari, to repel from de fruition of dat contentment, wi€ dey can bæ content, in steed of a tankful acceptanc^e, so ungrat^efully to abus^e; and dat to de spoil of demselvs and deir fellows. But wol^ely to prohibit dat wi€ God permittes, and, for de abus^e of soom, to debar all from de us^e of dis deligtful and healtful Recreation; is to doo^e as dat angri *Lacedæmonian,* wo commanded de Vin^es of his Countri to bæ grubbed up, becaus soom woold^e bæ drunk wit de fruit der^eof. Doo^e you not tink, hæ migt hav^e doon better, to cut doun de vic^e, and let de Vin^es grow?

Object. II.   I, but (dey repli^e) hou fall wæ bæ able to doo^e any good wit our unstable yunkers, so long as dos^e debost Baladmakers and Danc^e-makers [de voued vassals of *Asmodeus*] not content, wit deir own uncleannes to doo^e him homag^e and fealti, spend deir tim^e, and strain deir wits, to draw as many oder as dey can, into de sam^e condemnation: and de on^e wit obscen^e and filty woords, de oder wit immodest and fam^eles gestur^es, striv^e weider fall hav^e de precedenc^e, in leading deir silly proselyt^es hedlong into hell? But indeed de mat€ betwæn^e des^e twain is so uneqal, dat dis strif may soon^e bæ ended. It is not lik^e dat of de * two Sword-players, of wom^e de Proverb is, *Non melius commissus fuit cum Bitho Bacchius :* Nor dat of de † two Shepherds contending for de Masteri in extemporal poesi: wo did so eqaliz^e on^e anoder; dat *Palemon* knew not weider to prefer, but was fain to pas dis indifferent Sentenc^e, *Et vitulâ tu dignus; et hic.* - - -. But hær^e de ods is su€, dat an indifferent *Palemon* wil easily bæ resolved, and adjudg de *Calf* to de Baladers: wo dayly doo^e deir Master mu€ mor^e servic^e, dan deir mat^es doo^e: prostituting deir bas^e and pestilent mer€andiz^e, not on^ely at su€ publik Merriments; but also in privat houses, yea and openly in de stræt^es, and market-places: wer^e dey hav^e deir Factors, wo vent it boldly witout any blusing.

*Horat Sat. l. 1. Satyra 7.
† Menalcas & Dametas. Eclog. 3.

Ress. I.   For answer, It is tru^e dat dos^e you blam^e, ar de principal Arkitects

Arkiteꝭs of all ðe miſcief : ðey ar ðe Inventers and contri-
vers of ðe Plot : but it is ðeir ſordid Agents [ðe mercenary
Minſtrels] ðat put ðe ſtratagems of ðem bodᶜ in execution :
ðey ar ðe Inſtruments, to publiſ ðe filꬰy Songs of ðe onᶜ;
and to teaꞓe ðe filꬰy faſions of ðe oðer. And ðeſᶜ, it is in
your pouer ðat ar but inferior Magiſtratᶜs, or oðerwiſᶜ
men of wœrꬰ, to reform. If you findᶜ fault, ðat ðey ſay or
dœᶜ ðat wiꞓe is contrari to good manners, wiꞓe tendeꬰ to ðe
corrupting of yuꬰᶜ, or ðe offending of modeſt ears and eys;
haply ðey will bæ aſamed : but if you ſarply rebukᶜ ðem;
(knowing in wat caſᶜ ðe Law haꬰ left ðem) doubtles ðey
wil fear to offend eftſœnᶜs in ðat kindᶜ.

But (ꬰanks bæ to God) ðeſᶜ impurᶜ Buffons (weiðer it   *Reſp.II.*
bæ ðat ðey ar not nou permitted, as formerly, to defilᶜ ðe
Preſ; or ðat ðemſelvs ar, at laſt, aſamed of ðeir ſtalᶜ ribal-
dri ; or ðat ðe people, waxing morᶜ modeſt, wil noᶜ longer
endurᶜ it;) begin, mæ ꬰinks, to wear away; and ðerᶜ ariſeꬰ
in ðeir ſtæd a better generation : our *Marlows* ar turned into
Quarleſes. Haply ðey havᶜ found morᶜ, & morᶜ ſolid mirꬰ and
deligꬰ in honeſt conceipts, and witti Urbaniti; ðan in all
wanton and immodeſt jeſts, or any kindᶜ of obſcenᶜ ſcurri-
liti. For indædᶜ ðerᶜ is noᶜ truᶜ mirꬰ witout honeſti : and
ðerᶜforᶜ ðe experienced King-Preaꞓer joineꬰ ðem togoðer.
* *I know* (ſayꬰ he) *ðat ðerᶜ is noᶜ good wit ðe ſœns of men;*   * *Eccleſ.c.3.12.*
but for a man to Rejoicᶜ, and to dœᶜ Good in his lifᶜ.

And for ðe Dancᶜ-makers, even ðey alſo (weiðer it bæ
ðat ðey ar reſtrained by ðe pious Magiſtratᶜ, and ꞓekt by ðe
awful lookᶜs of auſterᶜ autoriti ; or ðat ðe people, growing
into a morᶜ civil carriagᶜ, begin to load ðeir ſlabbering
guizes; or ðat ðemſelvs ar ſo wearyed in ðeir foul ways,
ðat, likᶜ tired jadᶜs, ðey can goᶜ noᶜ furðer) giv nou noꬰing
ſo muꞓe caus of offencᶜ, as formerly ; wen modeſt maids and
matrons werᶜ oft times fain to ſit out, not knowing hou, for
ſamᶜ, to partakᶜ wiꬰ ðeir rudᶜ aſſociats.

Epilogus.

WEr^c^for^c^ (ingenuous and intelligent Readers) all tings rigtly weiged, der^c^ is no^c^ sufficient caus, dat *Wee* ʃoold^c^ wilfully depriv^c^ our selvs of des^c^ permitted Comforts; but rader tak^c^ heed^c^ dat wee provok^c^ not *God* to depriv^c^ us of dem: as de Ju^c^s oftentimes did wit deir wickednes and apostaci^c^; so * turning deir mirt into mourning,
* Vid. Ose 2. 15. &c. in c. 3. § 1.
and miseri. Let us not der^c^for^c^ bee lik^c^ dat † *faitles and stubborn generation*: [*a generation dat set not deir hart arigt, and wos^c^ spirit cleaved not stedfastly unto God*:] nor lik^c^ de profan^c^
† Psal. 78. 9.
godles headen: * *wo beeing past feeling, did giv demselvs over unto lasciviousnes; to woork all uncleannes, even wit greedines.*
* Ephes. 4. 19.
But let us consider dat wee are Kristians: *unto wom^c^ de grac^c^ of God hat^c^ appeered,* † *teacing us dat, denying ungodlines and and worldly lusts, wee ʃoold^c^ liv* (a) Sobriè, Justè, Piè, [*soberly, rigteously, and holily*] *in dis present world*: *holily* in respect of God, *rigteously* in respect of our neigbour, and *soberly* in respect of our selvs. Dis our Sobrieti, as at all tim^c^s, so ciefly in our Pastim^c^s, is to bee used: dat by Intemperanc^c^ and luxuri wee abus^c^ not our liberti, nor pollut^c^ our honest mirt, wit any kind^c^ of turpitud^c^ or Lasciviousnes: wic ar tings in demselvs so odious, dat by de common verdict bot^c^ of good and bad, of godly and profan^c^, dey ar condemned.
† Titus 2. 12. (a)
For Lasciviousnes in *Dancing*, derived from de wanton *Iones* to de *Romans*, in deir idle prosperiti, * even deir own Poet coold^c^ tax it, as an open enimi^c^ to Modesti, Castiti, and Civalri.
* Horat. Car. l. 3. Ode 6.

(b)

Motus doceri gaudet (b) *Ionicos*
Matura virgo: & fingitur artibus
Jam nunc: & incestos amores
De tenero meditatur ungui. &c.

Et mox ibidem.

Non his Juventus orta parentibus
Infecit æquor sanguine Punico. &c.

For

For Laciviousnes in *Singing*, dat † holy Fader doo't du's   † S. *Augustin.*
bewail it : *Quàm multi mali & luxuriosi scienter cantant digna*   *Exposit. Ps. 18.*
auribus suis & cordibus, novimus & dolemus. Sciunt enim se
cantare flagitia ; & tamen cantant tantò libentiùs, quantò im-
mundiùs : quoniam tantò se putant debere fieri lætiores, quantò
fuerint turpiores. De reason of dis complaint hæ givet in an
* oder plac' : *Talibus etenim turpitudinibus canticorum, animi*   * *Tom. 9. de de-*
humani illecti enervantur, & decidunt a virtute : & propter ip-   *cem Chordis.*
sas turpitudines postea sentiunt dolores : & cum magna amaritu-
dine digerunt, quod cum dulcedine temporali biberunt.

And for de lacivious *Autors* of dis Laciviousnes, [de de-
generated Cru' of deboo't Buffons] dat generous tru' Poet, in de person of *Urania*, doo't dus reproov' and exhort dem :

> † O Profan' *Writers, your lascivious* rhym'   † *Dubartas in*
> *Mak's our best Poets to bee bas'ly dæmed,*   *Urania : Qua-*
> *As Juglers, Jesters, and de scum of Tim' :*   *drain 44.*
> *Yea, wit de Vulgar, les dan des' estæmed.*

> *You mak' east' Clio a ligt wanton Minion,*
> *Mount Helicon a Stu's : your ribaldri*
> *Mak's prudent Parents [strict in deir opinion]*
> *To bar deir cildren reading Poëtri.*

> *De cain of Vers was at de first invented*
> *To handle onely sacred Mysteri's,*
> *Wit mor' respect : and noting els was cented,*
> *For long tim' after, in su'e Poësi's.*

> *So did my David, on de trembling strings*
> *Of his divin' Harp, onely sound his God :*
> *So mild'-souuld Moses to Jehovah sings*
> *Jacobs deliveranc' from d' Egyptians rod.*

> *So Deborah and Judit in de Camp,*
> *So Job', and Jeremi wit car's oppressed,*
> *In tun'ful Verses of a various stamp,*
> *Deir Joiz and Sigs divin'ly-sweet expressed. &c.*

To dis purpos' speaket * *Martyr* : first sewing de divin'   * *Locon. com-*
                              mun. Classis 3.
      R 3   original,   *C. 3. Parag. 25.*

original, and laudable Uſes of truᶜ Poëſi; and den inveying
againſt ᵭe ſamᶜful Apoſtaci of ſoom lewd Poetaſters : wo
having givn demſelvs over to all manner of luxuri and uncleannes, makᶜ no oder uſᶜ of ᵭeir Wit and Art, but to
proclaim ᵭeir own ſamᶜ, and, by ᵭeir alluring Carms, to
draw oders after dem into ᵭe ſamᶜ perdition. *Sciendum eſt*
veteres, & cum gratias Deo agerent, et cum ab eo aliquid impe-
trare niterentur, communibus votis carmina quædam ſolennia
conſueviſſe adhibere. Et ſane Poëſis initia ſua hinc habuit: eamq;
donum Deï fuiſſe non irem inficias : ſed id optàrim, ut pura ac
caſta inter homines retineretur. Id verò propterea dico, quoniam
immundi quidam et impuri homines illam fœdiſſimè conſpurcâ-
runt ; dum cantum et verſus ad laſcivas libidines, et quævis tur-
pia dejiciunt. Quorum carmina, ut elegantia et bene latina ſint ;
Chriſtianis tamen auribus ſunt prorſus indigna, neq; adoleſ-
centibus deberent ullo modo proponi : qui cum ad vitia ſatis
propenſionis habeant ; ad eos impellendos et inflammandos, novis
ignibus et arietibus non eſt opus. Verſus hujus generis, animorum
Sirenes jure dici poſſunt : quibus juvenes auſcultantes, vix fieri
poteſt quin naufragium faciant.

☞

† *In Martiali*
caſtrato.

Perditorum itaq; horum Nebulonum ſordes (ne preſtantes Ju-
ventutis Chriſtianæ indoles, diutius in perniciem inquinare que-
ant) ex illorum ſcriptis expurgare, († ſicuti jam factitari cœp-
tum eſt) opus ſanè eſſet Heroïcum, & Principibus dignum Chri-
ſtianis.

It werᶜ ᵭerefōrᶜ a happy ᵵing (ingenuous Readers) ᵭat
all ᵭeſᶜ dangerous ſtumbling-bloks (at wiᶜ wæ often ſæ
our cildren [our deareſt cildren] to ſtumble and fall) werᶜ
qitᶜ removed out of ᵭeir ways ; ᵭat in ᵭeir holſom and neceſſari Recreations, ᵭey migt, witout let, walk ſafᶜly and
uprigt. In ᵭe mean ſpacᶜ, (til ᵭis publik good may bæ happily effected) let us, in ᵭe fear of God, ſo muᶜe ᵭe morᶜ cir-
cumſpectly lookᶜ unto our footᶜ-ſteps ; leſt ᵭat, wiᶜ ſooldᶜ havᶜ
bæn for our good, bæ madᶜ unto us an occaſion of falling.
Let us in all our Sportᶜs, avoïd ᵭe fals deligts of Laſcivi-
ouſnes : wiᶜ dooᶜ ſo enervatᶜ and enfeeble ᵭe poners and fa-
cultiᶜs boᵵᶜ of body and mind ; ᵭat ᵭey wo ar oncᶜ infected
derᶜwiᵵ, dooᶜ hardly ever after proovᶜ good for any ᵵing : but

ar

ar an offenc' to God, a Scandal to good men, and, in ðe end,
Ruin to ðemſelvs : onſ'ly wiɛ ðis aduantag', ðat (lik' (c)
ðoſ' wo had ðeir harts woonded) ðey dy' lauging. Yea let
us, in our ɯol' converſation, eſ·eew evil and doo' good : let
us bɛ zelous in ðe ſervic' of God, abhorring Sacrileg' and
Superſtition : let us bɛ faitful in ðe loov of our neigbour,
abhorring Robberi and Oppreſſion : and let us ſo uſ' ðe
tranſitori Pleaſur's of ðis liſ' ; ðat wɛɛ loſ' not ðe perma-
nent joys of ðe liſ' to coom.

(c)

ANNOT.

(a) **S**obriè. † *Hæc tria perpetuò meditare adverbia Pauli :* † *Piſcator in*
Hæc tria ſunt vitæ regula ſancta tuæ. *locum.*

(b) *Motus Ionicos.* ı * *ſaltationes laſcivas & petulantes : inſtar* * *Coment: antiq*
Ionum, *qui mollem ſaltationem, membrorum geſtibus adinvenerunt.*
ɯie kind' of Laſcivioufnes, *Aþenæus* notet to bɛ ðen commonly
uſed, ɯen ðe win' is in, and ðe wit out. † *Ionicam ſaltabant inter pocula.* † *lib.* 14. *c.* 5.

(c) * *Ictu trajecta præcordia in præliis, riſum attuliſſe traditum* * *Ariſt. de Par-*
eſt. *tib. animal. lib.*
, *c.* 10.

3

FIⱢIS.